D1581626

Sports Geography

In this fully revised and updated edition of his discipline-defining text, John Bale comprehensively explores the relationships between sport, place, location and landscape. Drawing on sporting examples from around the world, the book demonstrates how geography is absolutely central to our understanding of modern sport. Key themes addressed throughout the book include:

- concepts of 'space' and 'place'
- the geographical diffusion of modern sport
- the economic impact of sport
- sport and the community
- cultural geographies of sport
- sport and the 'geographical imagination'.

Presenting a wealth of research data, a wide range of international case studies and a comprehensive guide to the literature, this accessible text will be indispensable reading for all students of sport, human geography and cultural studies.

John Bale is Professor of Sports Geography at Keele University and Visiting Professor of Sports Studies at Aarhus University, Denmark.

199 714

Sports Geography

Second Edition

John Bale

Routledge
Taylor & Francis Group

LONDON AND NEW YORK

First published 1989
by E & FN Spon
Second edition 2003
by Routledge, an imprint of Taylor & Francis
11 New Fetter Lane, London EC4P 4EE

Simultaneously published in the USA and Canada
by Routledge
29 West 35th Street, New York, NY 10001

Routledge is an imprint of the Taylor & Francis Group

© 2003 John Bale

Typeset in Times by Wearset Ltd, Boldon, Tyne and Wear
Printed and bound in Great Britain by St Edmundsbury Press,
Bury St Edmunds, Suffolk

British Library Cataloguing in Publication Data
A catalogue record for this book is available
from the British Library

Library of Congress Cataloging in Publication Data
Bale, John.
  Sports geography/John Bale. – 2nd ed.
    p. cm.
  Includes bibliographical references (p.) and index.
  1. Sports. 2. Sports–Regional disparities. 3. Human geography.
I. Title.
  GV706.8 B35 2002
  796–dc21
  2002068169

ISBN 0–419–25220–7 (hbk)
ISBN 0–419–25230–4 (pbk)

... in the next great Atlas to be produced by English mapmakers ... a map of the distribution of games throughout the world might be included. The inferences to be drawn from it are not within my power to draw; but they might be curious.

Edmund Blunden, *Cricket Country*, 1944

Sportsworld is a sweaty Oz you'll never find in a Geography book.

Robert Lipsyte, *Sportsworld*, 1976

He was in love with travelling, with running, with geography.

John Updike, *Rabbit Run*, 1964

Contents

Preface to first edition

In the preface to an *Introduction to Sport Studies* Harold Vanderzwaag and George Sheehan explained that the selection of sub-disciplines which made up each chapter of their book was undertaken in a somewhat arbitrary manner and was based largely on the content of courses being taught in the USA in the mid and late 1970s. The philosophy, sociology, history and psychology of sport were all dealt with but the geography of sport was not. They accepted that sports geography is another avenue for studying sport but they failed to embark on its exploration, believing that at the time there was a paucity of published work in this area.

The present book is written to show that this is no longer the case. It seeks to fill a substantial lacuna in the sports studies literature and is an initial attempt to draw together the principal foci from the existing literature on the geography of sports. It represents over a decade of academic involvement in the geographical dimensions of sport and a lifetime's activity as a sports enthusiast and participant.

When I started studying sport I tended to use it to teach geography. I found that allusions to sport, a pervasive feature of modern society, helped motivate my students and make my geography classes more interesting. I realise now that I was tending to devalue sport by reducing it to the level of a teaching gimmick. Sport is worthy of academic study in its own right and its geographical dimensions provide special insights not included in any other of the 'disciplines'.

This book is primarily intended for those following introductory sports studies courses in higher education. At the same time geography students might be interested in a book which deals with location, landscapes and regions, among other things. For geographers I hope that *Sports Geography* provides examples and insights of well-known geographical themes. In addition, a wide range of social scientists may use this book as a source of reference.

This book is not an encyclopaedia or gazetteer. Instead it is concerned with ideas, using specific facts to illustrate recurring themes in a variety of geographical contexts. Believing that geographers are essentially concerned with places I have included in each chapter vignettes which try to capture sport–place associations in an evocative way. The inclusion of several extracts from daily newspapers (and not always from the sports pages) serves to remind us that a geography of sport is all around us! I have tried to assist the readers of this book by providing detailed references and suggestions for further reading. Those using the book as a source of reference will be able to ignore the student-centred learning experiences, discussion topics and suggestions for projects, included as an Appendix, but all readers will probably benefit from having a good atlas close at hand, given the global nature of the illustrative material.

Many people have helped in the writing of this book. In particular I would like to thank John, Sandy, Dick, Pat, John and Jane for extravagant hospitality and good times while I was ostensibly involved in the academic study of sports in alien climes. As this book is a synthesis the names of a large number of other people are included in the pages which follow. Although I've never met most of them – and although they may never read this – I must thank all who have unwittingly provided ideas and information included in the maps, diagrams, tables and text in this book.

As in all productions of this kind thanks must go to the author's family. In my case, my parents supported an early interest in sports; today Ruth, Roderick and Anthony continue to support an ageing geography teacher cum sports enthusiast in diverse ways. Despite the help of all these people, the usual caveat applies.

Preface to second edition

The first edition of *Sports Geography* was generally well received and, over a decade since its publication, a second edition is long overdue. In recent years a substantial amount of writing has emerged which focuses on sports from a geographical perspective. Such written work has come from geographers but also from historians, sociologists and anthropologists whose approaches have reflected a geographical nuance. This new edition, while retaining much of the content found in the first edition, includes new material that updates the book by reflecting shifts in sports-geographical scholarship during the past decade.

The second edition does provide an introductory insight into what a geography of sport might look like but places greater emphasis on how the geographical treatment of sport has varied over time. I have tried to alert the reader to different 'traditions' of a geographical approach to sport, rooted mainly in changing emphases in geography itself. Hence, new material includes allusions not only to currently unfashionable notions such as environmental determinism (not covered in the first edition) but to areas of current geographic interest such as postmodernism and post-colonialism. In other words, there is no single geography of sport but a number of different such geographies, each situated in time and space.

It would be impossible to name all the friends and colleagues who have contributed to this second edition. In the 1980s it was easy to find a small number of key figures who had inspired and influenced my writing. That is no longer possible. Nevertheless, this remains an appropriate place to thank everyone who has contributed to the geographical study of sports and on whose work I have drawn in writing this book.

John Bale
Betley, Staffordshire

Acknowledgements

I am grateful to the following for permission to reproduce passages, illustrations and tables contained in this book: Bob Jones for Figure 2.4b; University of Texas Press for the quotes from the text by Al Reinert in *Rites of Fall: High School Football in Texas*, photographs by Geoff Winningham, text by Al Reinert, © 1979, on page 20; Hal Gillman for the passage on page 28; Eric Dunning for Table 3.1; R. Harisalo for Figure 3.1; Tony Mangan for the passage on pages 54–5; Ernst Jokl for Tables 4.1 and 4.2; Brian Rodgers for Figure 4.1; Frank Cass Publishers for Figures 4.3 and 4.6; Peterloyne for Figure 5.5; *The Miami Herald* (and Rex Walford for drawing my attention to) Figure 5.6; William Schaffer and Lawrence Davidson for Table 6.2; Geographical Association for Figure 6.6; Elsevier Science for Figure 6.7; Bob Adams for Figures 7.6 and 7.8; Collins Publishers and Simon Inglis for Figure 7.11; the *Guardian* and Matthew Engel for the passage on page 157; 'Gren' for the inspiration for Figure 8.2; A.G. Macdonnell and Macmillan Publishers for the passage on page 168.

Every effort has been made to trace copyright holders but I apologise for any unintended omission or neglect.

Chapter 1

Introduction

A well-known professor of geography has written that his subject is similar to the city of Los Angeles in that it sprawls over a large area, merges with its neighbours and has a central area that is difficult to find (Haggett 2001). However, it did not take him long to alert his readers to the fact that geography is basically concerned with three broad themes, namely (1) the location and spatiality of terrestrial phenomena, (2) human–environment relations, and (3) regional differentiation. Two recurring concepts in geography are therefore space and place. The subject is popularly associated with 'knowing where places are' or 'knowing what places are like'. Because the academic discipline of geography is a human construction, its character and content vary considerably between individual geographers and national 'schools' of geography. Some scholars are more concerned with physical than with human geography; some geographers adopt descriptive approaches, others are more analytical. But while it is common to resort to the old saw, 'geography is what geographers do', the two recurring concepts of space and place are rarely far away from the geographer's task.

The broad umbrella of geography has produced a number of subdisciplines. Indeed, some observers feel that geography is becoming an over-fragmented subject. The geographer Michael Dear (1988) has suggested that economic, social and political geography are the most important fields of geographical study. He also suggested that a geography of sport is not central to the structure and explanation of geographical knowledge. If one was to look at geographical dictionaries there might appear to be some merit in Dear's assumption. For example, it was only in the third edition of *The Dictionary of Human Geography* (Johnston, Gregory and Smith 1994) that the geography of sport earned a modest, but unsatisfactory, entry. However, Dear seems to have ignored that fact that sport is political, social and economic, and therefore is part of each of the three geographies that he prioritised. Additionally, Dear's view was challenged by the observation that 'the conditions predominating in any given field of study dictate which subdiscipline is more or less fruitful'. For example, 'the geography of the sport of soccer governs key aspects of political, social and economic conditions of Rio de Janeiro, rather than *vice versa*' (Scott and Simpson-Housley 1989). It has also been argued that insights about the workings of human society can often be found from the most marginal and surprising of sources. Hence, a case can readily be made for studying (what many regard as the 'marginal' phenomenon of) sport, which may be

> exceedingly helpful as we try to unravel the mysteries bound up in how geographical knowledge is constructed outside of the academy, and in how the everyday senses that people possess of themselves, their societies and their worlds have rolled into them sensations of bodies in movement through immediate surroundings as well as feelings of commonality sedimented in collective events, games, rituals and spectacles which so often embrace a sports component
>
> (Philo 1994, 2)

It should be added, however, that sports are significant not only as 'representations' of places and as 'rituals and spectacles', but also as examples of 'disciplinary mechanisms'.

The traditional neglect of sport by geographers (and of geography in sports studies) is paradoxical for several reasons. First, sport is a major aspect of economic, social and political life. While taking up huge amounts of space in the media it has also been the subject of significant political and environmental debates. Second, space and place – regarded by many as the two geographical fundamentals – are central to both geography and sport. Each is concerned with space and the way it is occupied; they both focus on the way people move and interact in geographic space; regions form a central feature of the organisation of sports; places are the means of identifying most sports teams; sport is affected by, and increasingly affects, the physical environment and landscape; sport is a world of territoriality and hierarchies. In short, sport – like geography – is a spatial science. Indeed, for one sport – orienteering – where map, compass and route-finding are all essential parts of the activity, it is difficult to know where the sport starts and the geography stops. It begs the question of whether an orienteer is 'doing' geography or sport.

In recent years geographical writing on sports has increased substantially. But sports-geographic writing has been undertaken in a wide range of disciplines and is found in often inaccessible and somewhat fugitive sources. The prime aim of the present book, therefore, is to draw together the major themes from a scattered literature in a coherent form. Although sport (like geography) is rather difficult to define (see Chapter 2), I tend to use the term in this book to describe the kinds of things written about on the sports pages of daily newspapers. In other words, I am more concerned with top-class, achievement-oriented sport than with sport as recreation.

However, because the distinction between these two levels of sport is blurred there is an inevitable overlap in terms of coverage and it must be noted that one reason for concentrating on serious sport is that recreational sport has received far more attention from academic geographers (Patmore 1970, 1983).

Although a geography of sport is widely thought of as a recent branch of both geography and sports studies, there are a number of antecedents to the present interest in sport, space and place. The late nineteenth-century humanistic geographer, Elisée Reclus (1876), briefly alluded to English cricket – which greatly impressed him – in his monumental *Universal Geography*. The founder of the modern Olympic Games, Baron Pierre de Coubertin, went further and in 1911 alluded to a 'Sporting Geography', noting that 'there is an athletic geography that may differ at times from a political geography' (in Müller 2000). Recognising that not all nations were nation states, he urged that nations, not countries, should compete in the Olympics. Other antecedents of modern sports geography will be alluded to in the following chapters.

The writing – or as one might say in the twenty-first century, the 'discourse' – of sports geography has been undertaken by a variety of authors. Some are Geographers with a capital G, that is professional Geographers whose work is published in Geographical journals and who present their work at Geographical conferences. These fall into two groups. First, there are those who have concentrated their academic attention on the study of sports. John Rooney, a Geographer at Oklahoma State University to whom I will refer later, is generally regarded as the 'father' of modern sports geography and is an example of a scholar who built his reputation on sports-geographic writing. The majority of his publications have been in this field of study. Second, there are many Geographers who have alluded to sport – almost in passing or in infrequent publications – and in so doing have provided fascinating insights about it. For such writers, sport is mainly used to illustrate geographical ideas that form the central focus of their academic work. An example is one of the major Geographers in the USA, Allen Pred. He would hardly be regarded as a geographer of sport, but in two of his major publications he has utilised sports to illustrate his broader themes (Pred 1981, 1995). The same applies to the late Peter Gould who was, during the 1970s–1990s, one of the premier geographers in north America. He used examples from sports to illustrate several quantitative geographical methods (Gould 1999, Gattrell and Gould 1979, Gould and Greenwalt 1981). Additionally, David Harvey (e.g. 2000), arguably the world's most famous geographer, has made at least some allusions to sport in his written work. The works of these, and other, scholars will be referred to in later chapters of this book.

However, some of best sports geography has been written by non-Geographers – academics in subjects such as History, Sociology or

Anthropology. A prime example is the cultural sociologist, Henning Eichberg (1998), whose work on sports space and the physical environment of sport have been of considerable influence in recent decades. Likewise, the anthropologist, Charles Springwood (1996), has brilliantly explored the baseball landscapes of two well-known American baseball places, Cooperstown and Dyersville, and provided fascinating insights into the 'meaning' of these places. A further example is Bartlett Giamatti (1989), the former President of Yale University whose sensitive treatment of the landscape of baseball makes his work a fine contribution to a cultural geography of sport. Finally, there are writers on sports-geographic themes who do not work within universities whose work should also be included within the discourse of sports geography. These range from respected journalists, architects and photographers, to 'zine' editors and members of the general public who contribute letters to them. Among them is Simon Inglis, whose substantial work on stadiums provides insights from an architect (1983) and a fan (2000).

As noted earlier, there is no one 'Sports Geography'. Its most prolific writers may have come from the USA, the UK, Canada, France, Australia, Italy and Sweden but this is not to say that in its broadest sense – and in its vernacular form in particular – it is solely a North American or European practice. In this book I will inevitably display a bias towards British examples, but I will not restrict myself to Europe and will try to include examples from as many continents of the world as possible. Integrating the literature on the geography of sport has been achieved by using broad theoretical frameworks in order to provide a structure, or skeleton, upon which the descriptive flesh of the real world can be draped. I do not seek in these pages to produce a theory of sports geography; if I have a conclusion it is that sport is becoming increasingly rational: more artificial, less like play and more like display. I argue that the geography of sport, its locations and landscapes, reflect these developments.

Perhaps the most obvious way to examine the geography of sport is to think of an individual sport (or sport *per se*) as originating at points in geographic space, spreading outwards from these initial areas to embrace regions, nations and in some cases the world, and hence forming a kind of regional pattern. During this period of geographical diffusion, which is still taking place in many sports, profound landscape changes have occurred, be they in the countryside or the city. Some landscapes have become sportscapes, so momentous has been the impact of sport. Today sporting attributes, be they the distribution or density of clubs for participation or the ability to 'produce' star players, is far from evenly spread over the face of the earth. However, such distributions are not randomly arranged either and for this reason sports regions (areas identifying strongly with particular sports) can be recognised. Within the sports landscapes of the modern world facilities for sport, or the way in which sporting activity is arranged, may be far from optimal. Their geographical sub-optimality may derive from the perspective of the profit-maximising sports entrepreneur or from that of the sports consumer. For this reason attempts can be made to produce geographically optimal or spatially equitable solutions to sports-geographic problems.

In brief, sports geography is concerned with the exploration of:

1   sports activity on the earth's surface and how the spatial distribution of sport has changed over time;
2   the changing character of the sports landscape and the symbiosis between the sports environment and those who participate in it; and
3   the making of prescriptions for spatial and environmental change in the sports environment.

Such explorations are undertaken at a variety of geographic scales, ranging from that of a sports stadium and the streets immediately around it to that of the world itself. In the chapters that follow, I include a number of 'vignettes' which serve to illustrate, in greater detail, examples of the sport–place nexus.

In Chapter 2 I outline how the geographical concepts of space and place are central not only to a definition of sport but also to an enhanced under-standing of sport's significance. The spatial character of sport helps distin-guish it from activities such as play, recreation and work. In addition, place not only influences sporting outcomes but also provides a social anchor to which clubs can relate. Chapter 3 examines the growth of sport, not simply historically but also geographically. Historians of sport have recognised that sports took time not only to grow but also to spread from place to place. The spatial perspective adds much to our knowledge of the history of sport, how sports grew and how innovations in sports spread from their points of origin. The geographical diffusion of sport graphically illustrates the roles of imperialism and globalisation at the same time; the role of sport in imperialism cannot be ignored. Chapter 4 deals with regional vari-ations in aspects of sports. This has been one of the most popular approaches to sports geography though it has become less significant in recent years. The sports region, i.e. an area identifying with a particular sport, is central to this approach and a focus on national differences in sport performance is frequently present when the world experiences festi-vals such as the Olympics or World Cup. Chapter 5 explores locational changes associated with sports and sports clubs. At the present time sports clubs are involved in a number of locational adjustments. Some relocate, be it to suburbs or to new regions; other clubs die out, a response perhaps to changing economic fortunes of the areas in which they are located; in other cases the balance of power in sport shifts from one region to another. Examples from several continents of the world are used to illustrate these themes. Welfare–geographical impacts of sport are introduced in Chapter 6 where I discuss the contributions, both positive – in terms of income and psychic benefits created by sports, for example – and negative – in terms of various kinds of sports pollution, for example.

Chapter 7 focuses on what I term the landscapes of sport. As sport has developed it has, in some cases, produced distinctive sportscapes – places designed specifically with sport in mind. In other cases the landscape impacts are temporary. Each of these examples is considered with evidence from sports on either side of the Atlantic. Chapter 8 examines what I term 'imaginative geographies of sport' – those images of sportsworld carried around in our heads or 'constructed' in texts of various kinds. Regional sports images may be stereotypes and it is incumbent upon the sports geographer to check their accuracy. This final chapter takes us into the world of the geographical imagination and brings sports geography nearer the realms of the humanities and cultural studies.

The aim of this book, as expressed earlier, is to draw together a scattered literature and in so doing to introduce students to a new perspective on both sport and geography. The present book is an introduction, but if it encourages either geographers or sports scientists to engage in further sports-geographic study it will have more than served its purpose.

Further reading

Readers of this book are likely to come from a variety of academic backgrounds. Those with a background in Geography may want to browse an extensive overview of Sports Studies. This can be done by consulting the essays in Jay Coakley and Eric Dunning (2000), *Handbook of Sports Studies*. Those with a background in Sports Studies wishing to explore current developments in Human Geography could read Paul Cloke, Philip Crang and Mark Goodwin (eds) (1999), *Introducing Human Geography*.

Chapter 2

The geographical bases of modern sport

Introduction

In the previous chapter I noted that space and place are two basic concepts that are central to both sport and geography. This chapter first examines different ways of looking at the term 'sport', then proceeds to review the ways in which space and place impinge on sport, and *vice versa*. Particular emphasis is placed on the significance of space in the organisation of sport and on the symbolic significance of sport-space. I examine the pervasiveness of place-pride, the widespread existence of the home-field advantage, and the links between sport, place and politics. But I first turn to a brief consideration of the nature and definition of sport itself.

The basic approach adopted in this book is that formulated by the German scholar, Henning Eichberg (1998). Instead of using the word 'sport' in an unqualified or uncritical way and hence losing its analytical power, Eichberg uses the words 'body culture' or 'movement culture' to describe different configurations of particular bodily activities. Take, for example, running. This can assume at least three forms. Children, and less usually adults, engage spontaneously in playful running in fields or forest or on a beach for no other reason than sheer enjoyment and freedom. What they are doing often means something only to them. They obtain sensual pleasure from such an experience and stop when they feel tired. The old English words of frolic, gambol and disport come to mind in relation to this kind of running. Close to such apparently free running in childhood is a Zen of running (Rohé 1974) associated with the 'new sports' movement of 1960s California or the 'jogging revolution' of the 1980s. In its ideal form, this kind of running is playful, spontaneous, free. It is difficult to think of being *made* or forced to play. Such running does not seek to break records or improve fitness. Eichberg sees it as an 'aproductive' form of movement culture.

A second configuration of running can be seen in the world of 'keep fit', 'sport for all', physical education and military training. Here the aim of running is fitness, health, hygiene or 'wellness'. It is not playful running but rather welfare running. It need not be confined in time and space but it often is, for example, in time slots on the school timetable for physical education and with the stopwatch being used to record performance in the interest of fitness. Other sites for welfare running are fitness studios, field-houses and gymnasiums. Here the running is used as a form of re-creation. The body is re-created so that it works better. To be sure, the aim is to achieve good health – but health with what purpose in mind? To look good, to be able to work longer hours, to save the state money in medical provision, to keep people off the streets and out of trouble? All these are welfare aspects of sport – a form of body culture that is concerned with the reproduction of a fit population.

Third, consider running as it is found in the Olympic 100-metres final. Here the aim is either to win or to improve one's performance, i.e. to achieve a personal record, something that places an emphasis on speed. The record can be seen a form of production which has to be increased over time as the result of the ideology of achievement which forms the basis of this kind of running. The Olympic 100 metres final cannot be run on a beach or in a field or on a running machine in an aerobics studio. It has to be undertaken on a very specifically designed track, precisely meas-ured and timed to one thousandth of a second. The track must be of a pre-scribed surface and there is no room for mistakes on the part of the athlete. It is a serious business. This can be called an 'achievement' model of body culture.

I have used running as an example here, but I could have just as easily used throwing, kicking a ball, hitting a shuttlecock, riding a bicycle or jumping. What is clear from Eichberg's 'trialectic' – and is of importance for the content of this book – is that the different kinds of body cultures described above require and produce different kinds of bodies and differ-ent kinds of places and spaces. The trialectic, therefore, seeks to resolve the problem of not only what kinds of bodies might exist but also what kinds of sites, sights, locations, landscapes and environments are found in the world of sport. The body of the 100 metre world record holder is clearly different from that of the jogger and the PE student. Likewise, the environments and spaces in which they run are also different.

In this book I will deal mainly with achievement sport and focus on the pyramid model (see Figure 2.1) that takes up the space on the sports pages of our newspapers. However, before proceeding with this I ought to point out that the three configurations within the trialectic are 'ideal types' (and not the 'real world') and they are static and discrete. Elements of one can be accommodated in – and perhaps take over – any of the others. For example, playfulness is not inevitably absent from achievement sport. Witness, for example, the antics of clown-like soccer players and other athletes who do manage to insert fun into what appears to be a deadly serious business. And playful running can sometimes become more serious

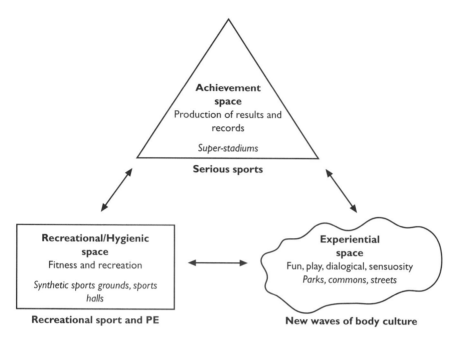

Figure 2.1 A body cultural trialectic (adapted from Eichberg 1998).

– or made more serious. The 'jogging boom', for example, soon became a world of road racing rather than simply running. While many serious sports have become dangerous and sports injuries have spawned the industry of sports medicine, others can improve fitness and health. So the model shown in Figure 2.1 has arrows between each configuration, indicating how one can merge with or influence the other.

Space and sport

Sport, as characterised by the achievement model, is almost invariably subjected to rigorously enforced spatial parameters. Recreation, leisure, play and games, on the other hand, are not. Rules specify precise spatial limits on sports activities. Recreation does not *require* carefully defined spatial contexts, such as 400-metre running tracks, pitches (as in soccer) of not more than 90 metres in width, wickets (in cricket) of 22 yards in length. Neither does it require specified courses, pitches, routes, greens and rinks (Figure 2.2). Even sports like orienteering, cross-country running and skiing, and canoeing possess artificially imposed spatial and temporal limits. As geographer Philip Wagner (1981) noted: 'There is nothing natural about a sports event.'

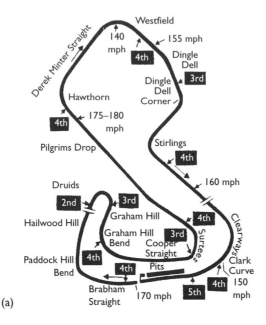

(a)

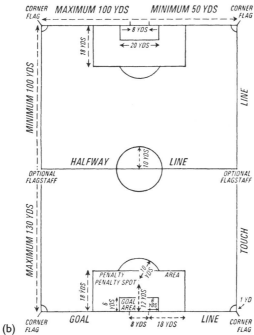

(b)

Figure 2.2 Unlike recreation and play, sport requires carefully defined spatial limits: (a) Brands Hatch Grand prix racing circuit; (b) spatial regulations for Association Football.

The kinds of spatial boundaries described above are obviously explicit boundaries, written into the rules and regulations which define the area of sporting activity. Virtually all sports are, in essence, struggles over space, but space that has carefully defined limits. Many sports have a very clear line demarcating where, exactly, the action can take place. Sport is subjected to 'territoriality' (Sack 1986) – an expression of human power over space – and I will return to the demarcation and segmentation of sports space in Chapter 7. A number of *implicit* boundaries also exist which are unmarked but readily recognisable. An attacking defender or a goalkeeper who wanders into the centre of the field are examples of athletes straying beyond an implicit boundary. Social as well as 'legal' factors may influence where, and where not, players are supposed to go within a game's spatial bounds. However, spatial (and temporal) positions at the start of a sports event often provide advantages or disadvantages to participants, reflecting the lack of total rationalism in the sportised environment. In track races involving confinement to lanes, it is generally regarded as a disadvantage to be allocated to the inside lane since the bends of a track are 'tighter' on the inside than the outside. In skiing, pistes become rutted and it is therefore better to be tenth than fortieth at the start in downhill ski events. Sometimes the spatial–temporal aspects of sports can be carried to apparently absurd extremes. For example, 5,000- and 10,000-metre track races are timed to 0.01 of a second, yet for this to be meaningful in record breaking, every running track would have to be exactly the same distance. If track lengths differ by only a few millimetres it can be argued that 0.01 seconds is too small an increment of time to be considered as a real improvement in, say, middle- or long-distance events. Similarly, space and distance can act as a kind of sporting fetish, as witnessed by the seeming obsession of a large number of people to run exactly 26 miles 385 yards, despite the fact that it is often more convenient and easier to run half or a quarter of this arbitrary distance.

Recreation and play are ubiquitous, but because of its spatial specificity sport is relatively localised. In many cases sport involves the dominance of territory or the mastery of distance; spatial infractions are punished and spatial progress is often a major objective (Wagner 1981). The concern in sport with spatiality means that spatial analytic techniques employed by geographers at a macro- or meso-level of geographical scale could also be applied at the micro-level of the field of play. It has been suggested that the geographer can view team sports as dynamic cases of carefully prescribed human behaviour within limited and bounded geographic spaces. Peter Gould and his associates produced maps showing players in 'interaction space'. Using a complex technique called multidimensional scaling, they constructed maps in which those players interacting with each other frequently are shown close together, while those passing to each other only a few times are far apart (Gattrell and Gould 1979, Gould and

Greenwalt 1981). New views of the conventional space of the playing area are obtained.

The spatial confinement which characterises – indeed, often defines – sport is also important socially. The compression of 'normal' social intercourse into the artificially created time and space limits of sports permits 'fluid interpersonal experience that would never occur so rapidly or within such permutations in real life' (Denney 1957). Such interpersonal relationships include the bringing together of representatives of different cultures, nations, races and classes. But despite the ability to promote an apparent degree of social bonding, the micro-spatial patterns of player locations in some team sports serve (literally and metaphorically) to put people in their place. For example, it has been shown in the USA, Britain and Australia that black players tend to occupy the less glamorous outfield, rather than infield, positions. It implies that black athletes are diverted into positions generally regarded as requiring non-thinking, but athletic, roles. The pioneering study of what has become known as 'stacking' was undertaken by the sports sociologists, John Loy and John McElvogue (1970), who observed that black baseball players were 'stacked' in particular parts of the field of play. They suggested that discrimination is positively related to centrality and in their study of baseball found that blacks occupied non-central (i.e. outfield) positions. Non-central roles were also performed by blacks in football.

Many studies have recorded similar findings to those of Loy and McElvogue. The pattern has been revealed in British and Australian sports. For example, Maguire (1988) showed that in the mid 1980s blacks accounted for only 7.7 per cent of all players in the English football league, but accounted for 13.5 per cent of all forwards. Indeed, of all black players 51.3 per cent were forwards. In Australian Rugby League Hallinan (1991) found that 60 per cent of Aboriginal players in New South Wales Rugby League teams were wingers or centres – like the forwards in English soccer, both non-central positions but ones requiring the stereotypical 'black' qualities of speed and physique. The emphasis on blacks having great speed is also revealed in stacking in English cricket where black cricketers are disproportionately given roles as fast/medium bowlers whereas whites predominate as batsmen (Malcolm 1997). Whatever the reasons, societal attitudes seem to manifest themselves in the players' spatial arrangement on the field of 'play'; blacks are often on the margins of society – and of sports, despite their disproportional presence. In other words, they are discriminated against on the basis of what is believed to be 'race' and the belief that there are important differences in ability between 'white' and 'black'. Although there may be a tendency in the twenty-first century for these spatial distinctions to be declining in significance, the spectre of 'race' continues to haunt the world of sport in several ways (see Chapter 4).

In a similar type of study of the micro-geographies enacted on the field of play, it has been suggested that the position of the captain in team sports might be expected to be central or defensive in order both to see and be seen. Some empirical support for this view has been obtained from work on soccer clubs in the English Football League (Murphy and Parker 1986).

Sport-space compresses normal space in that it brings together people who would normally be unlikely to meet. At the same time, it has been suggested that through sport 'a number of changes in spatial perception are experienced' (Murphy and White 1978). Such changes seem to include the perception of more details than usual, and an apparent increase in the size of the field of play occurring at peak moments during the sport experience. These examples serve to illustrate the practical significance of appreciating the spatial dimension at the micro-scale. However, such micro-scale relations may be symbolic of broader landscapes and it is to this theme that we now turn briefly.

Sport-space as symbol

The space upon which the sporting action is played-out sometimes evokes broader regional landscapes and environments. Big-time baseball in the USA has often been viewed as a vestige of the frontier. Ross (1973) draws a comparison between the baseball park, with its diamond within which most of the action takes place, and the outfield, which witnesses unpredictability and danger, and urban America, its hinterland and the frontier (Figure 2.3).

The spatial analogy between baseball and America itself is argued by some to be a major source of attraction of the game. In both baseball and nineteenth-century America conditions were the same inasmuch as both players and settlers were necessarily self-reliant; as Oriard (1976) puts it: 'The baseball space recreates frontier conditions.' Nostalgic imagery may also be drawn from other sports. For example, cricket in England has been said to serve as a metaphor for the ideal society, carrying with it to the industrial north nostalgic images of a mythical 'Merrie England' (Bale 1994). I take this subject further in Chapter 8; for the moment it is worth noting that, although the physical environment of both baseball and cricket can evoke a lost pastoral world, it may be equally true that the attractiveness of such sports lies in the fact that they are similar to, rather than different from, the day-to-day work of the male business worker with their divisions of labour, specialisation of roles and limited independence (Gelber 1983).

Whatever analogies are drawn between the geography of the sports place and the world outside the stadium, it is difficult to deny that space is central to sport. Because it is also central to geography the geographical

Figure 2.3 The baseball park can be regarded as a symbol of bygone America.

treatment of sport seems a natural enough field of study. But place as well as space is important to a fuller appreciation of modern sport and a number of significant aspects of place (that is, peopled space) and sport can now be reviewed.

Place attachment and sport

Apart from war, sport is one of the few things that binds people to place simply through ascription. Sport has become perhaps the main medium of collective identification in an era when bonding is more frequently a result of achievement. It is in spectator sports that 'the representative teams throw segmented units (i.e. schools, municipalities or nations) into clear-cut confrontations that occur much less frequently in other areas of social life' (Coleman 1960). Such segmental bonding contrasts with the functional bonding which characterises much day-to-day life. Eric Dunning (1981) elaborated on this distinction and highlighted its significance within the context of domestically pacified nation-states; where the state has established an effective monopoly on the right to use physical force, sport provides one of the few occasions on which large, complex, impersonal and predominantly functionally bonded units such as cities can unite as wholes. Similarly, at an international level, sporting events such as the World Cup and the Olympics, apart from providing occasions for limited international contests, are one of the few peacetime occasions when whole nations are able regularly to unite. If tension exists between cities and nations it is possible that this can spill over into the sporting event, producing conflict between either players or spectators. What is sometimes called 'war without weapons' can erupt into something nearer to the real thing.

At the intra-urban level of scale the catchment areas of supporters of particular clubs may be strongly associated with certain cultural variables, notably religion. In some cases religion influences where people live and as a result sharply demarcated regions of sport support can be identified. In Belfast in Northern Ireland this is classically illustrated where the Springfield Road has traditionally acted as a divide between the supporters of Linfield (Protestant) and those of Belfast Celtic (Catholic) soccer clubs. With the demise of the latter club, loyalties are now divided between Linfield and Glasgow Celtic (Table 2.1). In such cases sport serves to reinforce other cultural and geographic loyalties. Exactly the same thing happens at a regional scale. In the case of *pelota* in northern Spain and south-west France, the geographical distribution of the sport serves to reinforce the Basque culture as a visible feature of the landscape.

Place pride

Allied closely to place attachment is place pride. This is often generated by success in sport, be it by a national team or small-town high-school squad. At the city limits of many small American towns the welcoming billboard often proclaims the place's sporting achievements, however modest (Figure 2.4a). As with expressions of national loyalty (revealed in many countries through the display of national flags), such sport-induced

Table 2.1 Religion, location and football team support in West Belfast

Area	Per cent Catholic	Per cent supporting	
		Glasgow Celtic	Linfield
Clonard	98	73	0
Turf Lodge	99	63	0
Ladybrook	90	11	0
Shankhill	1	0	74
New Barnsley	12	11	63

Source: Boal 1970.

(a)

tokens of localism seem frequently to be spontaneous and unforced, though this is not to say that they are totally unattached to, and discouraged by, commercial as well as municipal interests. Such landscape artifacts are highly visible in some countries. In the USA, sport success is the most frequently cited form of culture found on the billboards or welcoming signs on the edges of US towns and cities (Zelinsky 1988). The fact that they are absent in others (e.g. Britain) is one small way in which national ideology acts as a filter through which the global phenomenon of modern sport passes, before appearing in the vernacular landscape. However, this does not mean that place pride through sport in the UK is not projected visually: it is often advertised in graffiti which acts either as a territorial marker indicating the spatial extent of a club's support, an assertion of power within its territory, or a defiant gesture by 'away' fans who wish to assert prestige in another club's territory (Figure 2.4b). Sometimes

(b)

Figure 2.4 The welcoming roadside sign and graffiti say the same thing: (a) The welcoming sign at Solon, Iowa, presents the success of the local high-school sports teams; (b) Graffiti on a wall in Stoke-on-Trent asserts the unlikely superiority of Stoke City over clubs from Merseyside.

such place pride can erupt into a kind of ritualised violence by representatives of either city or national teams.

Whether on billboard, bumper sticker or graffiti, the sentiment is essentially the same, namely pride in place through sport. The concern in Europe over the problem of football hooliganism has highlighted the presence of a perverse, rabid sense of localism, regionalism and nationalism. Consider, for example, the views of these self-confessed hooligans, taken from the early 1980s' work of David Robins (1981, 109):

> I am fighting for Darlington. Not the team – the town. I feel proud of the town and I want to defend it from people who say it's not very good

> I won't take verbal when we go away. I won't take it from a northerner. I followed this club for *years* ... and I'm not going away with the team for some dirty northern ponce to spit over me. If he spits all over me I'll cut his head with a wine-glass ... You do it for the reputation of the club

According to Williams *et al.* (1984), 'increasingly to be identifiably *English* at an England game on the continent is, for young fans, to experience the collective camaraderie ... and the power of an image which has most local fans and passersby recoiling in terror'. Indeed, at the local level it is the supporters who have become more the representatives of the areas the clubs are named after since few of the players can these days be described as 'home grown' (Pratt and Salter 1984).

Fan behaviour such as that described above is basically a masculine celebration of community, displaying strong forms of local identification and an equally strong tendency to denigrate other (opposing) communities by means of songs, chanting, graffiti, etc. It has therefore been suggested that solutions to the football hooligan 'problem' might work towards providing in such youths and young men 'forms of *local* identification, attachment and integration which are of a qualitatively different kind from those generated in the male-dominated public domain of the street' (Williams *et al.* 1984). Such forms would include the experiences and values of all community members and would emphasise knowledge of, and respect for, other cultures and other communities.

'Local memory' is a concept used by geographers Euan Hague and John Mercer (1998) to show how a sports club can be a source for what they term 'geographical memory'. For many people, they note, Raith Rovers, the local Scottish League football club in the town of Kirkaldy, 'is the prime *geographical* text of Kirkaldy'. Stories about the club are passed down from generation to generation. Being rooted in place, these are geographical memories, Raith Rovers triggering other memories of friends living in Kirkaldy. Stories of matches and cup wins are important parts in the construction of geographical memories. Such affection for place has been called 'topophilia' (Tuan 1974). Sports places provide a potent source of affection. Different senses – mainly sight but also smell, sound and nostalgia – contribute to a positive sense of place.

However, a relatively short step away from intense feelings of localism, regionalism and nationalism engendered by sports is the attitude of racism which sport can also encourage. Racial superiority can easily be read into sporting performance (one recalls the infamous Berlin Olympics as a 'laboratory' for the testing of racial 'theories') and in some countries – recently Italy – the football stadium is today the most easily observable forum for racial abuse – black players being regularly insulted from the stands and terraces. Even more sinister is the use of football stadiums as recruiting grounds by the fascist National Front and British Movement, though the success, in Britain, of the 'Kick Racism out of Football' campaign and related legal enactments cannot be denied.

Success in sport is not necessarily associated with violent outcomes. When Sunderland FC somewhat surprisingly beat the favourites, Leeds United, in the English FA Cup Final in 1973 there followed a period of increased industrial output and a reduction in the crime rate in the Wearside town. Not only had unfashionable Sunderland 'blown a raspberry' at the soccer establishment; place pride had been generated too. As one local resident put it, 'a not particularly glamorous town feels more proud of itself after a win of this sort' (quoted in Derrick and McRory 1973). Hague and Mercer (1998) recorded similar responses following Raith's victory in Scotland's Coca-Cola Cup in 1995. One of their respondents noted that 'when Raith Rovers won the Coca-Cola Cup it was like a fairy tale. It put Kirkaldy on the map for a while ... Everybody in Kirkaldy knew about the game and the result.' Sport had provided a kind of glue that had bonded the community together. A rather more quantitative assessment of the impact of soccer on the community showed that when São Paulo's most popular team won, production in the city increased by over 12 per cent, but when it lost the number of accidents increased by over 15 per cent (Lever 1981). Place pride is also boosted by sports success at the international level. The success of national teams or individuals in, say, the World Cup or the Olympics can generate 'psychic income' to residents back home. Brazil's first World Cup victory, for example, possessed great social and national significance, much of which was encapsulated by one of Brazil's finest players, Garrincha:

> While anyone could admire his football, Brazilians saw in his play the affirmation of Brazilian values over European and also popular values over those of the élite. For many people in Brazil there was no better sight than a six-foot, blond, superbly-coached and tactically-trained

European defender on a rigid calorie controlled diet being made to look like a fool by the devastating artistry of an undernourished, anarchic black winger with two twisted legs who would never have got past the medical exam in European soccer. In class terms, Garrincha was the semi-literate who could get by on his wits and cunning, able to put one over on the rich and the more powerful (Humphrey 1986).

On the outskirts of dozens of nondescript Texas towns, the resident boosters have erected billboards, usually artless but large, proudly announcing 'The Home of the Hutto Hippos' or 'Entering Panther Country'. Whenever possible these include a list of historical successes – 'Class 2A Bidistrict Champions 1964, State Semi-finals 1965' – painted in over the years like entries in an almanac's vintage seasons in the town's career. Positioned strategically in the last open curve of a farm market road, these handmade brags are as often as not the sole claim or welcome encountered on the threshold of a Texas town. Even approaching Gonzales, where the first battle of the Texas Revolution took place, the only notice posted anywhere by the townsfolk reads: 'This is Apache Territory, District Champions 1958.' It is a truer measure of their values than art or war or politics: the way they choose to declare themselves.

In most small Texas towns there are few enough ways to excite one's passion or ambition, to assert oneself. Life is bounded and determined by the land and the weather and the distant impositions of the government and God – both about equally predictable and final – which means life is physical and seasonal, elemental, stoical. It is commonplace by definition or as common, that is, as life in a place such as Texas can be. Full of their own rich yearnings, Texans have always seemed to struggle hardest against ordinariness, and for more than half a century now the basic stage and focus for that struggle has been on high-school football fields.

High-school football is the one thing that can both unify a Texas town and set it apart from the hundreds of other similarly rural and unremarkable Texas towns. Places like Nederland, Junction, or Hull-Daisetta can easily escape the notice of Rand McNally, for instance, but in Texas they are powers to be reckoned with a thousand miles away, denounced by far-flung boosters and politicians, spied on and worried about. Their success at high-school football is their one claim to recognition by the larger world, and thus it provides the clearest reflection of their own sense of worth. It is for many Texans the best indication of a town's vitality and pride, its sense of identity, and no one is more conscious of this than the men most concerned with the life of the town.

Vignette I High-school football in Texas (Source: Winningham and Reinert 1979). Writing in the 1920s in their classic book *Middletown*, the Lynds noted that it was the high-school basketball team which united the people of the town better than anything else. In rural, small-town Texas, the high-school football team serves the same purpose.

Sports undeniably foster localism, regionalism and nationalism. To this we can add an alternative interpretation which seeks to expose the ideological nature of sports when practised at the representative level. Local, regional and national attachments can be viewed as essentially conservative sentiments which divide the working class on the basis of place attachment, substituting place loyalty and hence reinforcing existing power relations in society. Although some sports like tennis or sailing are relatively class-exclusive, support for 'our team' may blur class differences in many sports. This view is elaborated by Young (1986, 10), as follows:

> In a conflict-ridden society in which each is the natural enemy of similarly situated competitors for jobs, land and resources, sexual access, and other scarce items, in which there are class antagonists and ethnic opponents, in which ever more people are impoverished, such solidarity activity is important to the masking of these antagonisms. When the home team beats the putative enemy with skill, genius, heroic acts or with deceit or trickery and guile, great delight, joy, and enthusiasm emerge and can be shared with those-present-on-our-side. Class antagonisms and ethnic hatred as well as gender and national hostilities with real conflicting interests can be assimilated to the harmless competition of sports. The structures of privilege, inequality, and oppression are left intact by such use of solidarity moments in sports.

Sport may be more appropriate than other forms of civic display in the fostering of community consensus (from the perspective of society's 'dominant classes') because of its serialised nature. Unlike many modern rituals such as coronations, carnivals and fairs, sport has an element of regular succession. Sport has a season and its contests are more continuous than other rituals. However, the representation of communities by sports teams and clubs may not necessarily have been authorised by the communities concerned. Alan Ingham (1987) and his co-workers have suggested that the 'community interest' may have been 'tutored' by big business and real estate speculators; I will return to this subject in Chapter 5. Indeed, the view that the sports team and the stadium provide a positive force for community life might be contested by that which sees it as 'a magnet for vice' and for the leading of 'indulgent and unproductive lives'. Negative aspects of sports are discussed further in Chapter 6.

Place, politics and sport

I have noted how, according to some observers, the ideological nature of sport seeks to defuse revolutionary fervour by uniting classes together in support of a place (represented by a sports team) or by promoting a place's political image or ideological integrity. I must stress that it is

Clemson: A Visual Vignette Clemson, South Carolina, is a small place of about 12,000 people, a university of about 16,000 students and a football stadium accommodating about 85,000 spectators. Clemson means football. The 'Tigers' were national champions in 1981 and the town lets you know this in no uncertain terms. In the 1970s the university, along with its athletic programme, adopted the now ubiquitous Tiger paw logo. This image adorns the Clemson townscape. Sport's contribution to pride in place can rarely have been so blatant yet it is not entirely untypical of the American scene. The Tiger paw logo is a popular icon of a latter day religion.

Main Street contains two of Clemson's three sports shops. Mr Knickerbocker claims to be the 'World's largest supplier of Clemson gifts'.

The Tiger paw adorns ... the local bank

... and the forecourt leading to Long John Silver's (fish restaurant).

politically defined places such as cities and nations which most frequently
define sports teams, and it is rare to find such teams representing physical–geographic or multi-national cultural units (though exceptions, such
as Ireland in rugby and the West Indies in cricket, do exist). Sports teams
most often represent either the nation state or the so-called 'local state'
(i.e. aspects of government at the sub-national scale such as local authorities). It is therefore difficult to understand the view, often expressed, that
sport is in some way independent of politics.

Consider briefly the more explicit ways in which sport and politics are
related. The impact of politics on sport (and vice versa) may occur as part
of either the state's external or internal relationships. If viewed as part of
its external relations or activities, i.e. its dealings with other states, sport
has an obvious role in international relations. In fact such sport–political
relations are not new. The ancient Greek Pan-Hellenic festivals which
contained sport-like activities, were vehicles for popularity, prestige and
power for city states; medieval jousting and tournaments kept national
armies in fighting trim; in the early nineteenth century the German Turner
and Slav *sokol* movements combined sport and politics in order to encourage Pan-German and Pan-Slav movements respectively; the late nineteenth century saw the genesis of the modern Olympic movement with de

Coubertin seeing the Games as promoting global peace and international co-operation, though paradoxically the Olympics may have only served to further politicise sports (e.g. through national teams, flags, anthems); and sport as a political tool was also stressed by the early twentieth-century workers' sports movement, which sought to develop working-class political consciousness through sport.

When the Nazis came to power in Germany, considerable tension existed about what type of body-cultural practices should be undertaken in schools and colleges. Many favoured the German style of Turner gymnastics which put emphasis on strengthening the individual in mainly rhythmic gymnastics. It was explicitly stated that this would prepare the youth of Germany for the next war. Sports Historian Arnd Krüger (1999) noted that PE students demonstrated their preference by ripping up stadium cinder tracks and planting oak trees in their place. For them, the track had been the instrument of British influence, the stopwatch a symbol of the pressure on individual athletes to race against each other rather than work together for the betterment of the German 'race'. The German oak stood for the Turner tradition of nationalistic gymnastics – or paramilitary training. This example demonstrates, in a small way, the political nature of body culture actually in the landscape.

Arguably the most significant site of the sport–politics nexus was at the Berlin Olympics of 1936. Initially Hitler was opposed to holding the Olympics in Germany but accepted them once he recognised the political propaganda that could be gained from them. Only 6 weeks after the PE students had planted the oak trees, they were uprooted and the track returned to its former use. Training young people for sports would lead to athletic success and be used to demonstrate the superiority of Aryanism. As the Olympics approached, the urban landscape of Berlin was sanitised in order to present a situation of normalcy during the period of the Olympics. Antisemitic leaflets and posters were temporarily banned, racist graffiti replaced with welcoming signs. The apparent benefits of National Socialism were presented to the world (Mandell 1971, Rürup 2000). In Riefenstahl's movie, 'Olympia', Hitler was normalised and presented as an enthusiastic sports spectator. Today nations continue to use success in sport as a means of propaganda, demonstrating the advantages of particular political systems over potential rivals or to achieve diplomatic recognition. I return to this subject in greater detail in Chapter 4.

A second way of viewing sport and politics is in some ways more contentious and refers to the state's internal activities. The state, be it national or local, clearly acts as a provider of sport. Many nation states today have Ministers of Sport and the state often plays a significant role in overall national expenditure on sport. The classic case is perhaps the former German Democratic Republic where at least 2 per cent of the Gross National Product was said to be spent on sport. At the local level, public expenditure by local authorities in Britain in 1982–1983 on sport-related activities amounted to about 30 per cent of the £836 million spent on all leisure activities (Kirby 1985). In many nations local municipalities may own major facilities such as stadiums and sports halls.

Place and performance

So far I have been largely concerned with the way in which performance in sports affects places, principally in the ways people respond to their team's success, or even simply to its presence. We now change the emphasis somewhat and consider ways in which place is important in influencing performance. Two approaches are adopted: first, by showing how the physical environment of a place may possess unique characteristics which influence sporting performance and, second, by looking at the apparent differences in performances by sports teams at 'home' and 'away' locations.

Although it will be stressed in Chapter 7 that there has been a gradual tendency towards a neutralisation of the effects of the physical environment on sports, it cannot be denied that physical factors continue to greatly affect – and in some cases determine – sporting events. Because the various elements of the physical environment – slope, relief, soil, vegetation, weather, etc. – vary geographically, specific places may be more affected (or affected in different ways) by the physical environment than others. This section considers some typical examples.

Regional differences in the physical environment clearly influence sporting performances. Temperature, wind, soil, rainfall and relief (to name a few factors) vary from place to place and affect sporting outcomes in a variety of ways (Lobozewicz 1981, Thornes 1977). Among the most dramatic influences of place on performance the 1968 Olympic Games held at high altitude in Mexico City. Spectacular performances were achieved in the sprints and jumps with extremely modest achievements in the longer distance running events. Events held at altitude are affected by a 7 per cent reduction in aerobic power and reduced wind resistance (Mackay 1976). In events such as long-distance running or cycle races, hot conditions can progressively produce dehydration, mineral loss and rising body temperatures. In events lasting several hours performance can be seriously impeded under such conditions. The London Olympic marathon of 1908 and the British Empire Games marathon of 1954 are well-known examples. In places where the opposite temperature conditions exist, speed and power events are performed poorly since human muscle functions best at 40–41°C.

Some sports require specific weather (and hence locational conditions) before they can even take place. Sailing and skiing are obvious examples. In other cases particular locations are more likely than others to experience weather conditions that will interfere with sport, either causing performances to be affected or influencing the comfort of the spectators (Figure 2.5). Such sports include outdoor tennis, football and field hockey. In Canada it has been shown that maximum attendance at tennis and golf course occurs when the temperature is 24°C (Paul 1972). Some places may be affected by changeable weather conditions that influence some competitors and not others (Thornes 1977). In golf, for example, players starting on a clear morning would have an obvious advantage over those struggling over a windy, rain-swept course later in the day. Any sport taking place in an area too small to allow all participants to take part at the same time is open to the possibility of a change in the weather affecting the participants unequally. But some places are more likely to experience such conditions than others. Ideally, many sports would be best

---

Although wind is a factor at all outdoor stadia, Atlanta and Fulton Co. Stadium experience conditions of prevailing home run weather, the result of beneficent breezes which constitute normal conditions for the areas and are associated with diurnal circulation patterns. These patterns are typically discussed at length in introductory physical geography courses. Because the winds involved are diurnal, home run weather is a diurnal phenomenon at both parks.

Atlanta, in addition to being the highest park in major league baseball (1050', 320 m), has live air. During the evening hours, air at higher elevations cools more rapidly than does air at lower elevations. Cooler, heavier air begins to flow downslope by gravity during the evening hours (cold air drainage), the evening breeze flowing from the higher elevations of the Appalachians toward the coastal plain. As it moves downslope, it passes through Atlanta, and over Atlanta Stadium, creating a steady breeze which favours hitters. The effects of home run weather at Atlanta can best be appreciated when player performance is considered. Two players, former Braves second baseman, Dave Johnson, and third baseman, Bob Horner, have benefited profoundly from Atlanta's home run weather.

Johnson hit 43 home runs while playing for the Braves during the 1974 season. This figure is more than double the number he hit while playing for other teams. To point out the effects of Atlanta home run weather on Johnson's performance, 29 of those 43 home runs were hit in Atlanta, in night games. Horner became an instant celebrity during his rookie season of 1978 when he hit 32 home runs in just 89 games. This greatly endeared him to the home town fans. If one was to project Horner's performance based upon 81 home dates and all games at night, he would be predicted to average about 38 home runs a year. However, if all games were played at night in Atlanta, he could conceivably produce 76 home runs a year.

Vignette 2 Home run winds (extracted from Gillman 1982).

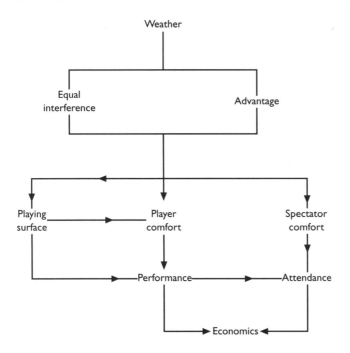

Figure 2.5 The effects of weather on sports (adapted from Thornes 1977).

undertaken on 'weatherless' days, a condition to which sports bureaucrats and planners seem to aspire (see Chapter 7).

It is not only a place's relief, climate and weather characteristics that may affect sporting outcomes. Soil type will influence the degree of bounce of a baseball or cricket ball, for example. It has been shown that the degree of bounce, registered by using a standard test of dropping a cricket ball on to the pitch from a height of 5 metres, varies directly with the percentage clay content of the soil. 'Thus, the pitches at Adelaide, Melbourne and Sydney, all with over 45 per cent clay, are classed as very fast. Brisbane with 73 per cent clay is exceptionally fast. In contrast, Nottingham and Leeds have been said to be moderately fast and Manchester easy paced' (Morgan 1976).

It has been shown by Shaw (1963) that a number of physical geographic factors influenced the games of the 1962 baseball World Series. Not only did each of the factors discussed above contribute to particular results but so did the micro-geographic surface features of individual pitches. For example, shots deflected by pebbles on the pitch can cost a team the game and the series! Physical geography obviously has great potential in the study of sports. Of course, place is also important in the effect it has on performance when considered from an economic perspective. Because economic, as well as physical, conditions vary from place to place we would expect levels of economic development to be associated with certain variations in sports performance. Likewise, we would expect different places to 'produce' differing quantities of superior sports performers, although this is not caused by climatic difference as Chapter 4 will show.

It will be obvious to followers of sport that in many team events a 'home field advantage' exists in which the home team is at an advantage over the opposition (Edwards 1979, Schwartz and Barsky 1977). Study any set of results involving top-level teams and more often than not home wins are found to occur more frequently than away wins. This seems to be common at both national and international levels and, in Britain, seems to have existed since the earliest days of the English Football League (Pollard 1986). Obviously, not all home teams win but as Table 2.2 clearly shows, away wins are much less frequent than those at home. In soccer in England and Wales, home wins tend to be about two-and-a-half times as common as away wins, though the ratio in Scotland is nearer one-and-a-half. In addition, point or goal scores tend to be bigger for home winners than away winners. This appears to be widely typical of North American professional and college teams and for British professional soccer and rugby teams (at least), details of which are shown in Table 2.2. These kinds of results are found in many other studies. For example, in over 6,000 European Cup soccer games involving four nations it was found that, on average, playing at home created an advantage of 0.47 goals per game or about one goal in six. In US gridiron football, on the other hand, the home advantage is thought to be about one point in twelve (Stefani 1985).

Some evidence also exists to show that the probability of winning forms a clear gradient according to distance from the home team's arena or city.

Table 2.2 Goals and points scored and conceded in American and British football

| | | Points/goals scored | |
		Home winners	Away winners
349 professional football	For	27.03	25.45
games, USA	Against	12.29	13.97
577 college football games,	For	30.25	26.84
USA	Against	11.13	12.95
600 Football League soccer	For	2.63	1.92
games, UK	Against	0.55	0.59
310 Southern League soccer	For	2.78	2.27
games, UK	Against	0.55	0.65
501 Rugby League games,	For	22.70	18.50
UK	Against	8.70	9.20

Sources: Edwards 1979 and Webb 1982.

This relationship is shown in Figure 2.6 for five university basketball teams in Philadelphia. It reveals that the proportion of home wins declines progressively with distance away from the home campus (A), taking in a neutral arena within Philadelphia (B), neutral courts outside the city (C) and finally in opponents' home courts (D). In British and French soccer it has been shown that 'local derby' games are less likely to produce a home advantage than in the matches played against teams who have travelled a greater distance to compete (Pollard 1986). Ravenel (1997) has shown that visiting teams located within 150 kilometres of their opponents were more likely to achieve a victory than those located further away (Table 2.3).

How are we to explain the undoubted presence of a home field advantage, especially in team sports? In part it might be thought to derive from certain aspects of territoriality, i.e. the identification with a specific place. After all, the home team will be more familiar than the opposition with the micro-geography of the field, the various locational cues like the billboards and architecture surrounding it, and even the actual size of the pitch, which can vary in sports like soccer and baseball. These are not the only kinds of possible explanations, however. Others might include the tiring effects of travelling to an away game for the visiting team, the bias of the referee in favour of the home team, and the social effect of a home audience, constantly reminding them that the team is representing a particular place. This final factor seems particularly plausible when differ-

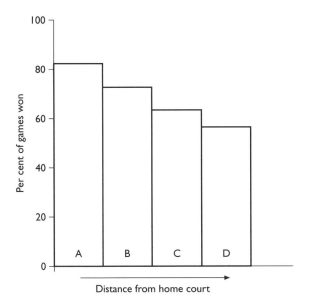

Figure 2.6 Percentage of games won and distance from home court. Big Five Basketball, 1952–66. Out-of-town opponents only (source of data: Schwartz and Barsky 1977).

Table 2.3 The 'derby effect' in French soccer 1945–1994

Location of visiting team	% of victories for visiting team
<150 km	25.1
150–400 km	20.5
400–800 km	19.0
>800 km	16.0

Source: Ravenel 1997.

ent kinds of sports and arenas are taken into account. An interesting American study by Barry Schwartz and Stephen Barsky (1977) tried to identify the key variables 'explaining' the home field advantage. They examined a number of sports, namely baseball, ice hockey, football and basketball, and found (contrary to some people's expectations) that the home advantage was least visible in the very sport which was most likely to have the least uniform playing areas and conditions, i.e. baseball. It was in ice hockey rinks and on basketball courts – where conditions are almost the same everywhere – that the home field advantage was most marked. This led Schwartz and Barsky to conclude that the home advantage was socially determined and was at its most pronounced when the social congregation before which a team performs is at its most intimate. They argued that sports events provide a forum for the local community to celebrate its existence. Subsequent studies have suggested that the home advantage will be greatest for well-established teams in small cities and in arenas located within the central city, since these will generate most intense local identification and pride. Two of the most placeless of sports (i.e. those where the micro-geography of the arenas are virtually the same), basketball and ice hockey, have been shown to possess the most substantial home field advantages (Schwartz and Barsky 1977). It has also been revealed that the home advantage is significantly greater in baseball games played in domed stadiums, playing environments where the effects of physical environment have been most neutralised (Zeller and Jurkovac 1989). The enhanced home advantage in domed stadiums was attributed to the closeness and involvement of the crowd.

A final example of the home advantage can be noted in the context of international sports. First, at European level it has been found that home advantage in Europe was, broadly speaking, less among clubs in north-west Europe; countries bordering the Mediterranean had much greater levels of home advantage. This was attributed, somewhat stereotypically, to the excessive passion and pressure from fans in those parts of Europe (Ravenel 1997). The cool and calm crowds of northern Europe were argued to have less influence on the outcome of a game than the passionate Latins of the south. As with the different effects of the crowd in different kinds of arenas, noted earlier, the crowd is still given great significance at the international scale.

A second international example of the home advantage is given by an examination of the Winter Olympics. In these games not only do teams and individuals represent nations (rather than cities) but some sports (e.g. ice skating) are judged on the basis of subjective judgement – that is, the awarding of points by judges rather than, say, the scoring of goals or points by players. Likewise, other sports (e.g. downhill skiing) include participants who are familiar with local conditions, whereas ice rinks are relatively homogeneous. British researchers sought to establish the home advantage in the Winter Olympics from 1908–1998 (Balmer *et al.* 2001). They discovered that when events were grouped according to whether they were subjectively assessed by judges or not, significantly greater home advantage was observed in the subjectively assessed events. That judges were scoring home competitors disproportionately higher than away competitors could, in part at least, be explained by the influence of the crowd. As expected, in sports with variable local conditions, a familiarity with local conditions was shown to have some 'home' effect, notably in alpine skiing. The proportion of points won by 'hosting nations' was least (though still present) in other events, typified by ice hockey.

Some final caveats need to be made at this stage in this review of home advantage studies. First, it may be that while the home advantage is present for most of the time, in decisive, end-of-season games, a paradoxical home field disadvantage exists. This hypothesis is based on the view that a supportive audience may have excessive expectations in key games which actually interfere with the execution of sufficiently skilful responses from players (Baumeister and Steinhilber 1984). The evidence for this hypothesis is mixed at the present time (and further research will be needed to test its validity). A second caveat is that the extent of a home advantage in non-team sports such as boxing, tennis or golf remains unclear. At the international level, national support may replace the local support found in most of the events that have been scrutinised by scholars involved in home-advantage studies. National identification with a particular competitor may be as potent as that at the local level. Finally, all studies of the home advantage have focused on top-class sports. It remains to be seen whether the same patterns exist as we move 'down' the sports hierarchy into amateur, high-school and recreational sports activities.

The kinds of findings described above strongly suggest that place is of importance in team sports. Whether such a fundamental geographical attribute as territoriality explains this in total is, of course, debatable, but it does seem to go part of the way towards explaining a common occurrence at sporting events.

Cross-cultural voyeurism

International sport remains one of the few live forms in which large numbers of people actually encounter and witness the feats of those of other lands. It seems that people have an almost innate fascination with the opposing team – especially if it comes from a foreign territory. In the late nineteenth century this curiosity about people from 'strange' places was satisfied to some extent by the emergence of international sports. For the cultural élites of the 1850s onward the same need was satisfied by upper-class cultural societies and organisations based on ethnography, anthropology and geography. The Royal Geographical Society was the place at which travellers' tales exposed the mysteries of far-away places with strange sounding names and where social élites vicariously encountered the exotica of Africa, Asia, North America and the European periphery. Popular and mass culture formalised its means to this end through the international exhibition (or exposition) and the Olympic Games (MacAloon 1981). At the 1904 Games in St. Louis, 'anthropology days' were held at which 'representatives from various peoples considered primitive and worthy of observation' (Mrozek 1983) were put into competition with one another. The organisers had expected the 'noble savages' to achieve outstanding performances in events which they had never encountered before. They were disappointed when they discovered that, according to Western norms, their performances were poor. This may have represented the apogee of the association of special sports with particular racial groups (an association for which a residual affection lingers on among some sports fans). Arguably, the early and continuing appeal of the Olympics is based in part, at least, on the continuing tradition of popular ethnography. At the 1984 Olympics in Los Angeles American television producers subconsciously recognised this by superimposing 'educational' captions describing, in an albeit ethnocentric way, individual countries as their teams marched into the Olympic Stadium. For example, Finland was described as being in northern Europe, as long, but not as wide, as Idaho.

Further reading

The geographical bases of sport can be followed further by reading Philip Wagner (1981), 'Sport: Culture and Geography'. A seminal British study by Ronald Frankenberg (1957), *Village on the Border*, explores the role of football (as well as religion and politics) in a small Welsh village; while, in a quite different way, football in small-town Texas is evocatively described – and illustrated with wonderful photographs – in Geoff Winningham and Al Reinert (1979), *Rites of Fall: High School Football in Texas*. Sport and a sense of place is dealt with in John Bale, *Landscapes of Modern Sport* (1994). Place attachment and its perversion into hooliganism is stressed in

Gary Armstrong, *Football Hooliganism*. Arguably the best book on weather and sport is the (hard to find) German language translation of the Polish original by Tadeusz Lobozewicz (1981), *Meteorologie im Sport*. There are a huge number of studies of the home field advantage. See, for example, the overview by John Edwards, 'The home advantage', in Jeffrey Goldstein (ed.) (1979), *Games and Play: Social and Psychological Perspectives*.

Chapter 3

The growth and globalisation of sports

The purpose of this chapter is to trace the geographical development of sport from its folk-game prototypes to its modern, global form. I first want to show how the antecedents of modern sport were regionally differentiated and possessed different characteristics from modern sports. The decline of folk-games was paralleled by the emergence of modern sports and local activities were replaced by national and later international organisations (bureaucracies) whose function was to control and administer them. In other words, the spatial margins of modern sports have been progressively extended away from the core areas at which they originated.

From the folk-game antecedents, modern achievement sport has emerged as a global system. The international diffusion of sport was associated with industrialisation and colonialism. Modern sport is, in many ways, a mirror of these two developments and the second half of this chapter explores aspects of the internationalisation of the sports ethos.

Folk origins

Regionally specific indigenous body cultures which can be described as folk games existed (and to some extent continue to exist) throughout the world. Dunning and Sheard (1979) have identified a number of character-istics of folk games that readily distinguish them from modern sports. These properties are shown in Table 3.1 and apply mainly to European pre-industrial games. This is a useful introductory categorisation but the extent to which it applies to non-Western games in tribal societies is debat-able. For example, fixed limits clearly existed for the ball games (played on stone courts) during the Mayan civilisation, and for some of the running tracks used by native Americans. It should also be noted that Table 3.1 presents a simple dualism and fails to allow for a 'third way', as in Eich-berg's approach noted in Chapter 1. It nevertheless provides a basic start-ing point for contrasting the 'pre-modern' with the 'modern'.

Folk games certainly seem to have originated in certain 'culture hearths', diffusing away from these cultural cores, and thereby modifying

Table 3.1 The structural properties of folk games and modern sports

Folk games	Modern sports
Diffuse, informal organisation implicit in the local social structure	Highly specific, formal organisation, institutionally differentiated at the local, regional, national and international levels
Simple and unwritten customary rules, legitimated by tradition	Formal and elaborate written rules legitimated by tradition worked out pragmatically and legitimated by rational-bureaucratic means
Fluctuating game pattern; tendency to change through long-term and, from the viewpoint of the participants, imperceptible drift	Change institutionalised through rational-bureaucratic channels
Regional variation of rules, size and shape of balls, etc.	National and international standardisation of rules, equipment, etc.
No fixed limits on territory, duration or numbers of participants	Played on a spatially limited area with clearly defined boundaries, within fixed time limits, and with a fixed number of participants, equalised between the contending teams
Strong influence of natural and social differences on the game pattern	Minimisation, principally by means of formal rules, of the influence of natural and social differences on the game pattern: norms of equality and 'fairness'
Low role differentiation (division of labour) among the players	High role differentiation (division of labour) among players
Loose distinction between playing and 'spectating' roles	Strict distinction between playing and spectating roles
Low structural differentiation; several 'game elements' rolled into one	High structural differentiation; specialisation around kicking, throwing, use of sticks, etc.
Informal social control by players themselves within the context of the ongoing game	Formal social control by officials who stand, as it were, 'outside' the game and who are appointed and certificated by central legislative bodies and empowered, when a breach of the rules occurs, to stop play and impose penalties graded according to the seriousness of the offence
High level of socially tolerated physical violence; emotional spontaneity; low restraint	Low level of socially tolerated violence; high emotional control; high restraint
Generation of relatively open and spontaneous form of pleasurable 'battle excitement'	Generation of more controlled and 'sublimated' form of 'battle excitement'

continued

Table 3.1 continued

Folk games	Modern sports
Emphasis on physical force as opposed to skill	Emphasis on skill as opposed to physical force
Strong communal pressure to participate; individual identity subordinate to group identity; test of identity in general	Individually chosen as a recreation; individual identity of greater importance relative to group identity; test of identity in relation to specific skill or set of skills
Locally meaningful contests only; relative equality of playing skills among sides; no chances for national reputations or money payment	National and international superimposed on local contests; emergence of élite players and teams; chance to establish national and international reputations, tendency to standardised terrain and 'monetisation' of sports

Source: Dunning and Sheard 1979.

their form. Smith (1972), for example, basing his conclusions on anthropological evidence, suggests that the ball-play concept among indigenous North Americans spread from meso-America and in doing so assumed a variety of different forms. Another example of the diffusion of pre-industrial sport can be provided from Europe where an antecedent of modern tennis called 'cache' existed in Picardy at the end of the thirteenth century. It is suggested by Gillmeister (1981) that the game spread to Holland where it was translated as *Kaetspel*, while the English 'cat's pellet' was a popular version of the Dutch name. The similarity of the names, first recorded in Picardy, and subsequently used in Scotland, Germany, Denmark, Spain and Colombia in South America ('juego de la chaza') led Gillmeister to conclude that the early French game of cache had diffused – and in doing so changed its form – between countries and continents (Figure 3.1). Tylor (1880), regarded by many as the 'father of modern anthropology', noted that while some simple games such as wrestling or throwing a ball had grown up independently in a number of separate geographic locations, others seemed so distinct and artificial that it was unlikely that their distinctiveness could be hit upon more than once. This, of course, is a classic exemplification of diffusionism, a term which in recent years has assumed somewhat negative and even racist connotations. However, Tylor argued that certain body-cultural activities could be traced from a common geographical centre and therefore be used to provide evidence of cultural diffusion. It was suggested, for example, that games of Polynesia and New Zealand diffused from Asia; likewise 'various forms of arrow throwing or shooting games show remarkably similar terminology, from Egypt, through Polynesia and much of the New World' (Jett 1971). Variations in types of folk games that were broadly similar but

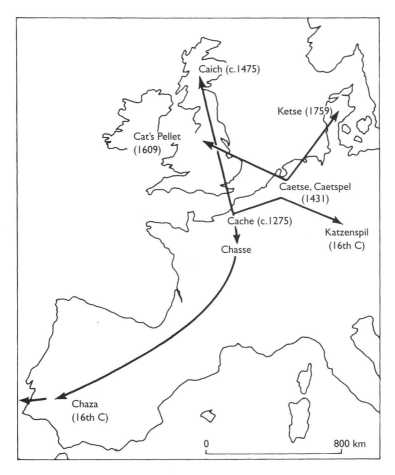

Figure 3.1 The migration of the Picardian game of cache (adapted from Gillmeister 1981).

lacked any standardised rules, any organising bureaucracy and any for-malised records meant that even if widespread and efficient international travel had existed, international competition would have been meaning-less. When, during the early colonial period, Europeans tried to compete in 'native' events, they invariably found that indigenous peoples could defeat them; when natives participated in European events, the Europeans usually won (e.g. Bale and Sang 1996). Folk body cultures and Western sports were not the same thing.

At a local scale, geographical differences were often found in pre-indus-trial sports. In England, for example, a wide variety of types of football could be found (Dunning 1971). It is clear, therefore, that before 1700 games similar in form to modern international sports such as football, hockey, cricket, lacrosse and tennis existed. This is not to say, however, that they provided the same functions. In some cases what are sports today were in earlier times essential skills, e.g. riding, skating, archery, skiing. In other cases modern sports have grown out of war-like activities such as fencing and kendo.

Folk games were still being played widely in Britain in the seventeenth and eighteenth centuries and in North America in the nineteenth. But between 1700 and 1900 their geographic specificity declined and they began to die out – though never totally so. Sport, bound by rules, precision, quantification, record-seeking and under bureaucratic control, increasingly came to mirror society at large. The transition from folk game to sport typically followed five stages, in total spanning less than a century and in some cases as little as 50 years. These phases were (a) the folk game stage, (b) the formation of clubs, (c) the establishment of a rule-making national bureaucracy, (d) the diffusion and adoption of the sport in other

---

At Llanwennog, an extensive parish below Lampeter, the inhabitants for football purposes were divided into the Bros and Blaenaus. . . . The Bros . . . occupied the high ground of the parish. They were nick-named 'Paddy Bros' from a tradition that they were descendants from Irish people. . . . The Blaenaus occupied the lowlands and, it may be presumed, were pure-bred Brythons . . . the match did not begin until about midday. . . . Then the whole of the Bros and Blaenaus, rich and poor, male and female, assembled on the turnpike road which divided the highlands from the lowlands. The ball . . . was thrown high in the air by a strong man, and when it fell Bros and Blaenaus scrambled for its possession, and a quarter of an hour frequently elapsed before the ball was got out from the struggling heap. . . . Then if the Bros . . . could succeed in taking the ball up the mountain to . . . Rhyddlan they won the day; while the Blaenaus were successful if they got the ball to their end of the parish. . . . The whole parish was the field of operations, and sometimes it would be dark before either party secured a victory. In the meantime, many kicks would be given and taken, so that on the following day the competitors would be unable to walk, and sometimes a kick on the shins would lead the two men concerned to abandon the game until they had decided which was the better pugilist. There do not appear to have been any rules. . .; and the art of football playing in the olden time seems to have been to reach the goal. When once the goal was reached, the victory was celebrated by loud hurrahs and the firing of guns, and was not disturbed until the following Christmas Day.

Vignette 3 A description of folk football in south-west Wales in the early 1880s (Dunning and Sheard 1979).

countries, (e) the formation of an international bureaucracy. It should not be assumed, however, that there was necessarily a 'seamless' merging or lack of overlap of folk and modern body cultures. The people who played folk activities cannot necessarily be assumed to have made an instant conversion to modern sports. In Africa, for example, some groups rejected modern body cultures and continued practising their own corporeal activities.

Some would suggest that in the Western world sport developed as a result of the reduction in working hours, and possibly also the emergence of the 'weekend'. However, as Theodore Zeldin (1977) points out, sports developed before working hours were reduced by law and, anyway, the working class was usually the last to participate in modern sports. Zeldin regards the emergence of sport as a reaction against the lack of free time rather than a cult associated with modern mass leisure. In similar vein Lewis Mumford (1973) suggested that perhaps sport began originally as 'a spontaneous reaction against the machine', though as we will see in Chapter 6, it has become increasingly machine-like. However, in a very general way, sport and industrialisation seem to be related. They both grew out of the changed outlook derived from the Newtonian revolution that stressed qualities that both sport and society were to embrace. As the eighteenth and nineteenth centuries progressed, bureaucracy, quantification, record breaking and the achievement principle became increasingly evident. It is these qualities, argues Allen Guttmann (1978), which characterise sports in contrast to their folk-game antecedents, though this is not to say that his widely accepted ideas have been uncontested (see, for example, Blake 1996). Additionally, time and space confinement increased in all walks of life. A time consciousness became imposed; there was a time for work and a time for leisure. In sport the growing regulation of day-to-day life was reflected in the standardisation of sports places and the imposition of specified time limits on various events. All this has been interpreted by some scholars as part of the hegemony of capitalism (Thrift 1981).

From local to national

According to Stovkis (1982), sailing and horse racing were strictly organised in seventeenth-century Holland with a specialised personnel to check violation of the rules. Other regulatory bodies existed elsewhere in sport prior to the widespread formation of clubs in team sports in the late nineteenth century. But such organisations were often set up to ensure a satisfactory basis for gambling; it was only later that the more amateur-oriented ethic of 'fair play' became the dominant reason for standardisation and hence the need for governing bodies. Prior to the nineteenth century there also existed a surprising degree of interregional, as opposed to merely intraregional, organisation and movement in sports. Horse racing was a case in point; the sports historian Dennis Brailsford (1987) has noted, for example, that in 1797 a horse based in the county of Somerset (in south-west England) competed at meetings in Dorset, Wiltshire, Worcestershire, Warwickshire, Northants and Leicestershire, all within the space of 3 months. Similar pre-nineteenth century national sporting activity also occurred in boxing and, to a somewhat more limited degree, in cricket. Of course, with the growth of the national transport network such inter-regional movement became commonplace.

Much eighteenth-century sport had been organised by private entrepreneurs who promoted contests between regional (and national) champions for what were often high financial rewards. By the mid-nineteenth century, however, their activities were being overtaken by those of the national governing bodies. A principal function of these organisations was not only to administer and arbitrate but also to uphold the amateur sports ethic which had its roots in the English universities and private schools. In Britain and North America national governing bodies grew most rapidly in number during the last quarter of the nineteenth century (Table 3.2). Associated with their growth was the emergence of national consciousness that replaced the local consciousness which had been associated with folk games. Switzerland possessed a national shooting federation as early as 1824 but this was as untypical of events on mainland Europe as were the pre-nineteenth century English organisations. The first national association was the Russian Gymnastics Society founded in 1883 (Riordan 1977), and by the end of the century many European states possessed a

Table 3.2 Early sports governing bodies in three countries

British national sports associations founded before 1870	
1750 Horse racing	1866 Athletics
1754 Golf	1866 Canoeing
1788 Cricket	1869 Swimming
1863 Football	

American national sports associations formed before 1880	
1868 Skating	1878 Swimming
1870 Horse racing	1879 Lacrosse
1871 Rowing	1879 Athletics
1875 Bowling	1879 Cricket
1876 Professional baseball	

German national sports associations formed before 1900	
1860 Gymnastics	1888 Skating
1883 Bowling	1891 Athletics
1884 Cycling	1897 Fencing
1887 Swimming	

Sources: Lewis (1968), Woeltz (1977) and others.

number of such bodies. Extremely rapid growth occurred in the development of British governing bodies into the 1900s, and at the present time shows little sign of slowing down.

The transition from folk game to sport was perhaps most dramatic when Europeans adopted and adapted a game that had been played by a native minority. Consider, for example, lacrosse (Metcalfe 1976, Vennum 1994). Until around the 1830s this was a game played by the indigenous nations of North America. The first white lacrosse club was set up in Montreal in 1839 or 1840. Rules, the vital requirement before inter-regional competition could commence, were formulated in Canada in 1867 and in the same year the National Lacrosse Association of Canada was formed. In 1868 the game took on an international aspect when the Mohawk Club of New York was formed. The US Amateur Lacrosse Association was formed in 1879 and the sport became formally internationalised with the establishment of the International Lacrosse Association in 1928. In less than 90 years an indigenous American folk game had become an international sport.

The example of football in England is similar. Here it was a case of one class rather than one ethnic group transforming a widespread native pastime. The folk games of football where village played village in a rough and tumble kind of way gradually became replaced by games between representatives of schools and universities and, in the 1850s, clubs. However, the game needed greater control and organisation; in 1863 the 'Cambridge rules' were formulated (Dunning 1971, Walvin 1975). In the same year the Football Association (so novel was such an organisation that the use of the adjective 'English' was not felt necessary) was formed and the game grew rapidly in popularity. Scottish and Welsh associations were set up in the 1870s and Irish, French, Dutch and Danish associations in the 1880s. In 1902 the International Football Federation was established to govern the sport at a global scale. A period of less than 60 years had elapsed between the folk-game stage and the formal internationalisation of what has become the world's most popular sport.

An ethnocentric overemphasis on events in Europe and North America obscures the fact that the codification and 'export' of sport was going on elsewhere in the world where a 'scientific world view' was being adopted. In Japan widespread indigenous martial and warlike pursuits were becoming sports following the Meiji restoration in 1868, of which classic examples are kendo and judo. The former had been a kind of swordsmanship that trained participants for war. The transformation of a weapon of war to a weapon for sport was encouraged by the Japanese government until the All Japan Kendo Federation was formed in 1928. The case of judo is perhaps more dramatic. Having studied the traditional Japanese martial arts and self-defence, Jigoru Kano integrated the best of these techniques into modern judo in 1882 (Hayashi 1972), at about the same time as the Europeans and North Americans were formalising many of their own folk games. In Japan Kano was establishing a ranking system (i.e. quantifying) in order to identify different exponents in judo (Harrison 1913). Twenty years after its formalisation, the sport was introduced to the USA and within 50 years it possessed an international federation.

The growth of modern sport has meant a growth in the number of individual sports. As we have seen, many possessed folk game antecedents. But others were invented from scratch. The origin of basketball, for example, can be pinpointed precisely, having been invented by J. Naismith in Springfield, Massachusetts in 1892 (Betts 1974). Likewise, volleyball was invented by W.J. Morgan in Holyoake, Massachusetts, in 1895. For these and more modern 'technosports' no folk game stage existed.

As new sports continue to grow, their acceptance as international phenomena seems to take much less time than their nineteenth-century equivalents. Trampolining is a case in point. Originally a circus act, American PE teachers and YMCA directors adapted the 'bouncing bed' for use with their gymnastics classes. After some years of research and development the 'Nissen trampoline' was patented in 1939 and subsequently produced en masse (Loken 1949). By 1948 trampolining was an official event at NCAA and AAU gymnastics meetings and by 1965 an international federation had been formed – a mere 26 years after the sport had been invented.

As sports grew and developed, their relative significance changed. New sports overtook others in popularity. In the 1870s and 1880s, for example, imported cricket was still a relatively popular sport in Canada, attracting as much media interest as indigenous lacrosse. After about 1900, however, interest in the 'home-grown' sport of ice hockey rapidly eclipsed both cricket and lacrosse, and it subsequently became Canada's national sport.

Although national associations had developed apace, the absence of any international bureaucracies before 1875 meant that international competition as we now know it could not take place because of different interpretations of rules and of amateur status. What did exist was the international sports entrepreneur who, like his national counterpart, engaged the skills of one champion against another. International sport of a private character involved considerable cash prizes. One entrepreneur, Jack Macdonald, brought the American, Deerfoot, to run for cash prizes against the best runners England had to offer. Professional scullers organised races for very high stakes. In speed skating Axel Paulsen won cash prizes in Britain, Holland, Norway, Sweden, Germany and Russia (Stovkis 1982).

In the last quarter of the nineteenth century the private ventures of the entrepreneurs were overtaken by those of the international organisations. The need to improve the regulation of international events was a prime

reason for their growth. The first sports to establish international governing bodies were the upper-class activities of yachting (1875) and horse
racing (1878). Sports which were attracting mass participation were also
controlled by people from the upper echelons of society. After all, considerable travel and international contact were required to set up such organisations, which revolved around the international social networks of the
leisured classes. Dates of formation of fifty-one international sports federations, for which data are available, are shown in Table. 3.3.

The significance of international sports bureaucracies was that the
sports system, like the economic system, had become a global system.
Standardisation of rules permitted movement internationally, the transfer
of sports personnel across national boundaries and meaningful international competition. What differences did exist in sport increasingly came
to result, not from local idiosyncrasies in the nature of sport-like activities,
but from national differences in sports ideology. Sport in Poland, Ohio,
was played according to the same rules as in Poland, Europe, but the
experience of sport in each place differed according to the national

Table 3.3 Dates of formation of 51 international sports federations

1875	Yachting	1928	Handball
1878	Horse racing	1928	Lacrosse
1881	Gymnastics	1929	Pelota
1886	Rugby Union	1931	Archery
1892	Rowing	1932	Basketball
1892	Ice skating	1933	Softball
1892	Cycling	1934	Badminton
1904	Association Football	1939	Ice yachting
1907	Shooting	1946	Boxing
1908	Swimming	1946	Water skiing
1908	Ice hockey	1947	Volleyball
1909	Cricket	1948	Rugby League
1911	Wrestling	1948	Modern pentathlon/biathlon
1912	Athletics	1951	Judo
1913	Tennis	1955	Bandy
1913	Fencing	1957	Luge
1920	Weightlifting	1959	Sub-aqua
1921	Equestrianism	1960	Netball
1922	Motor sport	1961	Ski bob
1923	Bobsleigh and tobogganing	1961	Orienteering
1923	Korfball	1962	Surfing
1924	Hockey	1965	Trampolining
1924	Canoeing	1967	Squash
1924	Roller skating	1968	Cycle polo
1924	Skiing	1970	Karate
1926	Table tennis		

Source: various, but mainly Arlott 1976.

ideological filters through which sports, their aims and their objectives, were interpreted. For example, in the USA the high school and college became a focus for top-level sport to a much greater extent than in much of Europe, where the club system evolved as the principal set-up for sport. In Britain the single-sport club contrasts with the multi-sport form of organisation more common in Europe.

Sport and innovation diffusion

The establishment of a modern sport in a particular place can be interpreted as the adoption of an innovation. Treating sports as innovations which diffused through time and across geographic space has produced at least two kinds of approach. The first is to seek general models which summarise the broad lineaments of geographical spread; the second is to look at the geographical history of sport by paying attention to the agents and agencies that carried sport to distant places and the barriers in the form of local resistance.

First, let me consider some very general patterns of sports diffusion, viewed geographically. Geographical innovation diffusion theory, based on the ideas of Swedish geographer Torsten Hägerstrand, comprises three broad ideas. First, it is assumed that innovations display a temporal and spatial pattern of adoption, rather than instantaneous transmission over space. Initially only a small number of potential adopters actually adopt the innovation. At a second stage a 'band wagon' effect is observed when the majority of adoptions occur, followed by a final period when the 'laggard' adopters finally succumb to the innovation. When plotted as a cumulative frequency curve (or adoption curve) this approximates to an S-shaped or logistic curve (Figure 3.2). A second characteristic of the theory is that the size of the adopting unit (i.e. town or country) is of importance.

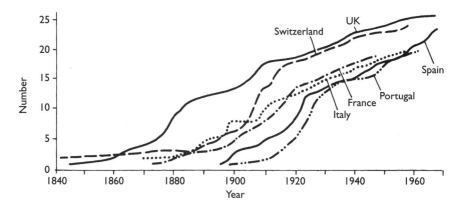

Figure 3.2 Adoption curves for Olympic sports in six European countries.

Large places adopt innovations before smaller places, the innovation 'trickling down' an economic hierarchy. A third theme is that distance from an existing adopter of the innovation acts as a basic barrier to adoption, implying some kind of imitative, contagious or 'neighbourhood' effect. Treating sport as an innovation (sport was indeed something new in time and space) means that we might expect its diffusion to exhibit evidence of both hierarchical and neighbourhood spread.

One way of identifying hierarchical diffusion of sport is to take all Olympic sports (using this collection as a surrogate for sport *per se*) and construct adoption curves for different countries over time. This is done by plotting the cumulative growth curves for the dates of formation of national associations for each Olympic sport in individual countries. Figure 3.2 illustrates the growth curves for sport (i.e. the total number of Olympic sports) for six European nations. Switzerland and the UK stand out as adopters of Olympic sports. Of course, in England certain non-Olympic sports had been adopted in the late eighteenth century and my dependence on Olympic sports therefore reduces somewhat the true relationship between sports development in the two countries. The fact remains, however, that Britain and Switzerland were the major industrial powers in Europe in the early nineteenth century. After 1860 the UK forged ahead in sport development and within 20 years had twice as many federations for Olympic sports as its nearest rival. France experienced the industrial revolution much later than Britain, some economic historians placing it as late as 1860. The development of its national sports federations was correspondingly slower. Although some sports such as football and athletics were adopted soon after the British precedent, sport *per se* was adopted much later in France. Likewise, Italy, Spain and Portugal were nations for whom industrialisation occurred at later dates, although in Italy the economy advanced more rapidly than those of the other two after the mid-1890s. A sharp upward turn in the growth curve for Italy's sport associations occurs at this time.

In the case of the Scandinavian nations there seems to be a remarkable similarity in the temporal pattern of growth of sport in a group of nations whose economic development has also run a parallel course. The notion of modern sport, interpreted here as the sum total of Olympic sports, seems undeniably to be associated with levels of economic development, interpreted in a Western sense. In American, European and Asian examples, the adoption curves for sport in the more economically advanced nations lie above those for the less economically advanced.

I now turn to the question of individual sports diffusing down an economic hierarchy. It seems that for some sports there is a marked correlation between the date of adoption (i.e. the date at which a national federation was set up) and the level of economic development. Consider, for example, the case of soccer in Europe. The first nation to adopt was

England in 1883. Figure 3.3 shows that subsequently the sport showed a tendency to 'trickle down' the European economic hierarchy: countries with large proportions of their male workforce in manufacturing at the turn of the century tended to adopt soccer earlier than those with smaller proportions. There were exceptions, Ireland being the most obvious, but the relationship between rank date of adoption and the rank level of economic development (as interpreted here) is clearly positive. Other examples of such diffusion exists and the example shown here is far from untypical (Bale 1984).

This chapter started with some examples of pre-industrial games spreading geographically from their source areas or 'culture hearths' to embrace continents and, indeed, move inter-continentally. I now return to this theme but in the context of modern sport. In Figure 3.2 it was shown that a characteristic of the temporal growth of sport was the S-shaped adoption curve. The fact that all countries did not adopt sports at the same time infers that some kind of barrier exists in the diffusion process. With pre-industrial games it seems reasonable to suggest that distance did present a fundamental barrier to the rapid spread of games, but evidence of a neigh-

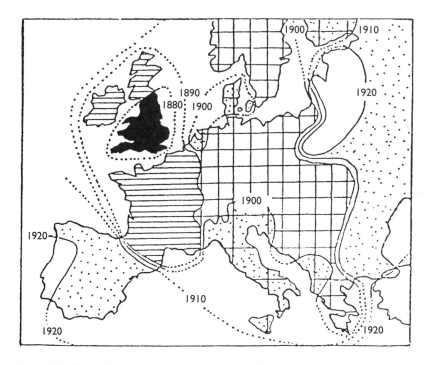

Figure 3.3 Generalised pattern of the spatial diffusion of track and field athletics in Europe (Bale 1980).

bourhood effect in modern sport is more problematic. This is because by the late nineteenth century, news about innovations such as sports could be spread rapidly – virtually instantaneously – from place to place. Yet evidence from maps showing the geographic growth of sport may be suggestive of a neighbourhood effect.

Before countries adopted sports (in the sense that they established national bureaucracies to administer them) they needed to have been made aware of them. It is the setting up of national sports federations rather than the introduction of the sport as such, that we mean by adoption in the present context. Before looking at adoption and the way in which a kind of geographical order seems to exist, I will first provide evidence for the importance of geographical proximity in the spread of knowledge of modern sports. For football in France, Holt (1981) argues that 'proximity to Britain [was] clearly important in the early years', and in its diffusion to France sport pursued 'predictable lines of penetration'. The sport entered France via the Channel port of Le Havre in 1872, adoption taking place in 1888 with the formation of a national association. Other examples can readily be cited of sports entering a country from their nearest neighbour: lacrosse from Canada to the USA, rugby from England to northern France, gymnastics from Czechoslovakia to Poland (the 'Sokol' quickly spread through all Slav countries after 1862), bullfighting from Spain to south-west France and gymnastics from Germany to Alsace in eastern France. In all these examples geographical proximity was of obvious importance in the diffusion of knowledge about particular sports. The role of proximity in subsequent diffusion to further neighbouring states remains unexplored, however.

I take track and field athletics as a sport that demonstrates the neighbourhood diffusion of sport in Europe. Track and field was another English sport, the Amateur Athletic Association (AAA) having been formed in 1880 and the Scottish AAA three years later (Figure 3.4). Two cross-channel nations, France and Belgium, had adopted it before 1890. Apart from Greece, where the first modern Olympics stimulated no doubt uncharacteristically (for that part of Europe) the early growth of modern sport, no country in eastern Europe had adopted track and field by 1900. The correlation between distance of national capital from London and the national date adoption is again positive, but not as strong as in the case off soccer (Bale 1980). By 1931 data collected by the international federation (the IAAF) suggested that one person in about 234,000 was a practising track and field athlete. Even though it was originally a British sport, by 1930 a defined 'athletics region' had emerged in Scandinavia and Germany. Sweden had over four times the continental average number of track and field athletes per head of the population. Despite the fact that the early adoption of athletics in Germany may have been retarded by the 'Turner' view that racing was fit only for animals (Mandell 1984), by 1930

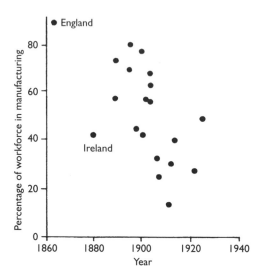

Figure 3.4 Pattern of hierarchical diffusion of football (soccer) in Europe (Bale 1980).

Germany, along with Finland and Estonia, had more than twice the continental per capita average number of athletes.

The patterns provided by the above examples are suggestive of a neighbourhood effect. Further support is provided at the national level, but before turning to examine this it is worth recording that in some cases sports changed their forms soon after crossing national boundaries: rather than being adopted they were adapted to new cultural or political ideologies. Such a phenomenon is well illustrated by the transformation of rugby into the 'gridiron' game in America (Reisman and Denny 1969), to 'Aussie' rules in Australia (Turner 1979) and to Gaelic football in Ireland where the rules were modified for explicitly political reasons (Mandle 1979). Once any new sport became established in a particular country, the diffusion process began to operate at the national level.

A pattern similar to that shown above at the international scale can be discerned at the national level. In pre-Victorian England, for example, cricket was still strongly concentrated in south-east England. The counties of Kent, Surrey, Hampshire and Essex had a quite disproportionate number of cricket clubs per head of the population, compared with the country as a whole. The south-east corner of the country tended to have at least four times as many clubs as the national per capita norm, while many of the counties to the north appeared to have less than half the national average (Bale 1981). The innovation (i.e. modern cricket) remained relatively localised until geographical interaction increased with the coming of the railway. This reduced the friction imposed by distance and the sport could grow by leapfrogging over geographic space to such an extent that in Yorkshire cricket clubs became so numerous as to exceed those in the southern counties where the modern game originated.

In the USA the modern rodeo had its origins, like English cricket, in folk culture. Early competitions grew out of work activities such as roping and riding. Not surprisingly the sport's 'culture hearth' lay in beef country and today the major area of rodeo activity lies west of the Mississippi (Jordan and Rowntree 1982). The Canadian boundary did not prevent the northward diffusion of the sport, the famous 'Calgary stampede' being established some 40 years after the first 'cowboy contests' in Nebraska. The Mexican border did, however, act as an impermeable barrier; in Mexico bullfighting established itself as a rival sport.

In 1945 the minority sport of American college soccer was still concentrated in the New England states, New York, Pennsylvania and Maryland. In the immediate post-war period college soccer diffused into the Ohio Valley area and began to penetrate the urban industrial centres of Ohio, Illinois and Indiana. By 1950 it had reached the South. Although still regionally concentrated, contagious or neighbourhood diffusion appears to have been the dominant process at work within, and from, the region in which it is most played. It is noteworthy that a major barrier to the adoption of soccer is found in Texas where by 1970 the sport had barely taken root. The reason for this seems most likely to be the tremendous emphasis placed on gridiron football in the Lone Star State, against which soccer has to overcome an almost insurmountable barrier in order to gain a footing. A similar example of a pattern of diffusion in which distance from the initial adopter and the date of adoption are clearly related is that of lacrosse in Canada. The first provincial lacrosse association was formed in 1856 in Montreal. Subsequently, adoption of the sport took place in Ottawa in 1862 before spreading to the provinces of Ontario (1863), Manitoba (1971) and British Columbia (1996). The first clubs in New Brunswick and Nova Scotia came in 1889 and 1890 respectively, and the sparsely populated province of Saskatchewan succumbed to lacrosse in the 1890s (Metcalfe 1976).

Sport diffusion as colonialism

The geographical diffusion model emphasises general patterns and stresses distance and economic potential ('size' of country or city) as barriers to the adoption of an innovation. The barriers tend to be emphasised at the expense of the carriers – and their motives. The basic barrier is seen as distance rather than a group of human beings who may be reluctant to adopt Anglo-Saxon or Western ideas. Such approaches may be read as examples of 'spatial determinism'. What is more, the operationalising of diffusion models to the growth of sport is not as simple as might be implied from the above. For example, the date of formation of a national federation as the definition of adoption may be illusory. This is because various associations may have acted as *de facto* national bureaucracies without possessing any official status. Hence, the date of formation of the first national governing body may be later than the date when the sport was first established.

Instead of looking for order in the spread of sports, an alternative approach is to focus on the individual human beings and various local institutions that were active in spreading sport from nation to nation. By doing so, the world of sport might appear more disorderly than the neat and tidy diffusion model suggests. I have already alluded to the role of businessmen in introducing football in many European countries. School-teachers and students did likewise. In looking beyond Europe, however, it is possible to see the introduction of sport as serving important social and political functions, something that is totally invisible in the patterns of diffusion noted above.

Sports historians have, in fact, documented the deeds of many of the proselytisers who took sports to many parts of the world. Scholars such as Tony Mangan (1986) have shown in illuminating detail the ways in which 'muscular Christians' took sport, along with school and Bible, to parts of Africa and Asia. The personalities and charisma of such people must frequently have been crucial in their success in planting many of the English private school sports in alien soil.

In some cases it seems likely that cultural conversion was unimportant in the carrying of a sport from one country to another. Hockey was introduced into the USA by Miss Constance Applebee, a member of the British School of Physical Education, who demonstrated it at a Harvard Summer School in 1911 (Tennyson 1959). In the case of basketball, the sport was introduced to Britain by Madame Osterberg who, having seen the game played while visiting America, introduced it to her teachers' college in London. Similarly, it could hardly be argued that the Scottish coffee planters who introduced golf to Malaya at the end of the nineteenth century (Butcher 1979) were intent on using their sport as a form of social control. More likely it created cultural exclusion rather than assimilation. The same could be said in the cases of the establishment of golf courses, tennis courts and horse racing tracks in colonial Africa and the Caribbean.

However, the notion that sport was introduced to places, both outside and inside their countries of origin, in order to divert revolutionary fervour or covertly to control potentially hostile elements in the host society is widely held. Indeed, there is explicit evidence that in some cases sport was introduced in order to teach discipline, reduce crime and encourage teamwork. This appears to have been the case with the introduction of soccer by English factory owners to Russia in the late nineteenth century (Riordan 1977). Missionaries in Kenya were quite frank about the social control function of sport. During the 1910s one wrote that:

> the game of football played in the afternoon, was played for moral benefit as much as recreational relief, ... to stiffen the backbone of these boys by teaching them manliness, good temper and unselfishness – qualities among others which have done so much to make a Britisher.
>
> (Quoted in Bale and Sang 1996, 77)

A particularly detailed study (Badenhorst and Rogerson 1985) of the introduction of sport as a means of social control indicates that, in the inter-war years, soccer was introduced on the Witwatersrand of South Africa with the aim of 'defusing Native passions', winning over 'the raw native' and 'channelling superfluous energies along proper lines'. White liberals and missionaries viewed sport as 'an agent for ameliorating the dilemmas associated with Black unemployment, crime and political radicalism'.

Such motives were undoubtedly true of many parts of the world and are a continuing element of government spending at the national scale. Stephen Jones (1987) suggests that in the inter-war period in Britain, the substantial government spending on sports facilities throughout the country served to act as an agent of social control. However, it should be pointed out that not all people, be they blacks on the Witwatersrand or alienated inner city youth in the 2000s, take part in sport. Indeed, the proportion of the national population which is interested in sports from the viewpoint of serious participation may be surprisingly small. For this reason the social control function of sport should not be overestimated. It can also be argued that participation in sport and political activism are not necessarily mutually exclusive. Finally, it might be reiterated that sports introduced to foreign countries may, in the first instance, have deliberately excluded the native population, and when indigenous elements did participate, they tended to be local social élites anyway. As with many other questions in both sport and geography, it is difficult to generalise, in this case about the role of sport *per se* as an agent of social control.

What is clear, however, is that the early years of the twentieth century witnessed the sportisation of the African body. African soldiers were being timed for cross country races as early as 1902 (Bale and Sang 1996). The role of the military, the missionary, the prison service and the plantation owner were all of importance in converting 'the African' into an image of 'the European'. The conversion or transformation of the 'native' into an athlete was a pervasive form of colonial rhetoric. During the 1920s and 1930s it became clear that another important function was served by the establishment of sport in the colonies. Natives from Africa, for

Today association football is the most popular game in the world, played in every quarter of the globe and for the most part disseminated in the recent past by British imperialist soldiers, teachers, traders and missionaries. Srinagar furnishes a delightful illustration of the introduction of soccer to a distant outpost of Empire through the medium of a self-righteous autocratic muscular missionary. The effort comprises a vignette of imperial self-confidence incorporating ethnocentricity, arrogance and determination in the face of indigenous religious customs and social habits. In 1891 Tyndale-Biscoe took a wife and a football to Kashmir. The football aroused no interest. Its reception by the assembled school was scarcely heartening as Tyndale-Biscoe recorded in his *Kashmir in Light and Shade*:

TB	This is a football.
Boys	What is the use of it?
TB	For playing a game.
Boys	Shall we receive any money if we play that game?
TB	No!
Boys	Then we shall not play that game.
Boys	What is it made of?
TB	Leather.
Boys	Take it away! Take it away!
TB	Why should I take it away?
Boys	Because it is jutha (unholy) we may not touch it, it is leather.
TB	I do not wish you to handle it. I want you to kick it ... and today you are going to learn how to kick it, boys.
Boys	We will not play that jutha game.

Despite his pupils' obduracy instruction about the pitch, positions and rules followed. The response was less than enthusiastic. As Tyndale-Biscoe has recorded: 'Before the end of school I perceived that there would be trouble, so I called the teachers together and explained to them my plans for the afternoon. They were to arm themselves with single-sticks, picket the streets leading from the school to the playground, and prevent any of the boys escaping en route. Everything was ready, so at 3 o'clock the porter had orders to open the school gate. The boys poured forth, and I brought up the rear with a hunting-crop. Then came the trouble; for once outside the school compound they thought they were going to escape; but they were mistaken. We shooed them down the streets like sheep on their way to the butchers. Such a dirty, smelling, cowardly crew you never saw. All were clothed in the long nightgown sort of garment I have described before, each boy carrying a fire-pot under his garment and so next to his body. This heating apparatus has from time immemorial taken the place of healthy exercise. We dared not drive them too fast for fear of their tripping (as several of them were wearing clogs) and falling with their fire-pots, which would have prevented their playing football for many days to come.'

The ground was reached, the sides were picked, the ball put in position, the whistle blown, and blown again. The boys were adamant. They had absolutely no intention of kicking 'an unholy ball'. Tyndale-Biscoe, for his part, had every intention that they should. The teachers were lined up with their sticks menacingly along each goal line, the boys were given five minutes to reflect on their decision. Five minutes passed. The master charged, sticks and voices raised, the game began.

Vignette 4 The introduction of soccer to Srinagar, Kashmir. Sport as an innovation was frequently resisted by indigenous peoples but the energies of the proselytisers invariably prevailed (Mangan 1986).

example, could be seen as 'raw material' for the 'mother country'. This was perhaps most notably explicated in France, where it was argued by the sports magazine *L'Auto* that explorers should be sent to colonial territories in Africa to find potential athletes for the French Olympic team (Deville-Danthu 1997). Since the early twentieth century, African athletes had competed for France in the Olympics, Boughéra El Ouafi, the 1928 Olympic marathon winner from Algeria being an example. This was achieved not only by shipping such athletes to Europe for training but in the changing of the African landscape itself. In contrast to the golf courses and tennis courts of the early colonial period that were intended primarily for the European settler class, the football fields and running tracks that were hacked out of the African landscape were also intended for the training of the native. This may have been undertaken for purposes of physical education but it also had athletic training in mind. The athletics tracks and the football fields, with their geometry and predictability, were as much symbols of colonialisation as were the mission station and the plantation. Colonisation by sport continues to this day. Global governing bodies are explicit in their colonising zeal. For example, the IAAF states that its aim is to 'help remove cultural and traditional barriers to participation in athletics'. African culture is therefore seen as something to 'remove' in order that Western forms of sport might take its place.

Evidence of resistance to the introduction of achievement sport is less apparent than one might expect (though see Vignette 4). Certain groups, such as the Maasai in Kenya, rejected conversion to Westernisation *per se*, rather than to sport in particular. In Europe, there was certainly resistance to English sports in parts of Germany and neighbouring countries that adopted non-competitive forms of gymnastics, placing more emphasis on performance than the result. The German 'Turner' movement placed emphasis on style rather than victory. An anti-sport ideology persisted in Germany into the 1930s, the gymnastic movement carrying 'volkisch' and military overtones. Eventually, however, the achievement model prevailed, even Hitler succumbing to its attractions as a form of political/national representation. Some evidence of anti-sport movements are found among some Islamic countries at the present time, yet such opposition is fiercely countered by those seeking to defy forces seen as conservatism. Hence, the role of the middle-distance runner, Hassiba Boulmerka of Algeria, can be seen as resistance – but against fundamentalism rather than a 'Western' institution (Morgan 1998).

Sport as globalisation

Globalisation includes colonialism but goes beyond it. In brief, globalisation reflects itself in sports through a huge range of activities and movements. Globalisation is the recruitment of sports workers from one country to another; it is the instant recognition of David Beckham or Michael Jordan in most countries of the world; it is the manufacture of footballs for use in Europe by young children in Pakistan; it is arriving at Singapore airport and seeing on sale souvenir scarves representing Manchester United and Bayern Munich. Sport is, in many ways, a paradigm of global culture.

Globalising changes that are occurring in sport are located and experienced at local, regional and global scales. It is possible to identify at least seven globalising tendencies in sports:

1   The increased involvement of global telecommunications companies, such as Disney and TimeWarner, in the control of the scheduling and production of sporting competitions. In addition, global corporations use sport as a marketing device and own sports franchises. For example, Disney owns ABC Sports, Eurosport, the Anaheim Angels baseball club and the Mighty Ducks ice hockey outfit.
2   The new international division of labour to produce sports equipment and apparel (e.g. sports shoes and footballs) in sweatshops in poor Asian countries, often using child labour and providing very low wages. Whereas in the mid-1960s Europe was the major producer of athletic footwear, producing about 260 million pairs of shoes, two decades later Asia was the global leader with an output of about 470 million, Europe's contribution having barely changed. While Nike's headquarters remain in the USA it has found that the optimal way of producing sports goods is to frequently switch countries if certain factories display inefficiency or poor standards (Donaghu and Barff 1990).
3   International sports organisations such as the International Olympic Committee, FIFA and the IAAF generating huge revenues by selling television rights to the Olympics, World Cup and World track and field championships to transnational corporations. I have already

alluded to the missionary zeal by which such organisations colonise new markets.

4   International sports management firms, such as the International Marketing Group, control athletes, promoting events in which their athletes compete, as well as producing the televising of those competitions. Additionally, such companies secure advertising and sponsorship for certain sports events.

5   Promoting national leagues and specific teams in markets overseas. Examples include the Chicago Bulls, Manchester United, the Brazilian national soccer team and New Zealand's All Blacks rugby team. Overseas exposure of such groups seeks to promote league and team-related merchandise.

6   The growth of foreign athletes in sports teams in most of Europe and north America. Not only has the international migration of athletes and the resulting permeability of national boundaries become more apparent, but the eligibility of athletes to compete for countries other than those of their birth has become commonplace. Consider the switch of tennis stars Greg Rusedski from Canada to the UK and Ilana Jokic from Australia (back) to Yugoslavia, and athletes Wilson Kipketer from Kenya to Denmark and Fiona May from the UK to Italy. These represent the tiny tip of a huge pyramid of 'floating' athletes for whom identity becomes somewhat blurred. Indeed, national identity becomes even more problematic when athletes may be seen representing their sponsors more than their nation.

7   The professionalisation of former amateur sports such as track and field and rowing (Wright 1999).

Achievement sport is a global phenomenon. Whereas a century ago many athletes were self-coached and half a century ago an athlete could be both a product and representative of a national system of 'sports production', today top athletes travel the world not only to compete but also to consult with doctors, coaches and take advantage of particular facilities. Top-level sport is no longer an individual activity; it has become 'totalised'.

Conclusion

Modern sport had its antecedents in the folk game prototypes of pre-industrial times. It would appear that both industrialisation and sport grew out of the changed outlook following the Newtonian revolution of the seventeenth century. Sport was no exception to the many aspects of culture affected by the desire for precision, quantification and the quest for records. As a generalisation, sport as a modern phenomenon had its roots in Britain and tended to diffuse from more advanced to advancing (in a Western economic sense) nations. The adoption of sport in general may be equated with Western notions of economic development, although this may not apply so well to individual sports. Indeed, some of the richest countries in the world (e.g. USA and Canada) have yet to adopt, to any degree, sports pioneered in England in the late eighteenth century.

Sports and sports innovations continue to diffuse over the face of the Earth. The numbers of clubs, federations and sports are all growing and it is difficult to know if such a trend will stop. Given the increasing treatment of sport as a commodity and the integration of sports into the global economic system, it is likely that sports entrepreneurs, as well as those who promote sport for its own sake, will continue actively to diffuse new sport-like practices for purposes of investment and profit. The distinction between sport and entertainment may disappear as 'trash sports', mediated by television, become increasingly prominent.

Further reading

The geographical growth of sport is implicit in a number of sports histories. That by Heiner Gillmeister (1997), *Tennis: A Cultural History*, illustrates not only the diffuse folk-traditions of tennis-like body cultures but also the sport's growth in Europe and America. An attempt to treat sports history as innovation diffusion is made by John Bale (1982), 'Sports history as innovation diffusion', *Canadian Journal of History of Sport*. Allen Guttmann (1994), *Games and Empires* is probably as good a place as any to begin an exploration of sport and colonialism. This can be fleshed out by reading J.A. Mangan (1986), *The Games Ethic and Imperialism*. A detailed geographical history of the development of a sport in Africa is John Bale and Joe Sang (1996), *Kenyan Running: Movement Culture, Geography and Global Change*. Two good books on sport and globalisation are Joseph Maguire (1999), *Global Sport*, and *Globalization and Sport* by Toby Miller, Geoffrey Lawrence, Jim McKay and David Rowe (2001).

Chapter 4

Regional dimensions

Introduction

The outcome of the different rates of adoption of sport, local tradition, alternative opportunities and other factors have produced a set of global, national and regional mosaics of sporting practice. In short, on a variety of scales sporting practices display marked spatial variations. There is a long tradition of exploring these variations, dating back, indirectly, to the late nineteenth and early twentieth century. By mid-century studies of the regional differences in sporting practice were quite common, and by the 1970s and 1980s such approaches were the most frequently found of sports geographic studies. They remain popular today, especially in the USA. This chapter seeks to provide an overview of approaches to studying regional differences in sporting attributes. Perhaps the most common approach has been to explore geographic variations in the 'production' of superior athletes and it is this that will form the main focus of this chapter.

Two broad approaches have been used in geographical studies of sport focusing on the identification of where superior athletes come from. Until the 1930s, such approaches were rooted in the geographical philosophy of environmental determinism. By the 1950s, however, a spatial analytic approach to sports geography had succeeded it, mirroring the trend within the broader field of human geography. Each of these approaches can be explored in turn.

Regions of human vigour

Early approaches to the study of differences in human performance, still not unknown today, adopted the philosophy of environmental determinism. This is the doctrine that human activities are controlled and determined by physical environmental factors such as topography, climate, relief, soil and vegetation. Cultural and historical factors were downplayed (even ignored) and the physical environment was given great explanatory significance. The most influential environmental determinists did not usually deal with the effect of environment on sporting ability and performance *per se*, but their views seem likely to have influenced sports personnel such as athletic trainers and coaches (see below). And the ideas of the most influential environmentalists, such as Ellen Semple and Ellsworth Huntington, seem to have attracted the interest of scholars involved in studying geographical variations in sporting success, notably Professor Ernst Jokl whose work I will discuss later. First, however, consideration will be given to the work of Semple and Huntington who can be read as latent geographers of sports.

Typical environmentalist thought was articulated in Semple's view that 'on the mountains she [i.e. the earth's surface] has given him [i.e. "man"] leg muscles of iron to climb the slope; along the coast she has left these weak and flabby' (Semple 1911). The writing of Ellsworth Huntington (1915) went somewhat further than that of Semple in explicating geographical variations in both the potential for athletic performance and performance itself. At the root of much of his work was his global map of 'climatic efficiency' and his willingness to engage in studies of variation in 'human vigour'. His map shows that north-west Europe and the north-east United States were the areas of greatest 'climatic efficiency'. Regions scoring low included those of central Africa and much of south America. Huntington also attempted to rank countries in order of the 'health and vigour' of their populations. He stated that out of 30 countries, those with the highest 'index of vigour' were New Zealand, the Netherlands and Australia; the lowest were Egypt and India.

Writers in sport seemed to have embraced environmental determinism early in the twentieth century if not before. In an article published in the *National Geographic Magazine* just after the First World War, it was confidently asserted that the sports in which people participated were determined by the physical environment in which they lived (Hildebrand 1919). A German writer noted that young cattle herders in the mountains of central Africa could quickly but effortlessly climb steep slopes, the nature of the terrain being the main determinant of their athleticism (Kna 1929). The climatic constraints imposed by the physical environment led some observers, such as the contributor to a Swedish sports encyclopaedia, to aver that 'it is not possible to make sports stars out of African negroes' (quoted in Goksøyr 1990). Based, presumably, on climatic factors, such a view was clearly racist. However, physical geographic factors were not only used to deny 'the African' an athleticism; at the same time physical environmental considerations were being applied to explain athletic success in northern Europe. During the 1920s and 1930s, Finland 'produced' a disproportionately large number of middle and long-distance runners. A French observer writing in the 1920s was succinct in his 'explanation' of the success of the outstanding Finnish runner, Paavo Nurmi. He wrote that 'Nurmi is a *product* of the Finnish twilight and cold' (quoted in

Raevuori 1997, 405, italics added). A German observer in the mid 1930s, waxing more lyrically about Finland's physical geography, claimed that:

All kinds of being in these stretches of land were capable *by nature* of special feats of endeavour.... Running is certainly in the blood of every Finn. When you see the clear, deep green forests, the wide open luxuriant plains..., the heights covered by massive clusters of trees and never ending light blue to the horizon with the lakes merging with the sky, one is overcome by an *involuntary* feeling of elation and because you don't have wings, you want to run. Nurmi and his friends ... began to run because there was a deep need, because a peculiar dreamlike scenery constantly *enticed them and pulled them* into the spell of its mysteries.

(Schumacher 1936, italics added)

Taking a slightly different position, the successes of African American athletes were explained by the environmental conditions of their fore-bears. The ability of black American sprinters resulted from the fact that 'not long ago [their] ability to sprint and jump was a life-and-death matter ... in the jungle' (Cromwell and Wesson 1941). One should not assume that such ways of seeing the physical environment as a causal agent has totally died out. Today, for example, the high relief of the East African nations of Kenya and Ethiopia is frequently used to 'explain' the success of long-distance runners from these two nations (see Bale and Sang 1996). Historical, cultural and social factors are totally ignored.

The environmentalist approach was also included in a novel paper by Harvey Lehman (1940), who sought to describe and explain the geographi-cal differences in the state 'production' of professional baseball players in the USA. I will return to his method of establishing the 'production' level of each state later in this chapter but at this stage simply note that a dis-proportionate number of pro baseball players was found to come from the southern states. The first 'causative factor' cited by Lehman for this pattern of pro player origins was 'the longer playing season which is to be found in the south' – a climatic variable typical of the environmental–deterministic mind-set. To be fair, however, Lehman acknowledged that other factors were of equal significance, thus muting the idea of mono-cau-sation.

By the 1950s environmental determinism was no longer a geographical orthodoxy. However, in terms of geographical studies of sports a concern with regional differentiation continued to exist, though considerable emphasis was placed on the search for *patterns* or generalisations. The prime mover in such studies was John Rooney of Oklahoma State Univer-sity who was to raise the image of a geography of sport and create, in the USA at least, a recognisable sub-discipline.

Analysing the Olympics

Before moving on to Rooney's approach it may be instructive to consider antecedents of his kind of analyses. National differences in sports performances have long been explored by analysing the results of the Olympic Games. Arguably still the world's greatest sports festival, the Olympic Games are *de jure* a competition between individuals, but media hype and government propaganda have combined to project the Olympics as contests between political and national ideologies. Essentially, an analysis of national and regional variations in success in the Olympics is an exercise in applied regional geography. In the popular press, sports journalists had started tabulating national 'winners' of the Olympics at least as early as 1928 (Lowe 1977). But it was really the 1936 'Games' at Berlin which generated the feeling that 'a stable of athletes ... became necessary for national standing'. Richard Mandell (1971), in his classic book *The Nazi Olympics*, noted that it was from 1936 that 'the better an athlete was as an athlete, the less he was allowed individualism and the more he was cast as an allegorical, ideological batterer'. The 1936 Olympics were billed as 'the struggle of the two titans, Germany and the United States', and a trend that was strengthened by the results of the 1936 Olympics was to view athletes increasingly as national assets in the 'production' of athletic performance, procurable like fighter planes, submarines or synthetic rubber factories (Mandell 1971). Such comments are invitations to social scientists to arrive at measures of Olympic 'success' which are more meaningful than the crude medal tally so frequently projected by the popular media. Indeed, although both Germany and USA were quick to point out that each had 'won' the 1936 Games, it needed a paper in the *Scientific Monthly* to emphasise that when population variations were taken into account the true 'winner' was Finland (quoted in Mandell 1971). In the post-war period a number of studies have attempted to measure Olympic 'success', to build models of national Olympic performance and to identify characteristics of the most 'successful' nations (Bale 1985).

Perhaps the most interesting and in-depth analysis of geographical variations in Olympic success was undertaken by Professor Ernst Jokl of the University of Kentucky, and his Finnish associates, into the 1952 Helsinki Olympics (Jokl *et al.* 1964). These Games were particularly interesting because they marked the entry of the Soviet Union into the Olympic arena and pitted that country against the traditional 'winner', the USA. However, what criteria should be used in assessing national performance at the Olympics? Jokl's approach was to reject the traditional medal tally and, instead, assign a number of points to each athlete in each final of each event. The success of each nation was measured by the number of points obtained by each of its competitors. Jokl's points system was calculated by using a formula derived from information theory. The formula was:

$$P = 100(1 - \log x/\log n)$$

where P is the number of points for a given nation, x is the placement of an athlete or team, and n is the number of contestants in the event. Hence first place (i.e. an Olympic Gold medal) received 100 points (the log of 1 being zero) while last place received no points (since log n/log n = 1). So, fourth place out of five contestants received fewer points (14) than the more praiseworthy fourth out of twenty contestants (54 points). This approach is clearly a vast improvement on simply a count of medals.

The definition of some of Jokl's terms are worthy of brief consideration. A nation's point share was defined as simply the number of points collected by the country's athletes, the participation rate as the number of participations in Olympic events per million inhabitants, the point rate as the number of points per million inhabitants, and the point level as the average number of points per participation. An important distinction is between the point rate and the point level. If we are considering the success of Olympic teams from each country then the point level is obviously more appropriate than the point rate, which measures success in relation to the population of the country as a whole.

On the basis of the 1952 Olympic results Jokl was able to reveal the global distribution of athletic performance on a continental and macro-regional basis. Consider in Table 4.1 the point rate criterion. In this case North America outscored the USSR. If the point level criterion is considered, however, the opposite is the case. In terms of team success (i.e. point level) the USSR was clearly more successful than any of the continents, though in terms of point rate both Europe and Oceania outperformed her. When participation and point rates were considered for

Table 4.1 Olympic participation and achievement of continents and regions, 1952

Continents and regions	Population (millions)	Participations	Participation rate	Point share	Point rate	Point level
North America	166	289	1.74	10,722	64.6	37.1
Middle America	51	131	2.57	2,269	44.5	17.3
South America	111	39	2.15	4,437	40.0	18.6
Europe	396	2,038	5.15	49,293	124.5	24.2
USSR	193	209	1.08	8,690	45.0	41.6
Africa	198	145	0.73	3,331	16.8	24.0
Asia	1,272	290	0.23	5,977	4.7	20.6
Oceania	13	86	6.62	2,601	200.1	30.2
Total	2,400	3,427	1.43	87,320	36.4	25.5

Source: Jokl et al. 1964.

Table 4.2 Olympic participation and achievement by temperature zones, 1952

Temperature zones	Population (millions)	Participations	Participation rate	Point share	Point rate	Point level
Cold	312	1,049	3.36	29,552	94.7	28.2
Cold and cool	246	417	1.70	14,979	60.9	35.9
Cool	401	1,395	3.48	32,472	81.0	23.3
Cool and warm	495	79	0.20	2,738	5.5	34.7
Warm	866	476	0.60	7,437	8.6	15.6
Warm and hot	64	11	0.20	146	2.3	13.3

Source: Jokl et al. 1964.

individual countries, however, it was found that little relationship existed between size of country and point level. Some very small countries were able to obtain high point scores, Jamaica on this criterion being almost as successful as the USA. Likewise, when Olympic achievement was related to the world's temperature zones it was found that it was possible that countries in hot regions could achieve success in sport, contrary to the environmentally determinist perspective prevailing at the time (see above). The differences between point score and different temperature zones are shown in Table 4.2. It is seen that the point rate, participation rate and point share for warm countries exceeded those for the cool and warm zones. Likewise, cold zones had a higher point rate than any other though these were the very zones, of course, which had long traditions of participation in the sports found in the Olympics and were generally the most wealthy. Even so, Jokl's method of analysis was surely better than simply examining the medal table; it is somewhat surprising, therefore, that it was not replicated for subsequent Olympic Games (Bale 2000).

Following the 1952 Olympics there was an ongoing argument about which countries in the world, communist or non-communist, were the most successful in the Olympics. This was typical of the Cold War decades and, as has been seen, it is possible to ascribe victory to various countries or ideological groups of nations depending on which indicators of 'success' are used. However, if Olympic success (and let me stress that only a tiny proportion of many nations' top athletes perform in the Olympics) is our concern then it does appear that communist countries did outperform non-communist states. In the 1976 Olympics at Montreal (the most recent to include both USA and USSR) six of the top ten countries in terms of Finnish sociologist Paavo Seppänen's (1981) 'success coefficient' were socialist. It is doubtful that even if the absent African nations which had boycotted in Canada had, in fact, participated, they would have featured in the top ten. What is more, despite the very different cultural backgrounds of the various socialist states, they had been more successful since adopting socialism than before doing so, although Albania and China must be excluded from this generalisation because they had not taken part in the Olympic Games before 1984.

Why should communist countries have done better in the Olympics than non-communist states? Part of the reason is that sport was regarded in such nations as a form of physical culture, rather than possessing the more recreational connotations of the West. In addition, the status of women was different under communism – sport being intended as much for women as for men. Furthermore, élite individuals were spotted early and enrolled in special sports schools, in much the same way as we cultivate talented young musicians. All this was undertaken with the state in full control of their national sports systems so that resources could be mobilised to a greater level of efficiency than in the West (Riordan 1977). As noted above, success in the Olympics can be measured in a variety of ways. The former communist states in general, and East Germany in particular, were the most successful Olympic nations on earth, though this does not necessarily mean that they 'produced' more world class athletes per capita than non-communist states (see below). Since the demolition of the Soviet 'empire' there has been a significant reduction in the dominance of eastern European states in the Olympics.

Sport for all or few?

In promoting sport, or individual sports, different nations may adopt different emphases. Some may feel that most of their ideological eggs lie in the welfare or mass-participatory sport basket and they therefore devote a considerable effort in engaging a large proportion of the population in sport, albeit at modest levels of performance when measured by the standards of the world's élite. In other countries sports ministries may feel that they ought to put a disproportionate amount of investment and effort into producing a small number of highly visible world-class performers. In yet other cases a truly egalitarian approach may be adopted, each individual being provided with the motivation and resources to maximise his or her own sporting prowess.

The various national attitudes to sport and its development can be conceptualised by using a variation of the well-known 'population pyramid' to describe diagrammatically the different theoretical 'outputs' of various sports systems. Different model situations can be outlined for four hypothetical countries. In the case of the *first* national model, facilities may be available for every individual to reach his or her potential in sports. Such an output possesses both a broad base and a narrow peak with both internationally successful participation and a broad mass of lower level, recreational participation. In Cratty's words (1973) such a country is at pains to 'remediate performance-blocking emotional problems in middle level competitors' so that few, if any, sporting stones are left unturned.

However, in this model it is important to decide whether it is being applied to a population across or within sports. We might feel at first that this model applied to the former German Democratic Republic, but Carr (1974) stressed that because some sports offer the possibility of accumulating more Olympic medals than others, the GDR had concentrated on those sports which were most likely to boost the national medal tally. Hence the model might have applied to swimming but not necessarily to sport *per se* in the GDR. The *second* model is what might be called a 'topped-off' pyramid. A broad base may exist but talent fails to rise to the top because of a lack of suitable facilities, inadequate training and support personnel or a political philosophy which stifles the development of a nation's athletic potential. Widespread mass-participatory sport but weakly developed top-class sport would characterise such a country. Maoist China might be cited as coming close to this model. The *third* model would be typified by a nation which put a good deal of emphasis on a few, élite athletes at the expense of widespread participation at the lower end of the pyramid. Cratty suggests that speed skating in the USA and diving in Canada are examples. To them could be added the case of long-distance running in Ethiopia. During parts of the 1980s, while the nation was starving, the Ethiopian men's senior and junior teams won world cross country championships.

It seems likely, however, that for most countries in the Western world the *fourth* model is most applicable. This takes natural wastage into account. If natural selection of superior athletes occurs and the less capable, physically or emotionally, fall by the wayside, only a few will rise to the top of the sports pyramid which will possess a steep upper slope. Britain and the USA are almost certainly overall examples of this system in which many potential champions are lost to sport despite relatively high levels of participation at the high-school stage. However, like the diffusion models in Chapter 3 and the central place model in Chapter 5, we need to ask whether these models can be operationalised in a real world context. Certainly, the actual construction of pyramids for sport *per se* would be difficult; it is, after all, well nigh impossible to compare a professional foot-baller with an international gymnast in terms of 'quality'. However, in individual sports where quantitative records of a country's athletes are kept we might be able to make some progress in comparing countries.

In sports like swimming, track and field, speed skating, weightlifting and others, we can construct 'rank-performance' curves for individual events, each curve representing one country (or region). Such curves could be applied to élite or mass sport, depending on the appropriateness and depth of the available data sets. As many countries do, in fact, compile in-depth data in the form of ranking lists for sports such as track and field and swimming, the slopes of such rank-performance curves and the identifica-tion of any marked changes in them might serve to provide real world examples of the nature of 'output' from the systems. A comparison of curves would be most meaningful for countries of similar population sizes. The approach can be used to illustrate in a dramatic way how Great Britain, in 1984, had been unable to achieve a level of output in one track and field event in comparison with two smaller countries, Sweden and Finland. The event in this case is the javelin throw and only the top ten in each country are graphed. Figure 4.1 shows how Britain's curve is much steeper than that for the other two, much smaller, countries. In terms of their available resources, Sweden and Finland have each been much more efficient than Britain in producing élite javelin throwers. Given suitable data, similar graphs could be drawn for all levels of sporting participation. The slopes of the curves will be a function of the kinds of factors discussed earlier in relation to the pyramid-type models.

Identifying sports regions

It is now time to return to the contribution of John Rooney whose name was mentioned earlier in this chapter. Widely thought of as the 'father' of modern sports geography, Rooney's significance in developing a particular

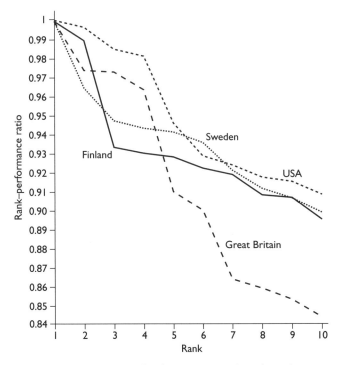

Figure 4.1 Rank–performance curves for four countries, based on their top ten javelin throwers, 1984. The rank–performance ratio is obtained by calculating each ranked athlete's best performance as a percentage of the first ranked.

style of 'sports geography' cannot be denied. Between the late 1960s and the mid-1990s Rooney published a large amount of material on geographical variations in sport in the United States. His work was climaxed with the publication of *An Atlas of American Sport*, co-authored with another pioneer of American sports geography, Richard Pillsbury (Rooney and Pillsbury 1992). This gigantic publication is arguably a testament to Rooney's style of sport geographic research. This section reviews Rooney's work and provides examples of studies that have been inspired by it. Before alluding to his work, however, it may be worth noting that several studies anticipated his approach: one was the aforementioned work by Jokl, another the little known (among geographers) paper by Lehman (1940), who sought to explain the geography of baseball player 'production'. Lehman's approach was closest to that of Rooney and I will briefly outline it.

In order to establish whether geographical variations existed in the origins (i.e. birthplaces) of professional baseball players in the USA, Lehman established the per capita 'production' of (white) baseball players per state. He did this by comparing percentage of the national total of players contributed by each state and compared this with the states' percentage share of the nation's white population. For example, California produced three times as many professionals as might have been expected on the basis of its white population. Other high levels of 'production' were found in the southern states. The location quotient of each state indicated the extent to which it deviated from what would be expected given its population. A score of more than one indicated that it produced more pro baseball players than its population would predict; a score below 1.0 that it produced less than would be expected.

Rooney's better known studies followed a very similar approach, though he was apparently unaware of Lehman's paper. Like Lehman, however, his work was mainly focused on the 'production' of superior athletes, though he did explore the distribution of facilities as well. His basic approach to the identification of 'hotbeds' of athletic productivity was to compare regional variations with the national per capita level of production. The national index was calculated as 1.0 and this provided a convenient yardstick against which regional levels could be compared. The per capita index was calculated by applying the following formula:

$$I = \frac{N}{P} \bigg/ \frac{1}{n}$$

where I is the index, N is the number of athletes or clubs in the sub-region (county or state) under consideration, P is the population of the sub-region and n is the number of people or clubs in the region per athlete or per club. For example, if there were 23,000 people per rugby club in

Britain as a whole, 1/n would be 1/23,000. If a particular county had a population of 900,000 and had 200 rugby clubs the formula would read:

$$I = \frac{200}{900,000} \bigg/ \frac{1}{23,000}$$

$$I = 5.11$$

In this case the county would have 5.11 times as many rugby clubs as the nation as a whole.

Regional variations in 'athletic production'

In a nation the size of the USA the ability of a region to 'produce' élite athletes varies tremendously. Consider, for example, the regional differences in the production of élite collegiate football players. Drawing on data from the NCAA Division I collegiate team rosters for the period 1968–1988, Rooney and Pillsbury (1992) noted that in the 1980s the per capita figure for Texas was 5.85, with a continuous belt of states stretching east to Georgia with indexes of over 1.91. Of the counties in Texas, 43.4 per cent had a per capita level of production of collegiate football players of more than 2.0. A belt of northern states stretching from Washington to Michigan, however, produced élite college ball players at less that 0.75 the national norm. In these and subsequent examples regions are said to be made up of contiguous states or counties of above a given average level of 'production'.

Rooney's approach was taken up in Europe and a rather more detailed consideration can be made of sports regions in the UK. Figure 4.2 exemplifies professional footballer and boxer regions in England and Wales on the basis of those counties with 1.3 or more times the national average per capita output. The map reveals that for football three regions and two outliers of high footballer productivity exist. The industrial north-east, long part of the folklore of British soccer, has counties such as Tyne and Wear, Cleveland and Durham with indices of 2.64, 2.31 and 1.75 respectively. Further south, Clwyd, Merseyside and Greater Manchester have 1.92, 2.22 and 1.39 times the national average per capita output. The third region is made up of Humberside (1.43) and South Yorkshire (2.34). The two outliers in industrial south Wales are West (2.54) and South (1.62) Glamorgan – showing that Wales can produce soccer as well as rugby players (Bale 1983).

The regions of above-average boxer production are similar in some respects to the soccer regions. Professional boxers and footballers tend to come from traditional areas of heavy industry which today have relatively high levels of unemployment. Undoubtedly the major region of boxing activity in terms of 'production' of boxers is South Wales, a region which has produced a long line of illustrious fighters over many years. In the early

Football

Boxing

Figure 4.2 Regions of England and Wales 'producing' more than 1.3 times the national per capita average number of professional footballers and boxers in the early 1980s (Bale 1985).

1980s very high per capita indices are found for South Glamorgan (4.25), Gwent (4.43), Mid Glamorgan (2.79) and West Glamorgan (2.75). A belt of industrial England running from West Yorkshire through South Yorkshire, Nottingham, Leicester and Northampton is another zone of high boxer productivity, the principal centre of activity in this region being Leicestershire and Nottinghamshire with respective indices of 2.41 and 1.55. For boxing three important outliers are worthy of mention. The metropolitan counties of Merseyside (2.41), Greater London (1.66) (the centre for the consumption of boxing) and the West Midlands (1.52) each produce at over one and a half times the national average. Interestingly, professional boxer production is noticeably absent from the major region of pro soccer player production, the north-east. Likewise, London's relative ability to produce boxers is not matched by its supply of footballers, even though output of the latter has increased dramatically over the last 40 years (Bale 1983).

In multi-event sports like track and field athletics different parts of the country appear to 'specialise' in the 'production' of different types of athletes. In Britain, for example, the south-east has been shown to have high per capita levels of sprinters, while the long-distance road runners tend to be most prolific in the north-west (Bale 1982). In the USA superior track and field athletes are mainly produced in high schools in the western states, a contiguous block of states from Arizona to Washington having per capita indexes of more than 2.0. However, marked differences exist in the 'type' of athlete produced. Sprinters are prominent in Texas while, at the state level, superior distance runners tend to be concentrated in west-coast schools (Rooney and Pillsbury 1992).

Explaining why such geographic variations should exist in the production of élite athletes is not easy. These days overly environmental deterministic 'explanations' tend to be avoided. The Texas football hotbed was attributed by Rooney (1974) to the traditions of rugged individualism and militarism. In some cases sport provides an escape route from the ghetto or dole queue – a perceived route to employment and upward social mobility. Undoubtedly a multivariate explanation lies behind the regional differences in athletic productivity, Yetman and Eitzen (1973) commenting that 'an unknown combination of variables predispose a county to overproduce or underproduce quality football players'. However, using multivariate statistical analysis of a number of social and economic variables they found that middle-class areas were highly productive but so too were those with large numbers of blacks. Simplistic economic explanations about regional variations in the production of professionals in boxing and football may well need complementing by approaches which include an awareness of traditional regional popular culture, since areas of similar economic character differ in their response to the labour market for various sportsmen.

A reasonably consistent finding from North American studies of regional variations in the 'production' of sports talent is that small towns produce relatively more professional sports personnel than large cities. The percentage 'production' of superior Canadian ice hockey players for each size category of community in comparison with the expected percentages on the basis of the number of boys born in each size category confirms this generalisation. For example, places of over 500,000 produced 18.9 per cent, of NHL players when it would be expected that they would produce 31.9 per cent; places of 1,000 to 2,499, however, produced 6.7 per cent compared with the expected 4.7 per cent (Curtis and Birch 1987).

Similar patterns have been found for American Olympic hockey players and, at the state level, American college football and basketball players. However, hockey players are under-represented from the very smallest places, those of under 1,000 people and in rural areas. In fact, it is the rural communities and the largest communities that are under-represented. The under-representation of the largest places might result from the large number of intervening opportunities for young people in large cities or from the fact that not enough teams exist in large cities to accommodate the latent talent which exists there. Rural places may be under-represented because of the lack of good facilities, lack of access to organised competition and the unavailability of good coaching. It is not known whether these kinds of relationships, common in some north American sports, are replicated in other countries and for other sports. Only further research will tell.

The kinds of study pioneered by Rooney at the national level can be applied at the international scale and compared with the kinds of 'geographical' approaches of Jokl and Seppänen (1981). Consider, for example, the frequently projected image that in Africa Kenya is a hotbed of élite athlete production. Since the Mexico City Olympics of 1968, Kenya has consistently 'produced' a string of famous high-achieving runners from 400 to 10,000 metres and, more recently, the marathon. Regional approaches to sports geography seem to be useful in exploring such stereotypes. Figure 4.3 shows the per capita variations in the production of African-class track and field athletes in Africa in 1993 ('African-class' defines those athletes ranked in the top 50 in Africa in any Olympic track and field event). Despite the global visibility of the Kenyan runners, it is South Africa that is, in fact, revealed as the major producer of superior African athletes. If gender differences are taken into account, however, Kenya emerges as the major producer of male athletes (index of 5.94), ahead of South Africa (4.37), though South Africa (7.28) easily outscores Kenya (3.10) if only female athletes are considered. Note the various 'regions' of above average athletic output; blocks of nations in east, west and north Africa contrast with the relatively 'empty' African core.

Dramatic variations in national differences in élite athlete production were noted for Europe during the period of state socialism in eastern Europe. Certain east European countries produced world-class athletes at extremely high per capita levels. For example, East Germany produced élite women swimmers at 32.31 times the continental norm and élite track and field athletes at 29.28 the continental figure (Figure 4.4). However, when nations' per capita scores were correlated with whether they were east or west of the infamous 'iron curtain', a very weak correlation was found to exist (Bale 1985).

A criticism of the kinds of studies noted above is that they exemplify overall 'production' of athletes and do not take into account the degree of diversification of that output. In certain multi-event sports like track and field, swimming, weightlifting or skating the diversification of a nation's output might be of more importance, not only for purposes of international comparison but also for the monitoring of national sports policy. Balance in sporting excellence might be the aim of many countries wishing to develop their sporting prowess. Diversification/specialisation can be measured in several ways. Take track and field as an example. The percentage of, for example, each state's (or nation's) top athletes in each event (100 metres, 200 metres, high jump, discus, etc.) is calculated and the following simple formula is applied:

$$SI = \sqrt{P1^2 + P2^2 + P3^2 + \ldots Pn^2}$$

where P1 is the total percentage number of athletes in event 1, P2 the

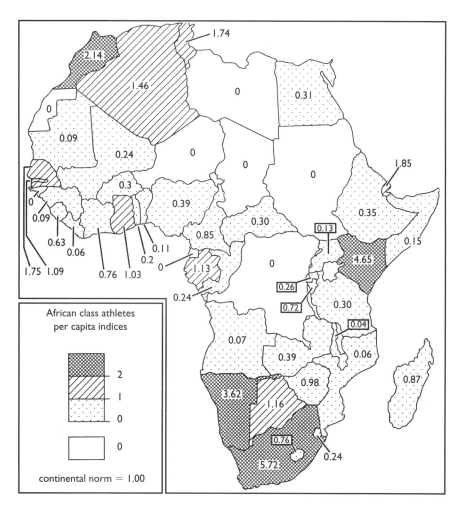

Figure 4.3 National variation in the per capita 'production' of world-class track and field athletes in Africa, 1992 (Bale and Sang 1996).

percentage in event 2, etc. The maximum score will always be 100, indicating extreme specialisation with all athletes in one event. The lowest score will depend on the number of events. When this is thirteen, the lowest score is 27.3; for eighteen it is 23.6. When used in the context of track and field the specialisation/diversification index is used in conjunction with the per capita index to reveal the location of different countries in 'success space'. Consider, for example, Figure 4.5 that compares the output of nations in Eastern Europe and the Americas in 1980 in terms of the numbers of world class track and field athletes per nation. The nearer the

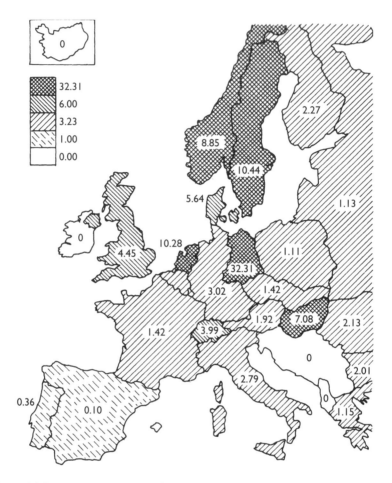

Figure 4.4 Per capita production of élite women swimmers in Europe, 1982. The European norm was 3.23 (Bale 1985).

top left-hand corner of the graph, the more 'successful' the country on the two criteria (diversification and per capita output) considered. Nations with high specialisation and low per capita score are found in the bottom right of the graph. An element of dynamism can be applied to the 'success space' graph by plotting the 'movement' within success space over time. Figure 4.6 shows how, in the case of Kenyan track and field, the national track and field output has been improving its per capita output but, at the same time, has been becoming more specialised with an increasing concentration of its output on long-distance runners (Bale and Sang 1996).

An additional approach is to use a method called combination analysis,

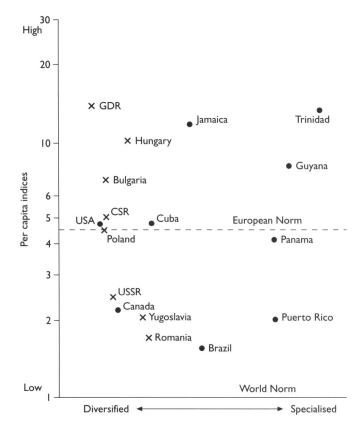

Figure 4.5 An application of the success–space matrix. Comparing the nations of the Americas and Eastern Europe in terms of world-class track and field athlete output in the 1980s.

a technique that seeks to classify nations (or any other areal unit) objectively according to the event-groups which are dominant or typical. For an example taken from track and field, a country might have a distinctive sprints–jumps combination and hence be designated an SJ nation. In order to classify each nation, their event group structures need to be compared with 'model' structures that describe specific situations. For example, a one-event nation would ideally have 100 per cent of its athletes in one event group and none in the other three. A two-event nation would have 50 per cent in each of two groups and none in the rest, a three-event nation would have 33.3 per cent for three groups and 0 for the fourth, and so on. So that comparison can be made easy, the event–group divisions are placed in rank order and in each case the squares of the deviations from the ideal structures are summed and divided by the number of event

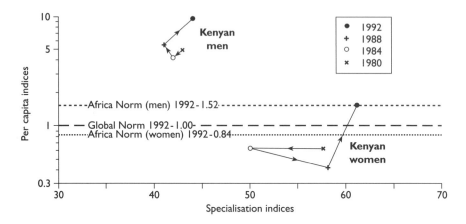

Figure 4.6 The movement of Kenyan track and field world-class athletes in 'success space', 1980–1992 (Bale and Sang 1996).

groups in each case. Each country is then classified according to the model structure it most closely resembles (Bale 1979).

Regions of interest and involvement

So far in this chapter I have been looking at regional variations in either the production of élite athletes or the performances of different nations in high-level competitive sports. There is another kind of regional variation, however: that found at the mass participatory level and concerned with variations in interest, participation or involvement. This section focuses on such differences, again at the international and national levels.

It is clear that considerable differences exist in the levels of recreational participation in sports between countries – even if the different definitions of what includes 'sport' poses a problem. In the 1970s for Norway and Sweden, for example, 50 and 30 per cent respectively of the national populations were claimed to participate in those nations' first ranked sports. In the UK and West Germany, it was revealed that only about 10 per cent take part in the most popular sporting activity (Rodgers 1977). However, this kind of information tells us little about the frequency and the intensity of participation; in order to introduce these characteristics into the study of international variations in sports, British geographer Brian Rodgers, defined three main indicators of participation:

1   the index of penetration, which defines the percentage of people who have ever played a particular sport;
2   the index of fidelity, which describes the number of adults who still

play a particular sport as a percentage of those who have ever played it; and

3 the index of intensity, which is the ratio between those who play it at all and those who participate regularly.

Sports played widely at schools tend to have high penetration levels. In the United Kingdom, for example, track and field athletics had a penetration index of 37; in France, on the other hand, it had an index of 15. However, the index of fidelity for this sport in these two countries was 8.1 and 7.3 respectively, while the indices of intensity were also similar: 36 for the UK and 33 for France. Figures for other sports are shown in Table 4.3.

Interesting though such data are, they cannot be used with very much reliability for comparing many countries because of incompatibility in data collected by different countries and the variation in the definition of sport. It might be possible to use the per capita approach described earlier in relation to the production of superior participants and apply it to the international scale by using data collected by international sports' governing bodies relating to club membership per country. Many such organisations keep quite precise records of club membership at the national scale. Of course, casual participation in sport by non-members would be excluded and such participation is likely to be sizeable.

We can return to the per capita approach by considering evidence and examples of regional differences in interest in different sports. Instead of the number of players 'produced' we can use numbers of clubs or, better still, numbers of club members, in order to highlight parts of the country which appear to place greater emphasis on some sports than others, given the caveat indicated above. Consider some examples from Britain shown in Figure 4.7. Tennis is clearly seen to be dominantly southern and suburban in location. Areas of limited emphasis on tennis are the great conurbations, London being an 'island' of relative inactivity, the Merseyside and Greater Manchester areas adjoining a 'lobe' of tennis underdevelopment in the industrial midlands. Tennis is a middle-class sport found in middle-class locations (i.e. broadly southern and suburban), but is not as strongly

Table 4.3 Indices of sports participation in UK and France, 1970s

Sport	Penetration		Fidelity		Intensity	
	France	UK	France	UK	France	UK
Athletics	15	37	7.3	8.1	36	33
Team sports	21	66	22	12	31	50
Swimming	36	50	55	12	13	52
Tennis	7.3	37	31	24	30	44

Source: Rodgers 1977.

Figure 4.7 Regions in England and Wales having more than 1.3 times the national average number of clubs in (a) tennis, (b) basketball, (c) cycling and (d) auto cycling in the early 1980s (adapted from Bale 1982).

localised in the south-east as many people think (compare Figures 4.7a and 4.7b). Basketball and cycling display clear patterns of Severnside–Wash and Lancashire–Essex axial spread respectively, but the pattern defies any obvious explanation. Auto cycling is dominantly peripheral and rural, located mainly in agricultural and non-urbanised areas where space is available for the noise and extensive courses which this sport demands.

Of course, the per capita approach to both the analysis of player production and popular, mass involvement is based upon only one variable, i.e. numbers of participants related to overall population. To obtain an indication of true intensity of involvement in a particular sport, a number of measures of involvement might be taken. For example, in the United States the Rooney–Adams golf involvement index involves a combination of per capita variables including facility supply, equipment purchases, golf magazine subscriptions, and support for the game in high school, to substantiate the premier status of the Midwest and Northeast as 'golfing regions'. By these criteria Iowa, Michigan, Minnesota, Wisconsin, New Hampshire and Connecticut are the leading golf states. Much of the south had very low involvement (Rooney 1986). Such an approach could obviously be applied to any number of sports, and as well as being of cultural geographic interest such findings are helpful in marketing sports equipment and facilities.

Cores and domains

In some cases it is possible to identify a kind of structure in sports regions. Figure 4.8 shows that for rugby union and golf the areas of greatest relative emphasis (i.e. those areas with more than twice the national per capita average number of clubs) are adjacent to, or surrounded by, areas of less emphasis but which still possess above-average levels of club provision (i.e. indices greater than 1.3). In other words, the sports region appears to possess a core and a domain, beyond which might be said to exist a sphere of sports activity within which the sport exists at lower densities and with less intense local involvement.

Three rugby cores are obvious from Figure 4.8a. First, several South Wales counties have very high per capita indices of over 3.5, confirming to a large degree the popular perception of rugby's geography (see Chapter 7). The South Wales rugby region extends across the border into the English county of Gloucester. Beyond this core, north-west Wales, Avon and Warwickshire constitute a domain of above-average rugby activity. The two other core regions are in south-east Scotland (the Border region has an index of 6.58, second only in Britain to Dyfed's 6.67) and Cornwall. In both cases a neighbouring domain exists. Two relatively isolated outliers of above-average rugby activity are found in the sparsely populated parts of north-west Scotland and in the 'rugger' county of Surrey. In terms of regional structure a similar pattern is found for golf (Figure 4.8b). The dominant core is central and south-eastern Scotland – the home of the game – where per capita scores exceed 4.0 in four of the Scottish regions. A minor regional core is found in north Wales with outliers of above-average, but not spectacular, emphasis in Cornwall and south-east suburban England.

(a)   (b)

Figure 4.8 Cores (heavy shading with per capita indices >2.0) and domains (light shading with indices of 1.3–1.99) for (a) rugby and (b) golf in Britain in the 1980s.

The distribution maps of sports preferences at the national scale are good examples of the geographical manifestation of popular culture. Tennis and rugby clubs, among others, are not simply dots on maps or parts of regional clusters, however. To many people they are the very things which distinguish their lifestyle from that of their regional (and sometimes local) neighbours. Association with such varying sports indicates that popular culture has not become homogenised; indeed, it may be one of the few such areas where a surprising degree of geographical variation continues to exist.

The patterns of player 'production' and of regional emphasis described so far are essentially snapshots taken at a point in time. It is now appropriate to begin to consider the dynamic nature of sports regions and provide examples of the way in which regional emphases change over time.

Patterns of regional change

It would be an oversimplification to suggest that sports regions such as those we have been looking at were static and never changed. We have already observed the ways in which sports diffused across continents and countries and, in many places, they are continuing to do so. Over time, subtle yet quite discernible changes take place in the geographical make-up of sports regions. In some cases the cores become intensified; in others they break up and the centre of the sport moves elsewhere.

In the case of British football (soccer) the traditional hotbed of player production has been the north of England (Bale 1983). In 1950 the northern region produced professional footballers at 2.45 times the national per capita norm (Figure 4.9). Within the region the county of Northumberland produced at a level of 3.97 the national average, while Durham (2.74), Tyne and Wear (2.49) and Cleveland (2.02) were also prolific producers. At this time the south-east of England had a per capita index of 0.39. In 1980 the north was still the major producer in relative terms but with a reduced index of 2.06 (Table 4.4). In addition, only two northern counties had per capita indices of greater than 2.0. The south-east of England, on the other hand, had increased its index to 0.69, with Greater London changing from a production level of only 0.38 times the national level in 1950 to one which was slightly higher (1.12) than the national norm 30 years later. When mapped, two things seemed to have been taking place. First, there was a growing convergence between the highest and lowest producers and, as a result, a southern shift in player production (see Table 4.4) so that by 1980 it was the south-east, not the north-west or Scotland that was, in absolute terms, the national centre of footballer production. The second thing that had been happening over the 30-year period was the growing metropolitanisation of player output. Instead of a north–south division in player production it had become clear that soccer players were increasingly coming from urban centres, irrespective of location.

Table 4.4 Per capita production of football league professionals by standard regions, 1950 and 1980

Region	1950		1980	
	Number	Index	Number	Index
North	293	2.45	205	2.06
North-west	315	1.26	288	1.40
Wales	154	1.49	116	1.29
Yorks/Humberside	254	1.40	200	1.28
Scotland	300	1.48	182	1.11
Northern Ireland	54	0.99	36	0.75
West Midlands	160	0.97	145	0.95
East Midlands	106	0.85	120	0.98
South-west	88	0.64	82	0.59
East Anglia	22	0.40	34	0.57
South-east	232	0.39	372	0.69

Source: Bale 1983.

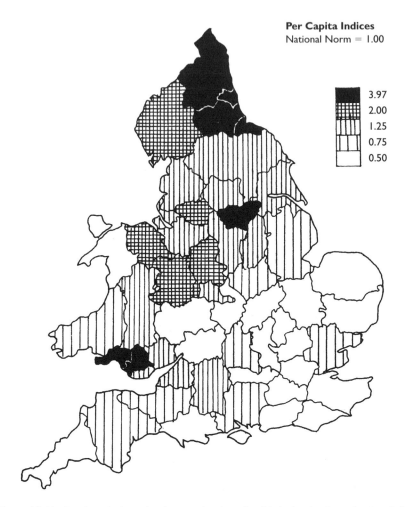

Figure 4.9 Regional variations in the production (by birthplace) of professional foot-ballers, England and Wales, 1950 (Bale 1984).

This growing regional convergence in soccer player production is prob-ably the result of a number of factors. Three can be considered seriously. First, as I will show in the next chapter, recruiting catchments in virtually all sports have been widening in recent decades. Soccer in Britain is no exception and recruitment from areas such as parts of the south, hitherto relatively untouched, may have contributed to that region's increased con-tribution. Second, football has always been a way out of a dole queue, and it is the cities which today form that repository of unemployed young men for whom sport can be an outlet. London was, at the time of this study, the single greatest centre of such unemployment; so too Merseyside had a major problem. Both have dramatically increased their contribution to British footballer output in recent decades. Third, it is in the south that the new entries to the Football League have been increasingly located. It is in the south that both economic opportunities in general, and football growth in particular, have developed in the 30-year period we have been considering. Connell (1985) notes, therefore, that the trend of changes in the distribution of professional footballers parallels changes in the national economy.

Conclusion

Sports regions can be identified for every sport. A huge number of sports regions exist, based on a vast number of criteria. For example, regions identified strongly with sporting animals rather than humans have been identified for Kildare, the centre of the Irish racing industry, based on the geographical distribution of stud fees (Lewis and McCarthy 1977). This chapter has illustrated a variety of ways of exploring place-to-place differences in sports, ranging from the Olympic Games to sport at the mass participatory level.

Just as environmental determinism was criticised during the 1930s, so the simple mapping of regional differences described in this chapter was critiqued in the 1980s. David Ley (1985), for example, noted that in such studies 'description takes place over interpretation'. There remains a place for such studies, however, in the world of national sports policies and recruiting practices of professional clubs. This is not to ignore, however, the need for the kind of interpretive studies for which Ley argued and these will be examined in later chapters.

Further reading

A key early work on geographical variations in sporting performance is Ernst Jokl (1964), *Medical Sociology and Cultural Anthropology of Sport and Physical Education*. Typical works in early sports-geographic writing are found in John Rooney (1974), *A Geography of American Sport: from Cabin Creek to Anaheim* and John Bale (1982), *Sport and Place*. Both these books are typified by the per capita approach and this genre of sports-geographic writing is climaxed in John Rooney and Richard Pillsbury (1992), *Atlas of American Sport*. Another excellent sports atlas is Daniel Mathieu and Jean Praicheux (1987), *Sports en France*. Approaches to geographical differences in performance and participation at the international scale include John Bale (1979), 'Track and field regions of Europe' and John Bale (1985), 'Towards a geography of international sport'.

Chapter 5

Sport and location

Ley's comments at the end of the last chapter were aimed at a positivist approach using quantification and seeking generalisation. This approach was prominent in geography during the 1970s and became almost synonymous with fields known as location theory and spatial analysis. Basically, this privileged 'space' as the prime geographic concept. A geography of sport could be viewed through this conceptual lens as patterns of points (e.g. sports facilities or clubs), movement (migration of players, journeys to spectate), hierarchies (clubs), or surfaces (variations in 'production' of players as shown in the last chapter). In this chapter I will deal with sports activities as points, hierarchies and movements.

Modern sport continues to adjust geographically, not only in the ways described in the last two chapters but also through processes of relocation and through the growth and decline in importance of different sport locations. Additional changes have occurred in the size of sport catchment areas, both in terms of spectators and of players. These adjustments are in part related to the continuing economic imperatives of modern sports and to the broader regional and national economic conditions within which sports find themselves. The present chapter illustrates a number of such locational adjustments but first describes some general location patterns in modern sports. One of geography's most famous theories – central place theory – very popular in the 1970s and is still significant as a conceptual base in theoretical and applied geography. Through this theoretical lens it can be observed that the location of sports outlets is arranged on a reasonably predictable basis. There are, of course, exceptions to such geographical rules, some sports outlets appearing to be in rather aberrant locations. However, the chapter goes on to stress that sports are becoming increasingly rational in terms of their locational patterns, resulting from the increasingly rational behaviour of sports entrepreneurs on the one hand, and the stresses and strains of the economic system within which the sports industries are embedded, on the other. Such developments seem to have produced four geographical outcomes, namely:

(a) sports club relocation at both the national and urban scales;

(b) changing national centres of success as a small number of sports clubs come to dominate regional markets for team sports and newly success-ful clubs emerge in economic growth areas with only tenuous sporting traditions;

(c) shifting geographic margins of viability with sports clubs going out of business as part of a downward economic spiral in declining economic regions; and

(d) widening spatial margins of recruitment of the raw materials of the sports industries, the athletes themselves.

Sports hierarchies

Central place theory is one of geography's most well-known contributions and we can apply it as an introduction to the location of sports. It can be conceived of as a normative model (i.e. what ought to be, according to certain built-in assumptions) to assist in the sensible location of a range of sports activities, ranging from, say, a top-level soccer club to a couple of recreational tennis courts. For our purposes we will call our model a sports place theory and describe it as follows:

- The main function of a sports place is to provide sports outlets for a surrounding hinterland. Sports places are therefore centrally located within their market areas.
- The greater the number of sports provided, the higher the order of the sports place.
- Low-order sports places provide sporting facilities that are used by small catchment areas; the threshold population needed for the via-bility of a low-order place is small.
- Higher order places are fewer in number and are more widely spaced. They have large population thresholds.
- A hierarchy of sports places exists in order to make as efficient as pos-sible the arrangement of sports opportunities for (a) consumers who wish to minimise their travel to obtain the sport they want and (b) producers of sport who must maintain a minimum threshold to survive.

An ideal spatial pattern for a sports system is shown in Figure 5.1. Here, sports teams or sports facilities able to draw on a regional catchment are located further apart than those catering for a district catchment which, in turn, are sited at more distant intervals than those only able to draw on a local sphere of influence. Each order of outlet has its own demand curve (or demand cone – the result of rotating a demand curve through 360 degrees) to create its trade area, represented ideally as a hexagon so that

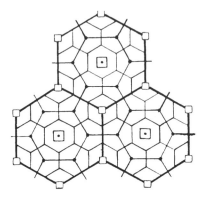

▣ Centre of regional catchment
☐ Centre of district catchment
• Centre of local catchment

Figure 5.1 Theoretical organisation of a sports system using the principles of central place theory.

no areas will be left unserved (as they would be in the case of less easily 'packed' circular trade areas).

In practice, such a classification is often used in the planning of recreational sports facilities, especially at the intra-urban scale. In urban areas recreational sports sites are chosen and provided with facilities to serve a surrounding hinterland of given size. Such facilities can be arranged as a hierarchy, each level serving a different size catchment. At the lowest level, for example, would be the playground possessing a sphere of influence of say, 800 metres in radius, and providing informal facilities for pre-sporting activities of 6 to 14 year olds. The second level of the hierarchy would be the playing field with a variety of sites for field and indoor sports. This might serve an area of about 2 km radius, while a third level might be made up of a top-level sports complex with athletic stadium and swimming pool included and designed to serve an entire community. Such a hierarchy would approximate to the tenets of central place theory.

Proximity to population is another major criterion frequently used in planning publicly funded sports facilities. For example, in Britain it is suggested that the threshold size for an eighteen-hole golf course should be 30,000 people, while 6 acres of playing fields should be provided for every 1,000 people. In the USA, baseball diamonds and tennis courts have respective thresholds of 6,000 and 2,000 people respectively (Ashworth 1984).

Public sports facilities should be as close to the potential users as possible in order to maximise pleasure from the sport experience and to

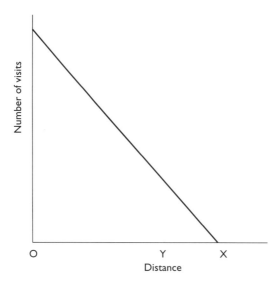

Figure 5.2 Spatial demand curve for sport.

minimise travel, and hence cost. The concentration of public sports outlets in areas of high-density population is therefore desirable on equity grounds. Of course, different criteria apply for private funded developments where profit, rather than population access, is crucial. In reality the spacing of sports outlets is far from uniform and the hexagonal pattern rarely observable. This is because of a variety of factors, not least the legacy of history and inertia, but also the physical nature of the landscape and the variability of the funding available for such developments. Several studies of professional sports have identified threshold populations above which a sports team will be regarded as a viable economic proposition. In the USA it has been suggested that a figure of one million fan visits per season is a critical threshold for a professional baseball franchise (Quirk 1973). Clearly, this figure is unlikely to be reached by many metropolitan areas.

Let me now return to the idea of a sports team's sphere of influence. This can be interpreted as a spatial demand curve which will decline with distance from a given sports outlet (this applies to both top-level and recreational sports) as potential 'consumers' are necessarily confronted with the increasing costs of overcoming the friction of distance. The slope of the curve will depend on a variety of factors, but beyond the point where it intersects the distance axis (at X in Figure 5.2) people will not find it worthwhile travelling to consume sport (either as spectators or as participants) at 0. This provides the potential for another facility to be located somewhere near X in order to serve those for whom travel to 0 is prohibitive. In planning for such provision there is always the danger, however, that the new facility, if located at Y, for example, would divert demand from 0 (Gratton and Taylor 1985). Such a situation could create problems in professional team sports where the slope of the spatial demand curve can change dramatically as the fortunes of the team change. In such a situation, spatial competition would exist; this is avoided in the United States sports industries (football, baseball, etc.) by assigning each team in the league an exclusive franchise to conduct league contests within some specific geographic area (Quirk 1973). This displays a degree of economic rationality absent in the major British team sports where a considerable degree of spatial competition for support exists.

In Britain it has been suggested by Sloane (1960) that those who run both football and cricket are motivated more by the maximisation of utility than profit. As Wiseman (1977) has put it, 'club directors are often fanatical supporters who find their involvement a rewarding hobby in itself'. As directors they are able to get the best seats at games and wine and dine their (often business) colleagues. A directorship is also good for prestige, image and business. Between 1978 and 1997 the overwhelming majority of Football League clubs operated with a profit marginally above or marginally below zero. This applied whether they achieved a high or low league position; no simple formula exists that relates financial success to success on the pitch (Szymanski and Kuypers 2000).

The central place approach to sports geography stresses what ought to exist given certain underlying assumptions and ideal circumstances. These include factors such an even population distribution, a homogeneous plane surface, and economic rationality. We have already indicated that in reality a number of irregularities exist which will make the real world different from that predicted by normative models. A vast number of physical, economic and social barriers will contribute to a distortion of the central place model. For example, in the British football and cricket industries, the spatial pattern is a virtual fossil of what existed at the start of the present century when conditions in Britain were totally different. In addition, sporting tastes vary from place to place: 9 per cent of the population support football in Carlisle in the north of England and only 1.5 per cent in Bournemouth in the south (Rivett 1975). In the case of ice hockey in North America, in a Canadian city of 3.5 million, attendance will average, all other things being equal, over 4,000 fans per game higher than in the United States (Noll 1974).

Much of the supply of sport, particularly at the recreational level, is made by the public sector whose resources vary dramatically over space. In such situations, what ought to exist is likely to be dramatically different from the pattern of sports facilities in the real world. Despite these 'aberrant' characteristics, however, a good deal of spatial order does appear to exist in the location pattern of sports. Let us consider initially the evidence for sports hierarchies, both in the form of provision by population size and in terms of the spatial arrangement of facilities or outlets.

First, if the case of football in France is examined, there is clearly a positive relationship between population of region and the number of clubs, as shown in Figure 5.3 (Ravenel 1997). Here the relationship appears to be quite strong but in other countries it may be weaker. In Britain, for example, places like Stoke, Bristol and Sheffield appear to continue to support more football league clubs than their population sizes justify. We might also expect bigger places being able to support more events than small places, and in many countries national championships of particular sports are always held in the national capital or largest city. It might also be expected that a relationship exists between the number of sports represented in a given area and that area's population size. This is clearly illustrated in the 1988 distribution of major sports franchises in the USA and the sizes of the top 37 metropolitan areas. New York, with a population of over 17 million, had nine franchises; lower down the hierarchy Pittsburgh with nearly 2.4 million had three; further down still, Salt Lake City, with a population of just over 1 million, had one franchise. While hierarchical order clearly does exist in the real world of sports, certain places with populations apparently big enough to support a professional sports team do not, in fact, have one. This provides the potential for relocation, a subject we return to in subsequent sections of this chapter.

It also seems logical that large cities not only contain more clubs but also contain the most successful clubs. Large cities possess the potential to

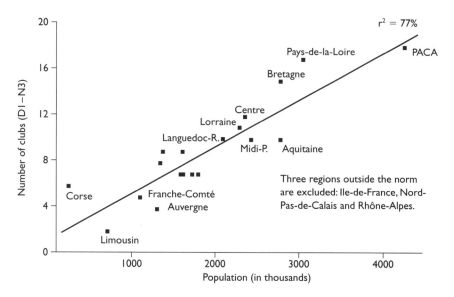

Figure 5.3 Population of regions and number of football clubs, France, 1994–5 (adapted from Ravenel 1998).

attract larger crowds; larger crowds bring in higher revenues which enable clubs to purchase better players – though it is not quite as simple as this because money, alone, cannot buy success. Figure 5.4 shows the relationship between performances and the population living within ten miles of a sample of English football league clubs' grounds. There is clearly a positive correlation between size of urban area and performance. However, it is rather weak and cannot explain why Manchester United and Liverpool, for example, have enjoyed such a high degree of success over a long period of time. Manchester United and Liverpool each have higher league positions than would be expected from the size of their catchment areas. What becomes important may be the effective management of distinctive capabilities such as tradition, reputation and what might seem to be idiosyncratic qualities such as well-loved architectural elements like the Kop at Liverpool. Teams in rural areas that are a long way from major conurbations are unlikely to be able to attract enough support to enable them to compete with big city clubs (Szymanski and Kuypers 2000).

Now let me consider some spatial implications of a central place approach. Where sports are arranged on a league basis, we find that minor leagues 'nest' with larger league areas, according to the pattern predicted in Figure 5.1. One of the few empirical attempts to map the spatial pattern of sports team support on a central place basis is shown in Figure 5.5, which illustrates the spatial organisation of Australian Rules football in Victoria. The territorial organisation of football under the auspices of the Victoria Football League affiliation shows areas enclosing the minor country leagues according to the centre of a main country league through

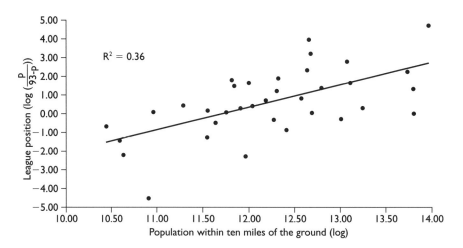

Figure 5.4 Relationship between club performance and population living within 10 miles of club grounds, 1991 (adapted from Szymanski and Kuypers 2000).

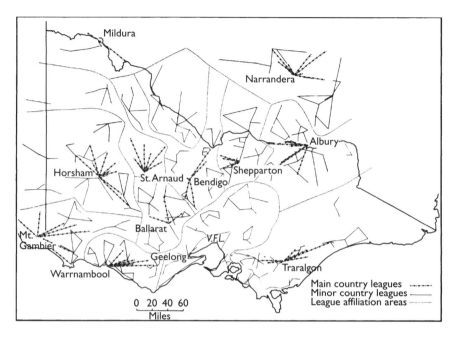

Figure 5.5 The territorial organisation of Australian Rules football in Victoria (Rimmer and Johnston 1967).

which they are administered. The minor leagues nest within the more spatially extensive major leagues. The spheres of influence were constructed by joining each team to others playing in the same competition (Rimmer and Johnston 1967).

An explicit application of a version of central place theory has been applied in Canada to explore the 'best location' for a new ice hockey franchise. Geographers Robert Geddert and Keith Semple (1987) pointed out that because some places supported activities larger than their population size suggests, the prescribed fixed size threshold needed to be modified. Their study investigated the premise that the city of Saskatoon had the potential to support a National Hockey league franchise even though its population threshold appeared too small. In support of their view it was argued that though its population, while being the threshold size, was one in which fan interest was extremely high. The region also displayed a long tradition of long-distance travel to Saskatoon by a large, affluent hinterland population. There were also minimal alternative entertainment options. It was concluded that many factors determine the success of ice hockey franchises. Hockey interest, team quality, competing sports options and the population of market areas statistically explained two-thirds in the variance in NHL attendances. The use of a central place approach to define the population parameter, when modified to take into account other factors, showed that Saskatoon was an appropriate location for a hockey franchise.

Periodic marketing of sport

Where a sports club operates from a 'home turf', spectators will travel to it. An alternative form of spatial organisation is for the sport to travel to the people in order to attract sufficient business to meet its threshold population. At the same time periodic marketing can be regarded as improving the welfare of sports consumers if it allows them access to sports they would otherwise be denied. Sport in its varied forms provides evidence of increased levels of periodic marketing in some cases and of decline in others.

The traditional way of marketing cricket in many English counties has been for the county clubs to engage in a tour of various grounds within their counties during the course of a season. A typical and traditional example is provided by the games of the county of Essex for the 1952 season. Their games were played at eight venues throughout the season. Although this incurred considerable transport costs it did ensure that people in various parts of the county had the chance of seeing their team play. However, such a form of organisation may be best suited to sports in which it is less easy to capitalise on a 'home field advantage' (see Chapter 2). The 1970s and 1980s witnessed a reduction in the number of locations at which mainly English county teams played. The Essex case is exemplary, with only half the number of grounds used in 1952 being frequented in 1979. However, in the cases of other clubs, an increase in the number of venues took place over the same period; indeed, nationally the number of venues has increased and this could be interpreted as providing improved welfare for cricket lovers nationwide. In this particular sport the increase in the number of venues has been a result of the growing number of one-day games.

Periodic marketing is most popular in other sports such as golf, tennis and automobile racing. The quadrennial marketing of the Olympics at geographically diverse venues might be regarded as an example, but the golf and tennis circuits are perhaps the best known cases. In the USA the PGA golf circuit was, in 1950, concentrated in twelve cities, found in California, Arizona and Texas. By 1970 the tour had expanded to take in 30 cities with the growth focused in Florida and the south-east in order to obtain good winter and spring playing conditions. Today, the location of the circuit is more or less driven by television. There are over 50 locations involved throughout the year with the tour starting in the west, moving on to Florida, then to the south-east for the Masters (Augusta), west to Texas, north for the summer and finally back to the south for an autumn finale (Rooney and Pillsbury 1992). Similar forms of spatial organisation are found in activities such as Grand Prix motor sports and other events lacking a 'home turf'. In some sports it is the actual event rather than a sequence of different events which moves from place to place. Car rallies are an example, but perhaps the most famous is the Tour de France cycle race, a mobile spectacle for a widely scattered rural population unable to support in live form other forms of professional spectator sport (Holt 1981).

Relocation

The movement of sports clubs from one location to another represents one of the most evident tendencies in sports in recent decades. Such locational change might be expected in situations where profit maximisation is the norm, sports club location taking place at two levels of scale. Movements at the intra- and inter-urban levels form the subject of this section. The former type – especially in the USA – invariably involves the suburbanisation of sports stadia while the latter might involve a trans-continental move. In Europe, locational change has occurred but has been less spatially dramatic. Each type of relocation reflects a growing economic rationalisation of the sports landscape. In north America, suburbanisation has been a frequent occurrence in recent decades. Such relocations are relatively easy in a US context since the move often involves staying within the league's (or cartel's) specified geographic area. Such moves illustrate that stadium location is obviously not synonymous with franchise relocation.

Before 1960 none of the 28 teams playing in the major baseball leagues or the national Football League played their home games anywhere but in a central city. By 1977 ten of the 53 professional baseball and football teams played in suburban locations, including eight which moved from a central city to a suburban community (Rosentraub and Nunn 1978). Luxurious new stadium complexes often characterise these suburban locales. In the 1970s the Dallas Cowboys, Detroit Lions, New York Giants, Capital Bullets and Anaheim's California Angels (formerly Los Angeles) and Rams were in the vanguard of the sports suburbanisation process (Muller 1981). Sports teams see the suburbs as newly accessible locations in times of freeways, by-passes and high levels of car ownership. The suburbs also possess a different image from the inner city; the Los Angeles Rams moved to Anaheim in 1980, in response to Orange County's more glamorous image, higher income population, and locational convenience for fans (Muller 1981). For the owners of the Rams, Anaheim was a much better investment risk than renovating the Coliseum Stadium in the Watts area of Los Angeles. As the Rams moved within the NFL's 75-mile territorial limit, it was not treated officially as a relocation at all but just a switch of stadium within a defined market area. The new location was also in a prosperous white neighbourhood – good for the sport's image. From the viewpoint of the suburban municipalities the presence of a professional sports team is seen to provide both economic and 'psychic' benefits. However, hard evidence of economic gains seems difficult to find since the benefits from newly located clubs tend to be spread over regions, rather than restricted to individual suburbs (Rosentraub 1977).

In Britain the intra-urban movement of professional football clubs was commonplace at the end of the nineteenth century. Among the most spectacular was the 15 kilometre trek of Arsenal from south-east London (Woolwich) to Islington, then at the northern limit of the metropolis. However, during much of the twentieth century relocation in UK football was almost non-existent. It took the Hillsborough disaster of 1989 and the subsequent government report to galvanise the British football industry into formulating a new map of British football. The Taylor Report (1990) recommended new, all-seat stadiums, and implied relocation to more expansive, suburban sites. As a result, British football has been on the move and a number of intra-urban relocations have taken place. A small number of these have been to greenfield sites, but most have been to brownfield sites as part of urban regeneration schemes. Typical examples

---

The National Football league Colts' move from Baltimore, on 29 March 1984, ended eight years of threats from the team's owner, Robert Irsay, to relocate his franchise to another city. However, not until February 1984 did the people of Baltimore genuinely fear they might lose the Colts. The franchise had existed in their city since 1953, and in only a few short years a relationship which Baltimore residents referred to as a 'love affair' ensued between community and 'its' team. Many times throughout this era the Baltimore press referred to the franchise/community relationship with nuptial-like analogies. That the Colts would end this 31-year-old marriage and sneak off to a little-known city in the Midwest seemed to Baltimore residents as not only disloyal, but mean-spirited as well. Baltimore's mayor Donald Schaeffer, whose tearful picture appeared on the front page of the city's newspaper lamented: 'I'm trying to retain what little dignity I have left in this matter. If the Colts had to sneak out of town at night, it degrades a great city ... I hate to see a man cry.' For the Baltimore community, Irsay's clandestine move added insult to injury. Not only did Irsay's disinvestment decision threaten Baltimore's business image but the Colts' fans also charged that the night-time gallop was intended to 'humiliate and degrade' them. In fact, two Baltimore Colts' fans filed a $US30 million law suit ($US5 million for compensatory damages and $US25 million for punitive damages) against Irsay on behalf of all Colts' season-ticket holders. The plaintiffs alleged the Colts' move caused them 'to suffer severe depression, severe physical and emotional disability, severe disturbance of mental and emotional tranquility and mental distress of a very serious kind'. Irsay's flight, however, was undoubtedly precipitated by more lucrative considerations.

Vignette 5 Some ramifications of franchise relocation; the case of the Baltimore Colts (Schimmel 1995).

include the stadiums associated with Stoke City, Sunderland, Middlesborough and Walsall. Another response to the Taylor Report was expansion *in situ*. Clubs like Manchester United, Liverpool and Arsenal have followed this route which is generally felt to be unsatisfactory.

While the clubs perceive the benefits of new relocations to be the occupation of less congested sites and more comfortable stadiums, the problem has tended to be whether existing fans would continue to identify with, and hence support, them some distance (again by British standards) from their historic origins. In Britain, local identification with a team can be stretched to the maximum even if relatively short distance moves are mooted. For example, a study of whether Chelsea Football Club in London would remain 'Chelsea' and continue to be perceived as such if it moved a few miles to Wormwood Scrubs revealed that the answer was a fairly emphatic 'no' (Bishop and Booth 1974). In the 1980s the London football club Charlton Athletic was forced to leave their home ground at The Valley and ground-share with Crystal Palace, 12 kilometres away. On the face of it, this may have been a rational decision, but sentiment for The Valley was strong and a successful local political movement was established to bring Charlton back home (Everitt 1991). Because of such a local sense of place, the majority of ground relocations have been over very small distances, often less than 1 kilometre. Such is the strength of attachment to soccer shown by British fans (see Chapter 7).

The notion of sharing a stadium with a not too distant neighbour has hardly become familiar in Britain but is widespread in many cities on mainland Europe. In Britain a few soccer clubs share their stadiums with rugby league. Yet it makes economic sense at a time when the finances of many British soccer clubs are precarious, to say the least. With grounds unused for the larger part of the week, they are a luxury which many clubs can ill afford.

In some cases it may not be the relocation of the club that is important in improving attendance, but the rearrangement of the league in which it plays so that it can benefit from the well-known 'local Derby' effect, i.e. the more local the opposition, the greater the attendance. Paradoxically, clubs in the lower divisions of the English Football League incur greater transport costs in order to fulfil their league commitments than the wealthier clubs in the higher divisions. This is because the clubs in the lower divisions tend to be more peripherally located. It has been shown that the lower the division, the more sensitive attendances are to the distances between the teams competing (Walker 1986); several commentators have therefore strongly recommended a return to the regionalisation of the lower divisions of the league.

The relocation of sports clubs assumes a rationality on the part of club owners (and consumers) which appears to be present in some countries but not in others, a reflection of differing national sporting ideologies. In the USA it is widely accepted that the owners of professional sports teams are in the business to maximise profits. As a result, dramatic transcontinental movements of sports clubs are not uncommon (Figure 5.6),

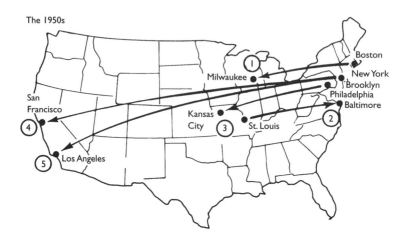

The 1950s

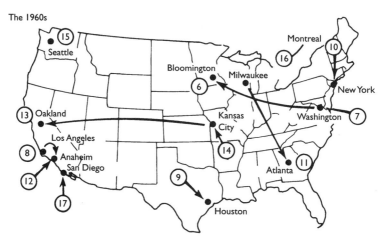

The 1960s

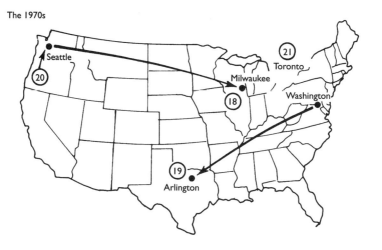

The 1970s

The 1950s

1. 1953 – Boston Braves (NL) move to Milwaukee
2. 1954 – St. Louis Browns (AL) move to Baltimore as the Orioles
3. 1955 – Philadelphia Athletics (AL) move to Kansas City
4. 1958 – New York Giants (NL) move to San Francisco
5. 1958 – Brooklyn Dodgers (NL) move to Los Angeles

The 1960s

6. 1961 – Washington Senators (AL) move Bloomington, Minn., as the Minnesota Twins
7. 1961 – Washington awarded AL expansion franchise, the Senators
8. 1961 – Los Angeles awarded AL expansion franchise, the Angels
9. 1962 – Houston awarded NL expansion franchise, the Colt .45s
10. 1962 – New York awarded NL expansion franchise, the Mets
11. 1966 – Milwaukee Braves (NL) move to Atlanta
12. 1966 – Los Angeles Angels (AL) move to Anaheim, become the California Angels
13. 1968 – Kansas City A's (AL) move to Oakland
14. 1969 – Kansas City awarded AL franchise, the Royals
15. 1969 – Seattle awarded AL franchise, the Pilots
16. 1969 – Montreal awarded NL franchise, the Expos
17. 1969 – San Diego awarded NL franchise, the Padres

The 1970s

18. 1970 – Seattle Pilots (AL) move to Milwaukee, become the Brewers
19. 1972 – Washington Senators (AL) move to Arlington, Texas, become the Texas Rangers
20. 1977 – Seattle awarded AL franchise, the Mariners
21. 1977 – Toronto awarded AL franchise, the Blue Jays

Figure 5.6 The locational dynamics of American baseball, 1953–85 (*Miami Herald*, 24 March 1985).

professional sports franchises making relocation decisions with a degree of regularity which would surprise the average British sports fan. We have seen how in Britain community solidarity and fan support have successfully countered the plans of some clubs to relocate. In the USA, however, fans rarely if ever oppose such moves with any degree of success and Ingham and Hardy (1984) are probably correct when they argue that 'when capital confronts community it is capital which wins the day'. Such a tendency is undeniably emerging in Britain at the present time, with moves towards relocation and the merging of football teams being mooted in cases where two existing clubs are sited relatively close to one another.

Because spectator sports are, by definition, market oriented, their owners might be expected to seek locations which have the largest market potential. Although we have seen that regional variations in demand do exist as a result of different tastes, the greatest returns are generally found in large cities. For example, in the early 1970s the after-tax profit of the most successful US baseball team was $1,075,000. That of the least successful was −$500,000. A major source of such disparities was estimated by economist Roger Noll (1974) to be the exclusivity of the geographical space afforded to each team – the regional franchise in the most lucrative markets (New York, Los Angeles and Chicago, for example) being immune from spatial competition, irrespective of the level of demand for the sport. Such a situation invites the possibility of the establishment of rival leagues, but the American experience suggests that established clubs tend to win such economic competitions and that new leagues can only succeed in new territory.

In the twentieth century in the USA there has been a broad economic and population shift to the west and south. The locational dynamics of US sports teams dramatically reflect this shift (see Figure 5.6). Some people date the decline of New York City to the mid-1950s when the Giants and the Dodgers left for the west coast and the affluence of California. We have already noted that in team sports the magic figure of one million fan visits is crucial for a team to break even. Hence, small-city teams rarely succeed in terms of profit even if grass roots interest is greatest in a relative sense. However, as Quirk (1973) has shown for US baseball relocations, though fan visits and profits may be high in the 'honeymoon' period immediately following a move, this can decline rapidly after a few years and induce further relocation. Such behaviour clearly demonstrates the significance of profit maximising behaviour in US sports. Indeed, it has been suggested that a logical extension of existing franchise movement would be to internationalise sports leagues into Japan and Mexico as well as Canada.

In the case of ice hockey it is not just large city dominance and the importance of profits, but also the presence of American control and ownership of the National Hockey League which helps explain the location pattern. In 1917 all North American professional ice hockey teams were in Canada. By the mid-1970s only three of the eighteen National Hockey League teams were in Canada and only five of the World Hockey Association's fourteen teams were so located. Kidd (1970) views such developments as part of the Americanisation of Canada and observes that 'not surprisingly this non-Canadian Organisation (i.e. The National Hockey League) has rarely acted in the best interest of the Canadian community. Given the commercialisation of the game its Americanisation is inevitable.' It is not grass roots interest but the television revenues which accrue from the more densely populated USA which are of greater locational significance.

Even in some sports which have been geographically organised according to the tenets of periodic marketing, commercial pressures have had the effect of increasing big-city dominance. In the case of the Tour de France, for example, recent years have witnessed places outside France bidding successfully to be stages in it. The mobile spectacle is no longer literally a tour of France but has taken in parts of Belgium and Germany. In 1987 West Berlin paid £1 million to stage the start, the riders not actually reaching France until the sixth stage.

Shifting centres of success

The locational changes such as those described so far might be most obviously associated with sports in which profit maximisation is the norm. This appears to be the case in American team sports, but in Britain the activities of those who run professional soccer and cricket appear to be more related to the maximisation of utility. Even so, certain geographical changes can be readily observed which suggest that even when the broad location pattern may be relatively static or fossilised, clubs in large cities and market areas tend to benefit from certain economic changes taking place both in the sport and in society at large. Success in sport is being increasingly associated with large cities and regional economic growth points. Let me illustrate these general tendencies with specific examples.

In Britain the removal of the maximum wage in soccer in the early 1960s meant that clubs in large population centres who could, all other things being equal, generate larger crowds, stood to gain from their in-built market potential. A bigger population meant bigger gates, which in turn produced the revenue to pay the newly spiralling wages of the best players. At the same time the general public was becoming more geographically mobile, car ownership and the motorway and by-pass networks increasing at the same time. Consumers could by-pass smaller clubs and head for the newly emerging super clubs which became locked into an upward spiral of success, being marketed to a more 'rational', discriminating consumer; old, local allegiances were dying. The overall result of these tendencies was that clubs in large cities obtained a greater share of their region's spectators. During the 1950s the share of the Football League's receipts going to the fifteen wealthiest clubs increased from 34 per cent in 1950 to 45 per cent in 1964 (Political and Economic Planning 1966). Table 5.1 shows dramatically how in the county of Lancashire the four giant clubs, Manchester United and City, Liverpool and Everton, received an increasing share of regional support during the period 1951–1971. I have already noted the positive correlation between the league standings of clubs and the populations of the areas in which they are located. What is more important to the present discussion, however, is that between 1968 and 1973 the relationship became progressively stronger – and has almost certainly continued to do so into the 2000s.

Growing 'primacy' in British sport is also exemplified by horse racing. As a result of decisions made by the Jockey Club and Horserace Betting Levy Board in 1980 certain courses, most of which are located in a ring around London, will receive help for capital projects such as the building of new stands. Others will obtain money for the course, stables and rooms while a lower tier of courses will be left to fend for themselves. In essence, the larger courses are subsidised and some of the smaller ones may have to close (Tomlinson 1986).

In some cases shifts in sports success may be associated with regional change in the economy. In Britain it would be tempting to link the growth of the East Anglian football clubs of Norwich and Ipswich with the growing affluence of that part of England. Likewise, the relative success of Aberdeen FC may be associated with the oil boom off the east coast of Scotland. Most graphically, perhaps, has been the broad southward shift of success in the English football scene shown by the 'southernness index' in Table 5.2. A technically more sophisticated and geographically more precise approach to exploring the southward shift of success in the English Football League was undertaken using centrographic statistics and plotting the changing geometric 'centre of success' on a map of England (Waylen and Snook 1990). It was established that, whereas in 1921 the centroid of Football League clubs was north of Derby, by 1987 it had shifted to the south-west of Leicester.

Table 5.1 Shifting shares of football support in Lancashire, 1951–71

Year	Total number of supporters watching games in Lancashire	Approximate percentage of supporters watching Man. City, Man. Utd., Everton and Liverpool
1951	7 million	40
1961	6 million	50
1971	5.5 million	66

Source: Rivett 1975.

Table 5.2 The southward shift of the English Football League, 1910–1990

Year	North	Midlands	South	Southernness index
1910	70	15	15	22.5
1930	64	18	18	27
1950	50	23	27	36.5
1970	41	27	32	45.5
1990	25	25	50	62.5

Source of data: *Rothman's Football Yearbook*, various editions.
Note: The 'index of southernness' ranges from 0 (all clubs in the north) to 100 (all in the south). It is calculated by applying the simple formula: $((N \times 0) + (M \times 1) + (S \times 2))/2$, where N, M and S are the percentages of clubs in the north, midlands and south respectively.

As areas of traditional industry decline and the tertiary sectors of the economy expand, so the location of sports clubs seems to adjust accordingly. In Portugal, for example, geographer Jorge Gaspar (1982) and his colleagues charted the changing geography of the Portuguese Football League. The proportion of league clubs within 50 km of Lisbon declined from 30 per cent in 1970 to 24 per cent in 1983. Clubs in the 'interior', on the other hand, increased in number, growing from 12 per cent of the total in 1970 to 17 per cent a decade later. Spectacular growth had especially taken place in Madeira and the Azores. Whereas at the start of the decade they had no league clubs, by 1980 they together had five.

Changing spatial margins of viability

The spatial dynamics of modern sports do not only involve the question of relocation. In some cases clubs disappear from the map altogether, the result of going out of business. This section looks at some of the geographical manifestations of such decline. The death of sports clubs may be caused by the supply of clubs exceeding the demand, as occurred in the early days of professional sports in the USA in the late nineteenth century. Of the 850 professional baseball clubs formed between 1869 and 1900, for example, only 50 lasted 6 years or more (Ingham *et al.* 1987). We have seen that this problem of over-supply can be solved by the practice of collusion between league members (or cartelisation). But the fact that places which at one time have accommodated professional sports teams no longer do so may also be related to changes in the economic structures of the nations or regions in which they are found. It is to this theme that we now turn.

Like any other industry which faces a decline in demand for its product, adjustments are made by firms going out of business. But there is a regional dimension. Of the league clubs in the British football industry which have been forced to leave the Football League since 1920 only two have been located south of one of Britain's most famous geographical divisions, the Tees–Exe line, separating older, industrial Britain from the more twentieth-century growth region of the south-east. The clubs which have left the league sound like a roll-call of the towns of the industrial revolution: for example, Aberdare, Merthyr Tydfil, Gateshead, Barrow, Accrington and New Brighton. The newcomers, on the other hand, include Wimbledon, High Wycombe, Shrewsbury, Bournemouth, Oxford, Cambridge, Peterborough and Ipswich. The Welsh historian, Gareth Williams (1983), has shown how in the years of the Great Depression in South Wales, it was principally those rugby clubs in the most severely depressed areas of the coalfield which suffered and went out of business while those in the somewhat more buoyant coastal areas remained viable. It should be noted that these were amateur, not professional, clubs, and decline and demise associated with economic conditions should not be thought of solely as affecting sports as business enterprises. Recession and depression will affect the ability of participants to take part in amateur as well as professional sports.

In professional sport, clubs at the economic margin and geographic periphery are often forced to sell their best young players in order to survive. Having paid something into the bank to reduce their overdrafts they buy a replacement player and are back to square one, hoping that more youngsters will make the grade. Stepney (1983) commented that 'this kind of asset stripping invariably angers supporters because it highlights the commercial imperatives of the game'. Those who stand to gain from the 'embourgeoisement' of football are the large, successful clubs in the bigger cities.

As already noted, clubs can go out of business because there has been too rapid an increase in the number of clubs and the demand for the sport has been more than satisfied. The British example of speedway racing in the 1950s illustrates how in such cases the spatial margins at which the sport is viable contract and hence reduce the distribution of the sport over geographic space. In the immediate post-war years speedway experienced a rapid rise in popularity. Towns throughout the UK adopted speedway racing teams; clubs were found from Cornwall to Scotland. By the 1950s speedway was becoming increasingly dominated by the Wimbledon team and results became rather predictable. Because uncertainty of outcome is regarded (by some economists) as essential in maintaining attendances at professional sports, interest in speedway began to decline in the mid-1950s. By 1957 the number of clubs had more than halved and the craze for speedway had passed its peak. But the clubs which closed down were not randomly located; they tended to be geographically peripheral and in small towns. The spatial margins to viability had contracted and what speedway racing remained was concentrated in the areas of greatest economic potential in the national space economy.

Decline and demise can be brought about also by the desire of club owners to switch their investment from sport to alternative, more profitable, land uses. If a new location is not found the club either merges with another or goes out of business. This form of asset stripping involves not the sale of players but the rejection of the sport altogether. The situation is most likely to arise when sports clubs are located at prestigious inner city sites on which alternative land uses are vastly more profitable. The single London borough of Fulham and Hammersmith possesses three professional soccer clubs, Chelsea, Fulham and Queens Park Rangers, whose sites are basically all owned by one property company. The commercial logic is to develop the sites and merge, or relocate the clubs. However, when the merger of Fulham and Queens Park Rangers was seriously proposed in early 1987, with a view to developing expensive residential accommodation on Fulham's riverside site (then valued at over £20 million) an alliance of local supporters' groups, the Football Association, Members of Parliament and other lobbyists succeeded in preventing such a move. However, the signs are clear; just as we have seen the decline of clubs in the north of England we may be witnessing pressure for decline and closure of clubs in the metropolis, but for different reasons.

Widening margins of recruitment

The final manifestation of growing rationality in the spatial organisation of sport is the more systematised methods used by sporting organisations (clubs and colleges) to recruit superior talent. A basic characteristic of folk games and early sport was their localness. Teams were mainly made of players from the neighbourhood of the club. Indeed, in folk games ascription (i.e. being a member of a village or town) was more important in qualifying for membership than was the achievement criterion, now a universal characteristic of modern sport. As seriousness, increased competitiveness and professionalism spread into sport, the catchment areas from which clubs drew their players increased.

Within individual countries the spatial margins of recruitment vary according to the resources of the various clubs or, in the USA, colleges. For example, in Britain the giant soccer clubs have the world as their recruiting oyster; clubs languishing in the lower reaches of the Third Division, on the other hand, tend to rely more on local talent. The same is true in the USA where big-time sports colleges out-recruit, in a spatial sense, the smaller colleges. Clubs in areas which produce an insufficient number of players to meet their own needs make do by recruiting from elsewhere. This tendency has existed for many years. For example, the English south-coast football team, Brighton and Hove Albion, imported what amounted to an entire team from Dundee in Scotland when they were formed in 1900 (Lowerson and Myerscough 1977). Indeed, Scotland has long been a source of soccer talent for English clubs, over 1,600 Scottish-born players having been lured south between 1946 and 1981 (Lay 1984). In Europe and North America the importation of players from outside the local area has rarely appeared to alienate support. As Korr (1978) has put it, in the context of the early days of the London soccer club, West Ham United, what the community wanted was not local representation on the field, but the chance to participate in a vicarious battle that would end in victory for their 'gladiator'. The intensification of professionalism (either implicit or explicit) and commercialism in sport, together with improved national and international modes of communication and a relaxation in restrictions on the international movement of sportsmen and women, has meant that in several sports the spatial margins of recruitment embrace almost the entire world – part of the process of globalisation noted in Chapter 3. This tendency can be illustrated with several examples.

The number of foreign players in British soccer increased dramatically during the 1980s and 1990s, following the lifting of restrictions on the international movement of labour within the European Union (Lanfranchi and Taylor 2001). However, movement was not one-way; in 1986 about 40 per cent of English league professionals had, at some time in their careers, played for foreign clubs, many in the USA and Asia, often near the end of their careers. A small number of younger players had been lured by the lire to Italy. In the early 1990s there were less than 20 footballers of non-British origin playing in the English Premier League; by 2000 there were 250. In the European context, the UK is not a major exporter of football talent. Players from the Scandinavian countries, where the professional game is less well developed, have been attracted to Germany, Italy, France and England, and South American and African players have also been recruited by the European clubs. In western Europe, the percentage of top-league players who are foreign often exceeds 30 per cent. In Belgium the figure is over 40 per cent. A relatively recent development has been the substantial recruitment of players from Africa (Figure 5.7). In 2000 over 5 per cent of western European top-division players were African (Bale 2002). This figure would be substantially higher if players whose parents were African was included.

In the USA a substantial number of foreign recruits have been drafted to both professional and college sports, the numbers increasing dramatically since the 1950s. Intercollegiate sports especially have witnessed the increase in overseas recruiting. Few foreigners were recruited in the 1950s; by the mid 1990s foreign recruits in NCAA (National Collegiate Athletic Association) schools alone totalled 8,851, amounting to an average of 10.5 foreign student athletes per institution (NCAA 1996). If non-NCAA colleges and universities were taken into account the overall figure would certainly be in excess of 10,000. For men the major sports that recruit

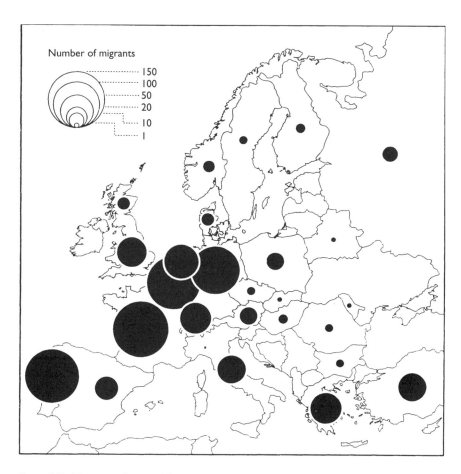

Number of migrants

150
100
50
20
10
1

Figure 5.7 African professional footballers in Europe, 2000 (source of data: Ricci 2000).

foreigners are soccer, tennis, ice hockey and track; for women tennis, track, volleyball and basketball attract most foreigners. In men's ice hockey over 25 per cent of student-athletes are from outside the USA. The major national supplier of foreign student-athletes to the campuses of US colleges is, not surprisingly, Canada which sends over 28 per cent of the total. Other important sources are the UK and Sweden. In certain sports, the widening margin of recruitment is graphically illustrated by the fact that in the mid 1960s Africa provided only 4 per cent of élite foreign track recruits; two decades later the respective figure was 30 per cent, with Kenya alone supplying over 10 per cent (Bale 1991).

As college sports in the USA become increasingly part of the entertainment business and the emphasis on winning becomes greater, so talent scouts have increased the spatial range over which they are prepared to recruit. Indeed, it may be actually cheaper to recruit overseas than to do so in the USA, given the right contacts or just good luck. A telephone call to Britain, for example, may be cheaper than scouring the whole of North America; in addition, out-of-state college fees are sometimes waived for foreigners, thus making their scholarships cheaper than those of in-state students. Although track and field is probably the best known of the college sports in which international recruiting takes place, similar trends have occurred in a number of other sports, notably in tennis and soccer. Even gridiron football has not been totally immune.

The growing internationalisation of recruiting has not been without reaction from the host countries. For example, in US baseball, rules were imposed in the mid 1970s to restrict major league clubs from increasing their signings from the Caribbean by assigning a quota to each club based on its previous usage of foreign athletes (Rupert 1980). In the case of English cricket, overseas migrants accounted for over 18 per cent of the registered county players (Maguire and Stead 1996). Various attempts have been made to limit the number of foreign players in many sports in Britain. With freedom of movement of labour enshrined in the European Union law, however, most such restrictions have proved abortive. In cricket, a sport where few European nations have players of a high standard, county teams are limited to one foreign player per team. In ice hockey a limit of three exists. US colleges have frequently demanded a reduction or even a ban on the recruiting of foreign student athletes, who have been perceived as competing at an unfair advantage over often younger American athletes and also taking away athletic scholarships from American citizens. The view that more mature recruits are at a competitive advantage over recently graduated high-school students has frequently been aired. Attempts to reduce the amount of 'athletic eligibility' for athletes recruited over the age of twenty have been partially successful in reducing the flow of such migrants, but a glance at recent results of the NCAA track and field championships, for example, shows that the contribution of foreigners remains significant.

As noted in Chapter 2, a somewhat more sinister phenomenon has been the attempts by athletes to assume the nationality of foreign countries in order to be able to compete at the highest levels. The infamous Zola Budd case is the best known; the Danish-Kenyan, Wilson Kipketer, is another example. By the late 1990s, however, what some have interpreted as 'sailing under flags of convenience' had become widespread in many sports. Such is the pressure to succeed by individuals, academic institutions and nations.

Conclusion

In large part, modern sport is part of the entertainment industry. As profit and commercialisation have become increasingly prevalent in Western sports, so sports clubs have engaged in a number of geographical readjustments. Clubs relocate to more profitable locations; success in sports shifts to the growth points in the national space economy; spatial margins of viability of sports clubs reflect growth and decline in regional economies and the desire for success induces clubs to widen their geographical areas of recruitment. It seems likely that sport will continue to adjust geographically in response to the increasing seriousness with which it is taken. This chapter has dealt with the locational implications of such a trend but given the increased significance of sport it would be unsurprising if it has not also had significant economic–geographical and landscape impacts. It is to these subjects that we turn in the next two chapters.

Further reading

A detailed spatial analysis of modern sports has yet to be written, but much of the economic geography of sports can be teased out of the work of Roger Noll and Andrew Zimbalist (eds) (1997), *Sports, Jobs and Taxes: The Economic Impact of Sports Teams and Stadiums*. Much of sports-geographic interest in a UK football context is also found in Stefan Szymanski and Tim Kuypers (2000), *Winners and Losers: The Business Strategy of Football*. Some papers which deal with the location and relocation issues raised in this chapter include Jonathon Comer and Tracy Newsome (1996), 'Recent patterns of professional sports facility construction in North America', and Bruce Walker (1986), 'The demand for professional league football and the success of football league teams; some city size effects'. On international sports–worker migration see, John Bale and Joseph Maguire (eds) (1994), *The Global Sports Arena*. Other works on this theme include John Bale (1991), *The Brawn Drain: Foreign Student-Athletes in American Universities*, and Pierre Lanfranchi and Matthew Taylor (2001), *Moving with the Ball*. A useful website on stadium geographies is ⟨http://garnet.acns.fsu.edu/~tchapin/stadia/stad-ref.html⟩.

Chapter 6

Sport and welfare geography

Introduction

Having considered some locational tendencies of modern sports I now want to outline the economic and social impacts that sporting locations have on the people, communities and landscapes in which they are found. Such impacts are not necessarily positive; indeed, one of the most publicised spin-offs of sports events is the large number of negative impacts generated by British football (soccer) stadiums. In this chapter the geographical spill-overs of sports, positive and negative, are described and mapped, and solutions to the negative impacts are considered. I also return to some of the ideas discussed in the previous chapter in my consideration of catchment areas of fans or 'fandoms'. In most respects this chapter adopts a more welfare-oriented approach to sports geography than previously, as it is noted that what might be sporting 'goods' for some people may be 'bads' for others.

Positive effects of sports facilities and events

Positive effects of sports facilities and events range from increased employment and income to people simply 'feeling good' about themselves, in the city or region in which an event/facility is located. A substantial amount of research has been undertaken into the economic–geographic impact of sports on cities, mainly in North America. However, given the global nature of modern sports and the international hosting of global sports events, few nations remain immune from sporting celebrations. The French geographer, Jean Gottman (1974) suggested that historical religious pilgrimages have been replaced by modern international flows to such rites as the Olympic Games, the World Cup, national championships, cup finals and even smaller events. Gottman believed that such sporting occasions are among 'the important components of the centrality of large cities'; the mega-structures which often contain them are not only symbolic of, and contribute to, the life and personality of places but, more importantly from an economic perspective, enlarge the movement of transients between cities and hence contribute to the wealth and economic dominance (positive spill-overs). As noted above, such focal points for major sports events are not restricted to the Occident or the 'developed' world. Indeed, the desire of 'Third World' nations to host mega-events is gradually being satisfied. Rio de Janeiro possesses the largest stadium in the world, Mexico City has hosted the Olympics and two World Cup competitions, Kingston, Jamaica and Kuala Lumpur, Malaysia, have accommodated the Commonwealth Games. Almost every 'Third World' capital, from Suva to Santiago, houses a National Stadium, without which they would not be real capitals and without which they cannot assert themselves in the world of international sport (Figure 6.1).

Stadium construction in many modern cities results, therefore, from more than simply a desire to improve facilities for spectator sports. Lipsitz (1984) argues that the Dodger Stadium in Los Angeles, for example, drew attention to the city's transition from a regional centre to a national metropolis while the Houston Astrodome, built as an anchor for a hotel

Figure 6.1 Although smaller than the stadiums of many small colleges in the USA, the National Stadium in Fiji is a symbol of nationhood and an assertion of modernity.

and convention centre complex, proved sufficiently newsworthy to advertise the growth of that city. Likewise, the Superdome in New Orleans and the Skydome in Toronto set the stage for tourist-based growth programmes for the cities' downtown areas. In Europe, the Globe and the Millennium Stadium have done much to promote Stockholm and Cardiff respectively (Pred 1995; Jones 2001).

To accommodate the transients who move to sporting rituals, transport, lodgings and many other services need to be provided. Existing businesses often increase their revenues from sports events; employment is created for the construction of stadiums and other facilities; travel agents set themselves up in business to specialise in sports tourism. The movements which are generated by sports events tend to contradict the view that the Internet, telephone and television have eliminated the desire for geographical interaction. Consider the economic benefits of, say, football to a large urban area. At the stadium itself, spectators spend money on tickets, concessions of various kinds, e.g. food, replica shirts, memorabilia, programmes and parking. In addition, and in the USA in particular, a visit to a football game is often part of a visit to a city. Hence, lodgings, fuel for vehicles, shopping, outside-stadium parking, taxis, chartered buses, public buses and eating are all part of the expenditure generated by sport. Near British soccer grounds, pubs and other retail outlets may increase their revenue by as much as 500 per cent on match days (though as we shall see later, some actually lose money on such occasions).

Even quite small sporting events can generate substantial amounts of revenue for the communities within which they are located. If these take place annually they become regular injections of income for the local economic system. Take, for example, a relatively modest event that occurs annually in Peterborough, Ontario, in Canada. The Peterborough Church League Atom Hockey Tournament has a 23-year history and is probably the largest recurrent sporting event in the Peterborough community. Today it attracts 3,000 players, coaches and spectators for 4 days of competitive ice hockey and associated social activities. Because competitors come from all over Ontario, parts of Quebec and the north-eastern USA, a considerable amount of money is spent on, for example, accommodation, meals, parking, gasoline, drink and souvenirs. In 1982 over $165,000 was spent in these ways (Table 6.1).

Other examples illustrate the impact of bigger sports events on local economies. Football at the University of Wisconsin at Madison is typical of American big-time college sports. The Greater Madison Chamber of Commerce attempted to establish the expenditure in Dane County by out-of-county football fans who came to watch Wisconsin games during the six weekends of football activity in 1975. Parents of students (who may have come to Dane anyway) were excluded but it was estimated that football visitors alone spent $4,680,000 during the period concerned. Restaurants

Table 6.1 Summary of total expenditure for the Peterborough Church League Atom
Hockey Tournament, 1982

Distant teams	$130,637
Local teams	11,374
Spectators	2,704
Players' and spectators' children	8,481
Households supplying billets	2,666
Tournament team entry forms	9,303
Total	$165,165

Source: Marsh 1984.

and bars were the major beneficiaries of this spending but owners of many
other retail outlets also gained. If locals and parent visitors were included
the direct impact of football was estimated at a staggering $6,315,000. It
was estimated that if indirect impacts (that is, spending by the recipients of
the dollars generated by football) were included the total would exceed
$13 million (Cady 1978)! More detailed analyses have been undertaken
into the expenditures generated by the Atlanta Falcons football team for
the seasons 1966, 1972 and 1984. Attending Falcons' home games over
321,000 times in 1984, fans introduced nearly $12 million into the city's
economic system. The nature of this expenditure is shown in Table 6.2.

It is possible, of course, that money spent by local fans would have been
spent in Atlanta anyway, but if it is assumed that the 96,000 out-of-town
fans brought new money into the Atlanta economic system it is clearly an

Table 6.2 Summary of expenditures by Atlanta Falcons' fans and visitors, 1984

Objects of expenditure	Sources of expenditure (thousands of dollars)				
	Local fans	Out-of-town fans	Teams	Visiting press	Total
Tickets	5,040	2,160			7,200
Concessions	658	282			940
Parking	168	82			250
Food and drink	453	1,092	32	30	1,607
Other entertainment		322	6	9	337
Lodging		750	74	64	888
Gasoline	110	272			382
Shopping		239			239
Parking	37	15			52
Buses	47	11	16		74
Taxi				9	9
TOTAL	6,513	5,225	128	112	11,978

Source: Schaffer and Davidson, 1985.

economic advantage. Furthermore, visiting press and visiting teams will spend money in the city in a variety of ways. In addition to the expenditures shown in Table 6.2, we must include the purchases and payments made by the Falcons football outfit itself. For many services an overwhelming proportion of expenditures and payments is made locally (e.g. transportation, construction, eating and drinking, employee payments) and in 1984 the total local expenditures made by the Falcons exceeded $15,051,000. However, this is not the end of the story because all this money is in turn spent by those who receive it and, in turn, by those who receive it from them so that the initial injection of money into the system is increased by a multiplier effect. The precise value of the multiplier will depend on the proportion of any increment of additional income spent in the local system, with allowances being made for 'leakages' out of the local economy. When the multiplier works its way through the Atlanta system, Schaffer and Davidson (1985) estimated that the extra money brought into Atlanta by the Falcons in 1984 amounted to $24.7 million. Of this, $17.3 million was spent locally and stimulated economic activity valued at $37.1 million. All this activity resulted in $16 million in incomes to local households while the local and state governments obtained revenues which together exceeded $4.6 million. If the multiplier applied to a 17-year period of their presence in Atlanta, the $291 million spent by the Falcons and out-of-town fans stimulated $640.6 million in revenues and incomes to businesses, households and local governments.

In addition to the revenues and incomes generated by sports, the local community will inevitably be involved in expenditure to attract and provide for those attending sports events. The ratio between revenue and expenditure is therefore of importance. Such ratios will vary considerably depending on the extent to which fans make use of various local facilities. For example, when ratios of revenues to expenditures by non-residents attending spectator sports were calculated for the city of San Diego in California it was found that the city received 3.36 times more than it spent on sports visitors if they enjoyed hotel accommodation. However, the revenue/expenditure ratio varied considerably if other forms of accommodation were used. For a rented cottage it was 2.50 and for day trippers it was 1.66. In a sense, of course, the accommodation is a surrogate for income and the city naturally earns less if sports spectators stay at camp sites or are day trippers (Murphy 1985).

In addition to the quantifiable benefits brought to cities through sports we have already noted that local pride and morale are boosted, sometimes merely through the presence – let alone the success – of sports clubs (see Chapter 2). In addition, a city itself obtains increasing publicity (what amounts to free advertising) through a professional sports club's media coverage. Other economic benefits include the possible generation of extra employment, new recreational opportunities for local residents, especially if going to a sports event replaces less desirable activities, and the possible generation of interests in sports among young people (Okner 1974).

We should not underestimate these external benefits of sports simply because we cannot quantify them. Many cities feel that they are not in the 'first division' or the 'big league' unless they have a professional sports team or (in America) a public stadium. As *The Economist* newspaper put it in relation to the possibility of the Minnesota Twins baseball outfit leaving Minneapolis, 'a publicly owned domed stadium is a symbol of municipal machismo'. Faced with the possible loss of the team, unsold tickets for home games were bought up by 'phantom ticket holders' made up of civic-minded citizens, city councillors and local businesses – even though the seats themselves were never filled!

The presence of really major sporting events can have a huge impact on entire regions, many negative (see below). The Olympic Games, for example, generate vast flows of international tourist traffic which stimulate the need for new hotels, parks, roads and various other aspects of regional infrastructure. For the Munich Olympics of 1972 the Federal German government, the State of Bavaria and the city of Munich pooled enough investment to produce a new mass transportation system for the entire region, subsequently inducing the growth of population through migration into the region (Geipel 1981). The 2002 Commonwealth Games was seen as a focus for the regeneration of east Manchester, leading to an increase in tourists and trade. £170 million was spent on new sports venues including the stadium, accommodation for Manchester City Football club after the games. £5 million was spent on cosmetic support for the city and the publicity associated with the events was felt to enhance the city's image. Such events not only induce massive tourist flows at the time of their occurrence but a permanent expansion of tourist business may also have been generated by these special events (Williams and Zelinsky 1970). At the level of the Olympics the expenditure before the event takes place runs into tens of millions. Even the promotion of the city during the bidding stage can run into several millions.

Such events involve regional, national and international bodies in the course of their organisation. Such bodies are, in effect, interest groups, each group being made up of 'actors' whose motives may differ. The different perspectives held by each group can have locational implications and can lead to public controversy and conflict. For example, in the planning of downhill events in the winter Olympics, the need for proposed sites to meet Olympic standards may conflict with the conservation or development needs of local or regional government or other interest groups. The infrastructure required for the development of such events is determined by several groups. Those involved following the selection of Calgary, Alberta, for the 1988 Winter Olympics are shown in Table 6.3. Interest groups, each with their own values and attitudes, are also

Table 6.3 Key 'actors' involved in the development of the downhill events for the winter Olympics, 1988

Actors	Involvement
Calgary Olympic Development Association	Responsible to International Olympic Committee for organising games, including selection of venues
International Ski Federation	Responsible for deciding if proposed sites meet Olympic standards
The Provincial Government	Control of the terms and conditions in which ski areas will be developed; also closely involved with the promotion of the Olympics
Private sector	Expected to undertake the development and operation of ski facilities; several consortia contended for the site of the Games
Other private/public sector interest groups	Lobbying or otherwise working towards influencing the outcome of the selection process

Based on Sadler 1983.

principal actors at the national and local scale. In British soccer, local community groups, football supporters' clubs, local political parties and major developers are each pitched against each other when a club is faced with closure, relocation or merger. Analogous interest groups are evident in similar situations in North America and in some cases such sports developments serve to satisfy both the political ambitions of local mayors and city governments, and the economic ambitions of real estate and property developers.

Some sports facilities, designed ostensibly for special events such as the Olympic Games or World Cup, or simply for general use, can develop over time a sufficient mystique to become tourist attractions in their own right. They can continue in their primary roles as sporting venues but can also generate additional revenue as tourist foci. In some cases such revenue is generated 'off season' when the venue is not being used for sport; in other cases tours and visits are arranged during the sports season on non-game days. Many stadiums, for example, offer guided tours; the Holmenkollen ski jump in Oslo offers tours by lift to the top of the ski jump to view Oslo and the land and sea beyond, as well as having an excellent ski museum and memorabilia outlet as part of a ski complex. Other examples of sports venues that have become part of the tourist itinerary include the Berlin Olympic stadium, the Wimbledon tennis complex and the Athens Olympic stadium for the 1896 games. Such attempts at revenue generation show that in modern sport every possibility that encourages spending is explored. It is hardly surprising, there-fore, that sporting facilities are sometimes termed 'tradiums' rather than stadiums (see Chapter 7).

A more radical view of events such as the Olympics is to see them as being dominated by economics, profit and multinational corporations. Although it is possible to demonstrate that sport does indeed contribute to the urban economy in a significant way, the question of whether the bene-fits of successfully attracting a professional club to a new location out-weigh the costs of getting the club there remains problematic. This equation is, of course, magnified when one is exploring the cost/benefit ratio of an event like the Olympics. This problem assumes all the more importance when it is realised that in the USA the majority of sports facili-ties are publicly owned. It seems that the attraction of a stadium is seen by city boosters as being a focus for urban regeneration and improved image. This flies in the face of available evidence. Marxist geographer David Harvey (2000) has noted for Baltimore:

> To improve the city, nearly half a billion dollars went into building sports stadiums for teams (one of which was lured from Cleveland) that pay several million a year to star players watched by fans paying exorbitant ticket prices. This is a common enough story across the United States (the National Football League – deserving welfare clients – calculates that $3.8 billion of largely public money will be poured into new NFL stadiums between 1992 and 2002). The state spends $5 million building a special light rail stop for the football stadium that will be used no more than twenty days a year.

The Olympic Games, while undoubtedly stimulating considerable changes in land use and transport infrastructure, can also be seen as leaving limited benefits. This has been called the 'bourgeois playground' legacy – facilities to be enjoyed mainly by the more privileged section of society (Lenskyj 2000). Studies of stadium developments and relocation in the USA have indicated that publicly financed stadiums are bad invest-ments (Euchner 1993; Baade 1995). It is suggested that unless teams are willing to finance a significantly greater proportion of the costs for new sta-diums, the city will almost certainly end up an economic loser. Euchner (1993) dismisses the rhetoric of indirect benefits and the economic effects of being a major city. An examination of the costs and benefits of moving the Texas Rangers baseball network to the city of Arlington, located between the boom cities of Dallas and Fort Worth in Texas, showed that a major initial cost item was the stadium, together with the necessary parking and roadways. In addition, there was the need to pay compensa-tion to the minor league team that already existed there and to purchase the broadcast rights of the Rangers' games. Finally, there would be the ongoing interest payments on stadium bonds (Rosentraub 1977). In order to attract the Rangers from Washington (where they had been the Senators) to Arlington, Rosentraub estimated that the total cost involved was at least $44 million over a 30-year period. The revenue projected over the same period would come from the media networks, food and drink sales, parking, gate receipts, etc. This amount was estimated at $22 million – about half the cost estimate. The financial commitments which brought the Rangers from Washington to Texas amounted to about $36 per family in Arlington per annum. This analysis ignored the kinds of multiplier effects examined earlier for a single year for the Atlanta Falcons' football games, and the psychic benefits which virtually defy quantitative measurement. Nevertheless, the cost to Arlington's local government – and hence the local taxpayer – of attracting a professional sports franchise was substantial, though somewhat less than Seattle's $60 million facility and New York's $100 million expenditure to keep the Yankees there.

Some have argued that the resurgence of downtown St Louis was stimulated by the construction of the Busch Stadium. Its creation, along with parking lots, stores and restaurants, has replaced ramshackle and marginal business establishments. Central-area oriented sports facilities may make an important contribution to the urban tax base since the increased revenues from sport and its associated land uses help to offset the loss of inner-city tax revenue resulting from the suburbanisation of activities such as offices and manufacturing and of middle- and upper-income residents (Lipsitz 1984). An alternative view of such inner city sports complexes is that they are extravagant examples of urban monumentalism and greed. For example, the Busch Stadium probably did more for the Anheuser–Busch brewing company (who own the St Louis Cardinals baseball team) than for the people of St. Louis; no slum housing was cleared or new residences built accompanying the construction of the stadium (Lipsitz 1984). Likewise the 1976 loss-making Montreal Olympics were taking place at the same time as the largest stock of slum housing in Canada and the continued discharge of untreated effluent into the St Lawrence River were being ignored (Ley 1983).

In Britain's geography of stadiums, suburban and inner-city redevelopments have developed significantly since the Taylor Report into the Hillsborough disaster of 1989. At Hillsborough nearly 100 people were killed when crushing resulted from spectators, who arrived late, charging into an enclosure that was already full. The report into this disaster led to a new generation of stadiums in Britain. In the context of this chapter, three kinds of new stadiums were constructed. These were: redeveloped stadiums on existing sites, new stadium development on greenfield sites, and new stadium development on brownfield sites. Additionally, both new and redeveloped stadiums commenced ground sharing, usually with a club from a sport other than football. Although some relatively long-distance moves were mooted (e.g. Wimbledon's suggested move to Dublin), most were over extremely short distances, seemingly demonstrating the power of place in Britain's most revered team sport. Though these stadiums contrast greatly with their antecedents in terms of design, they are not always treated with affection; as I will show in the following section they may generate nuisances for those who live in the cities that they represent.

Fandoms

The physical artifacts which sport has given to the landscape are obvious impacts which are there for all to see; in many cases they will remain as permanent features of the landscape. However, many of sport's contributions to the landscape are temporary or irregular but do, nevertheless, have a considerable impact on both people and places. This section deals with the spectator journeys to sports events which produce flows of humanity reaching peak intensity as the site of the sporting action approaches. The area over which a team draws its support is called a fan region or fandom, the size of which varies from club to club. In general, however, three factors may be said to be of prime importance in defining a fandom's spatial extent. First, as was noted in Chapter 4, is the size of the city in which it is located; second, the existing quality of the club's performance since supporters are somewhat responsive to the win/loss record of their team; and, third, the quality of the opposition. The fandom over which a club exerts its influence may be doubled during a period of a week if its opponents change from being a bottom to a top-of-division club. Other factors affecting attendances include local intervening sporting, and other, opportunities, the nature of the facilities at the ground and the weather (Thornes 1983). When investigated empirically, the fan region can vary in size according to the method of delimitation which is adopted. For example, the fandoms shown in Figure 6.2 are based on what might be termed a sample of 'hard core' supporters who said that they would be likely to attend a majority of home matches. Other surveys reveal that in the English Premier division, one fan in six travels more than 50 miles to support their team – in the case of Liverpool the figure is almost one-half (Sir Norman Chester Centre 1995). Over half of Manchester United's season ticket holders live outside the local area. These figures are certainly less than that for top-flight USA pro football if the data generated by the previously mentioned survey of the Atlanta Braves is typical. In 1984 local fans alone had an average journey-to-spectate distance of 18 miles and one-quarter of all fans came from outside the greater Atlanta area. Again, it is worth reminding ourselves that, given a spatial elasticity of demand for sport, this figure will vary somewhat from game to game. Also, the precise slope of the distance decay curve will be affected by the same kinds of factors influencing the spatial extent of the fandom.

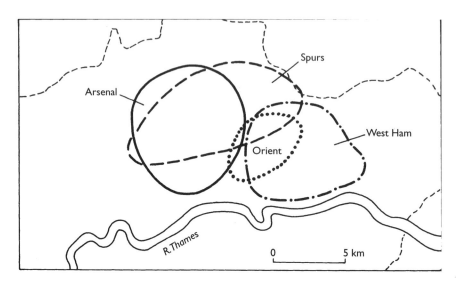

Figure 6.2 Fandoms of North London football clubs in the early 1980s based on inter-
views with 100 home supporters from each club and plotting the distribution
of fans who said that they would be likely to attend the majority of home
matches (Thornes 1983).

It is therefore within the fandom that periodic landscape impacts are felt
in the form of considerable movements of people across geographic space.
However, in the twenty-first century, support for a sports team does not
necessarily involve any physical movement from home to stadium. The
game can be brought to the home by means of television and in the USA,
where televising of live games is the norm, the size of the fan region is
more a function of the spatial extent of television penetration of the
team's games.

Some sports clubs are supported nationally, even internationally.
When Manchester United soccer team play their matches, supporters
from all over the UK converge in order to lend support. In the USA
the support for the New York Yankees and Los Angeles Dodgers
baseball teams reaches around 50 per cent of the college population in
parts of far-away Texas and Tennessee respectively, the result not only of
their playing success but also of their locations in media centres and the
resulting large amount of media attention paid them (Shelley and Cartin
1984). The presence of fandoms which are separated from the home town
of the team by many thousands of miles are a possibility given live television coverage of games. In Britain such coverage has been vigorously
resisted by the Football League. Should it become widespread in football,
the national sport, it seems likely to create even more problems (see

Chapter 4) for the small clubs who already find it difficult to survive, without instantaneous transmission of games played by Liverpool or Manchester United.

I have tried to show that fans and economic activities benefit from accessibility to sport. But some people incur negative impacts as a result, not of their accessibility, but because of their proximity to sport. Unlike the fans, such people are often consuming more sport than they would freely choose; they are victims of negative externalities of sport, a subject I now consider.

Negative impacts

The previous section showed how the presence of a sports team may bring benefits to the area, region or nation within which it is located. However, the multiplier effects which a new sports facility may bring to a locality will work backwards if the facility should decide to move elsewhere. Franchises are mobile but communities are not. When the Rams left Watts for Anaheim, the Los Angeles Coliseum lost $750,000 in rent since the Rams were the major tenant. Watts lost its income derived from the presence of the Rams and their fans. It also lost whatever civic pride the team provided. As Alan Ingham and his associates have put it, the Rams' relocation served to 'materially and symbolically exacerbate the community deformation process' (Ingham *et al.* 1987). Losing a professional sports team may not only threaten the community's financial and psychological well-being but also serves to highlight how a facility with few alternative uses can become an economic (and local political) liability.

However, the most obvious negative impacts inflicted by sports are those that might be best described as sport-induced nuisances. It is the journey to spectate that directly and indirectly provides a major impact on urban areas. The journey to a football ground, in many countries often undertaken by car, is just one of what might be termed 'stages' in the spectating experience. Three of these – the journey to spectate, the in-stadium experience, and the journey home – possess the potential for major environmental impacts. The other two (Figure 6.3), recollection and anticipation, are also important because it is upon these that the journey to the next game in part depends. If the recollection is satisfactory it is the best publicity a destination can achieve, for it promotes return visits (Murphy 1985). Bad experiences, such as a boring game, a bad performance by the fans' team, harassment from hooligans or police, or congestion and parking difficulties en route to the game may reduce the level of anticipation for a future visit. Such bad experiences are often cited as at least a partial contribution to the post-war decline (from over 40 million in 1949 to less than 18 million in 1986) in the numbers attending Football League matches in England.

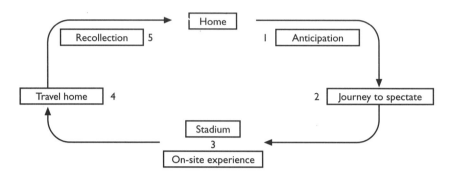

Figure 6.3 The five stages of the sports spectator's experience (adapted from Clawson and Knetsch 1966).

Negative spill-overs affecting the areas proximate to sports events are not a new phenomenon. After a visit to a New York racetrack in 1842 it was felt that the 'crowd and dust and the danger and the difficulty of getting on and off the course with a carriage are scarcely compensated by any pleasure to be gained from the amusement' (Barth 1980). In Britain the negative aspects of football were felt in city centres in the years around the start of the present century. The destruction of virtually every street-lamp around Hampden was the way the *Glasgow Herald* described the aftermath of the 1909 Scottish Cup Final. Less desirable spill-overs from British soccer were widely felt around many football grounds at the turn of the century (Inglis 1983).

The basic theoretical background for an examination of spill-over effects comes from welfare economics by way of welfare geography (Smith 1977). For the purposes of this chapter welfare geography can be viewed as the spatial and environmental effects of 'goods' and 'bads' which spill over from a sports facility into an adjacent community. Respectively, they are known as positive or negative spill-overs. They are 'external' to their sources and are thus also termed 'externalities'.

Generally, people residing or operating businesses within an external-ity's spatial field can be said to suffer from proximity to the source of an externality and benefit from accessibility to it. Such a relationship is shown in Figure 6.4. Here the vertical axis measures costs and benefits, the horizontal axis shows distance. S is the sports facility (say, a stadium). Two graphs, each declining with distance from the stadium, denote positive and negative spill-overs respectively. Beyond point L positive spill-overs exceed negative effects. Beyond N no negative effects are felt and beyond P neither positive or negative effects are found. An attempt to verify the relationship between the positive and negative externality curves, as shown in Figure 6.4, can be illustrated by data taken from a study of the perceived impact of three sports facilities in Peterborough, Ontario. A sample of residents living within a kilometre of each facility was asked if they perceived the facilities to generate negative and/or positive spill-overs. As Figure 6.5 shows, in the nearest sample of respondents to a facility (those in the 0–250 metre band), the number claiming that they perceived positive effects virtually matches that of those noting negative effects. Further away from the facilities the gap between the percentages perceiving positive effects and those perceiving negative effects increases. The numbers perceiving negative effects decline more steeply than those seeing the facilities' effects as positive. I should stress, however, that positive and negative externality curves do not always conform to the relationships shown in Figures 6.4 and 6.5.

Bad experiences of a sports event – sport as nuisance – has been researched mainly in the context of the British football industry. Several studies have explored the nuisances of football matches, as perceived by residents living in proximity to them. Two main dimensions are explored in such studies. These are the spatial extent of the nuisance, i.e. how far away from the stadium nuisances are perceived to 'spill over' from it (as, for example, in Figure 6.5), and the nature of the individual nuisances and their relative importance to those who perceive them.

Before considering the nature of sport-induced nuisances it is worth noting that in the case of Britain's most popular sport, the general public tends to over-estimate the extent of such effects. In Britain the football stadium is stigmatised by many people as a noxious facility. Figure 6.6 compares the responses of a sample of the British public who thought that

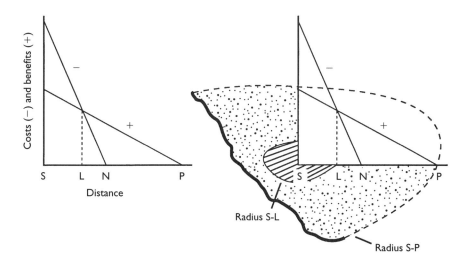

Figure 6.4 Positive and negative externality effects for a sports facility.

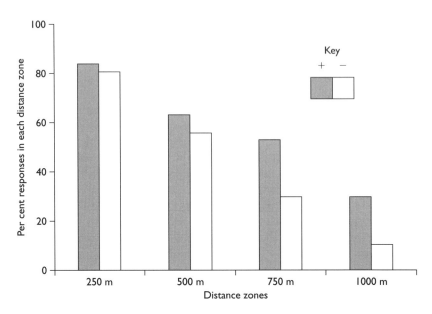

Figure 6.5 Positive and negative perceptions of the effects of three sports facilities in Peterborough, Ontario (after Maurice 1994).

they would experience match-day nuisances if they lived near a football stadium (graph A) with a sample of residents who actually experienced such nuisances, living as they did within 1.5 kilometres of a Football League ground (graph B). Of the former sample, over 90 per cent thought that they would suffer football-induced nuisance if they lived within 0.5 kilometres of a football ground. About half felt that these would be 'serious nuisances'. Over 25 per cent thought that they would consume such nuisances if they lived between 1 and 1.5 kilometres from the stadium. In the case of those who actually lived in proximity to stadiums the responses were much lower. For those living within 0.5 kilometres, only slightly more than half experienced nuisances, less than 20 per cent serious nuisances. Only about 5 per cent experienced nuisances if they lived in the outer zone. Obviously, there will be considerable differences in nuisance consumption between different grounds (Bale 1990).

The popular press might lead readers to believe that vandalism and hooliganism were the major problems associated with British football. However, several surveys suggest that not only are other nuisances such as traffic congestion and parked cars perceived as serious by more local residents (Table 6.4) but they are also perceived as such over a wider geographical area. Put in more explicit geographic terms, while a general 'nuisance field' can be identified there are spatial variations in the extent

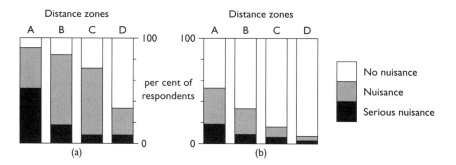

Figure 6.6 Expected (a) and actual (b) perceptions of nuisance living within 1.5 kilometres of selected English football stadiums (Bale 1990).

of individual sport-generated impacts that go to make up the overall nuisance. The impact of some nuisances is very localised and perceived by a small number of people, while that for others is more widespread and felt by many residents. Such patterns have been shown to be typical of many British clubs. While a distance decay pattern has been the traditional model used to represent such nuisances, a recent development, in Britain at least, has been the growth of nuisance outliers, some distance away from football grounds. In recent decades England's soccer supporters have become what amounted to a mobile 'nuisance field', taking trouble with them to various European venues. The areas around stadiums in several capital cities temporarily became latter-day landscapes of fear.

The traffic and parking impacts that are perceived by most stadium communities as nuisances reflect the frequent inability of existing road networks to handle the traffic which stadiums generate. This even applies to newer stadiums, often located close to a club's previous 'home'. Central city located stadiums can overtax the already-congested streets of the downtown and increase the off-street parking problem. Central city traffic congestion can be at least partially overcome, however, by special access

Table 6.4 Ranking of main problems, as perceived by residents according to distance from 'the Dell', Southampton in the 1980s

Zone A (0–500 metres)	Zone B (500–1,000 metres)	Zone C (1,000–1,500 metres)
Traffic	Parked cars	Parked cars
Pedestrians	Traffic	Traffic
Parked cars	Pedestrians	Hooligans
Hooligans	Hooligans	Pedestrians
Noise	Noise	Noise

Based on Humphreys *et al.* 1983.

ramps to the facility and by the construction of new parking lots (often, again, at the expense of inner city low-income housing), by peripheral parking with mass transit shuttle service to the sports facility, or by effi- cient subway access.

The main impacts generated by travel in relation to sports events tend to be felt after the events because crowds try to leave within a consider- ably shorter space of time than they take in arriving. It is common for over half the spectators to arrive at least an hour before kick-off. In really big events the first spectators arrive many hours before the start. The concen- tration of 40,000 or more people leaving a stadium at once may put serious strains on public transport. Suggestions to reduce such pressure include direct footways linking stadiums with railway stations, extra mass transit systems, park and ride programmes and post-match entertainment avail- able in the stadium to aid the spreading of departures over a longer time period (Saunders 1972).

The costs of sport-induced nuisances to those who unwillingly consume them are difficult to estimate. Traditionally the community benefited from a major sports stadium because rateable values (taxes) were high and the necessity for public services was low, thus creating savings to the rate- payers. Police were traditionally mainly deployed inside football grounds, the clubs bearing the costs of such policing.

As football clubs in England have sought to diversify their activities for financial gain, it has been possible to compare the spill-overs from football with those from other stadium-based events. Spill-over effects from non- sports events that are held at sports facilities have been shown to be less than those effects generated by football. For example, a study of stadium spill-overs generated by Ipswich FC's Portman Road ground revealed that although occasional large-scale rock concerts increased the noise nuisance, football-induced nuisances were regarded by nuisances by a larger number of local residents (Chase and Healey 1995). The general nuisance fields of football matches and rock concerts are shown in Figure 6.7.

It would be erroneous to assume that new, suburban stadiums have necessarily eliminated the nuisance effects so well documented for older facilities, located amid residential areas. For the Scottish football club of St Johnstone, a new location in suburban Perth failed to eliminate foot- ball-generated nuisances. However, because about three-quarters of the new stadium's externality field comprises non-residential areas, the number of people who experience such nuisances is less than it was at the club's former inner city stadium (Mason and Moncrieff 1993).

During the past two decades the policing of soccer matches outside grounds has increased dramatically as police have enforced the segrega- tion of home and visiting fans. The costs of such police work is borne by tax payers. Whereas previously retail outlets near grounds increased their revenues on match days, today many put up shutters in order to prevent

a) Football matches   b) Rock concerts

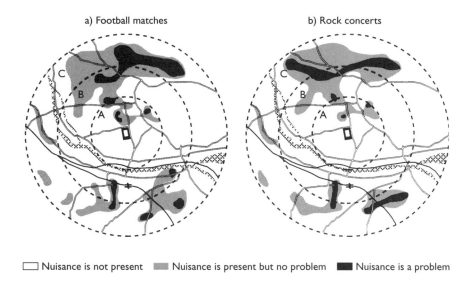

☐ Nuisance is not present   ▨ Nuisance is present but no problem   ■ Nuisance is a problem

Figure 6.7 General nuisance fields for football matches and rock concerts at Portman Road, Ipswich (reprinted from *Applied Geography*, 15, J. Chase and M. Healey, 'The spatial externality effects of football matches and rock concerts', pp. 18–34, © 1995, with permission from Elsevier Science).

entry. The costs of nervous stress imposed on local residents is difficult, if not impossible, to quantify. In addition, the community around the ground will incur costs resulting from traffic delays, the loss of car parking space and the use of streets for children's play. All these nuisances rarely result in compensation, except, possibly, in the reduced cost of housing. The effect on house prices of different sports facilities can be illustrated by an early 1970s study that estimated that a £5,000 house located within 10 miles of central London would, on average, experience a reduction in price of about 2.5 per cent as a result of its next-to-stadium location (Bowen 1974). More expensive houses would suffer greater percentage reductions – a £20,000 house by as much as almost 12 per cent (Figure 6.8). Some sportscapes, on the other hand, have a price-enhancing effect. The classic example is the golf-course effect, estimated for the early 1970s to increase the price of a £5,000 house by about 14 per cent. For playing fields the effect is rather different. For the cheapest category of house the effect of being next to a playing field is price-enhancing but for the more expensive categories it is seen to be price-reducing. Though house prices have risen dramatically since the 1970s, the relationships shown in Figure 6.8 are likely to be about the same.

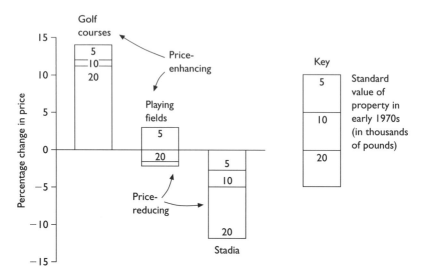

Figure 6.8 Percentage change in prices of three types of property within 10 miles of Central London when located next to different sports facilities (adapted from Bowen 1974).

One way of eliminating negative spill-over effects is to locate the noxious sports facility in areas within which the externalities can be spread out over non-residential areas. Suburban locations may be the answer, though in Britain, as we have seen in Chapter 4, suburbanward movement has not even started to approach the extent reached in the USA. Where this has taken place amid complementary land use, sports facilities may be starting to have an impact on urban morphology, encouraging as they do the potential for increased growth and polynucleation of the urban area. Given such expansion, the central area of cities often becomes run-down. At the same time, 'leisure zones' develop around the new stadiums. For example, around Stoke City's new Britannia Stadium, built on a 'brownfield' site, adjacent land users are a Holiday Inn, a health club and a public house.

Sport induces nuisances beyond the immediate impact of the stadium. At a macro-level, in the case of the notorious Montreal Olympics, it has been suggested that the benefit/cost ratio was less than 1.0, resulting from the fact that the apartments in the Olympic village were never occupied (Loy *et al.* 1978). Indeed, the Montreal Games resulted in the postponement of housing, environmental and public transport projects and reductions in the social service budgets (Kidd 1979). Geographer Kris Olds (1998) points to the negative housing impact of the Winter Olympics at Calgary, Alberta in 1998. During the construction phase of the Games 740 tenants were displaced from apartment complexes, several dozen long-term residential hotel dwellers were relocated from their rooms to make way for Olympic visitors and about 1,450 students were temporarily displaced from residences in two educational institutions.

The negative impacts on the environment (e.g. congestion, crowding) were anticipated by the state of Colorado as being so serious that a decision was made not to bid for the Winter Olympics of 1976. The argument against state subsidisation of the Games was that 'the Olympics would serve only to increase developer pressures in Colorado, creating that congestion the absence of which was one of the state's great

---

Highbury Community Association was formed in 1997 amid fears that Arsenal F.C.'s development ambitions may lead to the demolition of a row of homes on Highbury Hill adjacent to the stadium. In late 1997 Islington Borough Council was to produce a planning brief to guide any future development of Highbury Stadium. Highbury Community Association actively engaged in the consultation process arising from the formulation of the brief. They held a series of meetings with the assistant Director of Planning and convened several public meetings. The Association also used the services of consultants to support their case.

Within a year the Community Association had grown to over 550 members. Regular newsletters are produced to keep everyone abreast of issues of interest and concern. Aside from stadium-related matters the newsletters cover a range of issues including planning applications, environmental issues, community events and regeneration proposals. The Association has also been effective in attracting considerable media interest and a balanced debate about Arsenal's expansion plans. In addition to newspaper articles and radio programmes, the issue was the subject on Channel 4's 'Nothing but the Truth' series.

The Association also networks extensively with other voluntary and community organisations and participates on a range of committees. The Association has become involved in wider neighbourhood issues and is ... able to do this because of the increasing skill and awareness level amongst its members.

Due in no small way to the efforts of the Highbury Community Association, Arsenal F.C. appear to have accepted that the redevelopment of Highbury Stadium is no longer a viable option in the way it was originally conceived. It now appreciates the community's feelings and has recognised that it may have to consider sites for possible relocation rather than bring any further disruption to the lives of local people. In any case, it will not be able to ignore the feelings of the local community when it finally makes its decision.

Vignette 6 Community involvement in contesting the ambitions of a major British football club (Source: Federation of Stadium Communities 1999).

virtues' (Cox 1979). The case of the 1980 Winter Olympics is referred to by Shinnick (1979) who reminds us of the way local residents at Lake Placid viewed with considerable alarm and hostility the suggestion that the Olympic village be converted into a prison once the games had finished.

Given the negative impacts that clearly accompany the establishment of new sports facilities or sports events, a number of oppositional organisations have emerged to contest such projects. In Toronto, for example, a group called 'Bread not Circuses' is vigorously opposing Toronto's bid for the 2008 Olympics. In Britain the Federation of Stadium Communities, formed after the Hillsborough disaster, seeks to advise local activist groups about strategies to work to reduce sports-induced nuisances (Vignette 6). At a global scale an anti-golf movement has been established to counter the negative ecological effects of golf (see Chapter 6).

Conclusion

This chapter has demonstrated that sporting activities can create what are widely regarded as positive spill-overs, such as new employment, the provision of infrastructure and local economic multipliers. From another perspective it can be argued that this simply represents the increased packaging and commodification of sport. We have also seen that sport can create a number of negative externalities, both in terms of the costs it imposes on those who unwillingly consume more sport than they would freely choose, and in terms of its ecological effects. I have touched upon some of the landscape impacts of sport in this chapter and implicitly, in my discussion of relocation and suburbanisation, in earlier chapters also. The chapter which follows considers in a more explicit way the kinds of landscapes and environments within which sports take place. It takes into account certain ecological dimensions of sports but also illustrates the gradual transformation from landscape to sportscape and explores the impact such changes have on the sporting experience.

Further reading

A review of many of the ideas in the chapter, in the context of British football, is John Bale (2001), *Sport, Space and the City*. A range of views of the modern stadium, views from a variety of disciplinary perspectives, is found in John Bale and Olof Moen (1995), *The Stadium and the City*. On the political contestation of mega-sports events see Helen Lenskyj (2000), *Inside the Olympic Industry: Power Politics and Activism* and for a guide to local activism in the UK context see Federation of Stadium Communities (1999), *Stadium Communities Handbook*. On the various impacts of sports mega-events see selected articles in the special issue of *International Review for the Sociology of Sport*, 35, 3, 2000.

Chapter 7

Sites, sights and the senses in sports

Inevitably, the growth and continuing locational adjustments made by modern sports have created significant changes in the landscape. Some landscape changes are, as we have seen from the previous chapter, temporary in nature. The colours (and sometimes chaos) which marathon runners, cyclists and football spectators bring to the landscape disappear after a few hours. This chapter is more concerned with the permanent landscape impacts which sports have created. Golf courses, race tracks and stadiums are obvious examples. The sports landscape is approached initially by considering two broad tendencies which have characterised its evolution. These are (a) the gradual artificialisation of the sports environment, and (b) the increasing spatial confinement of the sites within which sport is practised. This chapter illustrates these two trends with examples from several sports and concludes with a consideration of whether such developments have, in any way, affected the overall sporting experience. The chapter is therefore rather more humanistic than those which have preceded it, dealing as it does with such notions as 'feelings' and 'values'.

From landscape to sportscape

I have already noted that the folk game antecedents of modern sports were played on rough terrain without any standardised spatial limits. Commons, streets and fields – landscapes designed with things other than sports in mind – constituted the environment in which sport-like activities were found. In the late 1500s and 1600s, however, there emerged a number of artificial and spatially confined sporting milieux in which the nobility practised games like tennis and physical recreations such as riding, gymnastics and fencing. For example, as many as 250 ball courts were said to exist in Paris in 1596, although in 1615 London had only fourteen ('Real' tennis is a modern-day legacy of such activities). Indoor riding halls were popular in much of Europe as a form of 'social geometry' which swept through the sport-like activities of the well-to-do, a sporting analogy of the landscape garden. Of course, the notion of the tennis 'court' may be interpreted not only as an area for sport but also as a way of marking the territorial bounds of the nobility at the expense of the commoners.

In Europe the court-oriented games began to lose their attraction from the end of the eighteenth century. Revolution and industry induced changes in the sport environment and, perhaps as a reaction to industrialisation, sports and recreations saw a shift into the open air; a sort of 'green revolution' was taking place in sports. Gymnastics took to the fields and woods, and later to the *Turnplatz* (the sites of German *Turn* 'gymnastics'). Sports played in the open air were showing increasing popularity: cricket in England, golf in Scotland, steeplechasing, rowing and swimming all having an impact on the outdoor environment. The indoor sports declined, so much so that only one of the indoor riding schools (that at Vienna) survived. During the nineteenth century a series of developments took place which moved sports back indoors. Sport palaces and gymnastics halls made a return but by the late nineteenth century we again see a swing to outdoor activities – cycling and later motor sports, but also the continuation and intensification of the 'English' games of soccer, rugby and cricket. At the end of the century we witness the emergence of the modern stadium and the indoor swimming pool.

It is clear that what has been described in the previous paragraphs amounts to a cyclic interpretation of the evolution of the sports landscape, in contrast to a 'linear' interpretation which would infer a gradual transition from folk games to the highly confined and artificial environments of much of the present-day sports landscape. This cyclic approach derives from the work of Eichberg (1998) who, drawing on his idea of the trialectic (see Chapter 2), sees present-day sport moving in three different directions in terms of its relationships with the landscape and environment. First, there are the continued tendencies to confine and artificialise the sporting environment. Synthetic tracks, Astroturf, concrete and domed stadiums and similar manifestations of modern technology make up industrial culture's technologised sportscape. Second, there has been a growth of 'keep-fit' movements (which may include sport-like activities) but also through various forms of statutory (in schools) and commercialised forms of physical education such as aerobic studios and 'fun running'. In such cases, however, they often tend towards the competitiveness and quantification found in achievement sport and frequently show a tendency towards the basic ethos of sport. This is noticeable in the creeping sportisation of the National Curriculum for Physical Education in the UK. Many such activities are often found in gymnasiums, windowless sport halls and keep-fit studios. A third movement, however, does reject both competition and a special sport environment. This represents a return to the neutralisation of space so that physical activities can be undertaken without recourse to specialist sites. Yoga and tai-chi, running uncompetitively and the emergence of skateboarding that reclaims urban spaces, could each be cited as postmodern examples of body cultures that defy neat categorisation. Such activities could be regarded as a reaction against the specialised sportscapes of modern industrial culture.

Confinement and artifice

Let me now look in a little more detail at the ways in which sports have become increasingly more spatially confined and have been 'played' on increasingly artificial surfaces, accepting that at the same time there have been countercurrents as noted above. In the early days of modern sport racing took place on open country, cricket on fields with unmarked boundaries, golf on coastal dunes, gymnastics in fields, football often on unenclosed land behind public houses and boxing inside the public houses. Sport was part of an existing landscape. Gradually, however, the emphasis shifted back to artificial landscapes (which had never totally disappeared) as spatial limits came to dominate the sporting scene. Sports became increasingly refined and ordered in both time and space, mirroring the growing economic rationality of the world of work. Artifice and spatial confinement, though present in the 1600s, grew rapidly to characterise sports in the late nineteenth century. Whereas in the eighteenth century cricket games usually had to wait for their fields until after the first haymaking, hence determining the latitudinal location of the season's first games (Brailsford 1987), by Victorian times the role of the groundsman (the leading cricket scientists of the time) had become paramount (Sandiford 1984). Pitches became increasingly tended in order to reduce the chance element in the bounce of the ball. The first cinder running track was built in London in 1837; the first enclosed race course and artificial ice rink in the 1870s, the first floodlights at football in 1878; the touchline followed in 1882; cricket boundaries were first established in 1885 and the dead ball line in rugby in 1891. It was an era of artifice, spatial delimitation and ordering in the world of sport. And as an increasing number of spectators became prepared to pay to watch team sports, banks and terraces were constructed around the pitches. The spatial separation of players from spectators and the identification of specific sites (to be filled and emptied at specified times) for sports, marked the end of folk games.

In the twentieth century, sportscapes – monocultural sites given over solely to sport, rather than multifunctional landscapes – have increasingly tended to characterise the sports environment. The trend towards specifically designed sportscapes started in the nineteenth century. New materials had changed the shape of the stadium and 'turf science' had modified the texture of the surface; fields became carpets and parks became concrete bowls (Figure 7.1). Most sports require artificial settings although the degree to which the natural environment needs to be changed varies. Even

Figure 7.1 (Above) Overgrown rugby field in a cleared forest near Suva, Fiji and (below) the synthetic surface of Lewis Field [sic] at Oklahoma State University, Stillwater, USA.

in sports like sailing and canoeing, in which only buoys or markers are used, it is not 'nature' which sets the challenge for the sports participant as it is for the outdoor recreationist. Instead, 'sport in all its varied forms needs specific kinds of places ... and such places must be made' (Wagner 1981).

One interpretation of the manufactured nature of sports places is that, because they are purpose-built 'with an overwhelming amount of concrete rather than just pure, uncontaminated, unmanipulated nature', they (and therefore all sports) are inclined to be anti-nature. Galtung (1984) stresses that this tendency results from the 'near-laboratory settings in which the unidimensionality of competitive sports can unfold itself under controlled conditions. Pure nature has too much variation in it; too much "noise".' The following examples of the stadium, ski-jump and golf course illustrate such a tendency in the transition from landscape to sportscape.

The stadium

The sports stadium has emerged as a spatially confined and increasingly artificial element of the landscape through a period of just over 100 years, involving four stages of development (Figure 7.2). In folk games (stage 1) no spatial limits were imposed and games were played on terrain that was usually used for other purposes. Players mixed and mingled with spectators in a rough and tumble game with no standardised rules. Following the imposition of rules, spatial limits (enclosure) were placed on the area of play (stage 2). These limits served not only to standardise the playing space but also to separate players from spectators. The imposition of the touch line in soccer in 1882 marked the end of the folk game tradition, as fans were now formally separated from players by an unambiguous straight line. Players and spectators now 'knew their place' but spectators were allowed to wander round the playing area and were not committed to specific places. In the late nineteenth century it was recognised that what were to become stadium-based sports could be comodified and people were required to pay money to watch. Initially only the principal clubs would have had enclosed fields. At first the pitch was simply roped off but subsequently pavilions, embankments, grandstands and turnstiles were required; social segregation was enforced as those willing to pay more were accommodated in superior style which, in the first instance, was simply a converted terrace (stage 3). The field was becoming a monocultural space, used for sport only and in many cases a particular sport only. In Britain football grounds, for example, gradually became used for nothing but football.

The date of commencement of each stage in Figure 7.2 varied, of course, from sport to sport. In the early twentieth century, wooden structures costing in the USA about $60,000 gradually gave way to fireproof stadiums

Stages	Environment
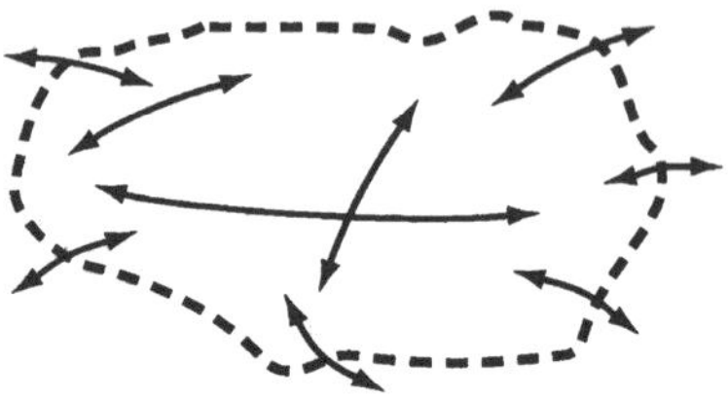	**Permeable boundaries; weak rules of exclusion** No spatial limits; uneven terrain; spatial interaction between 'players' and 'spectators'; diversified land use.
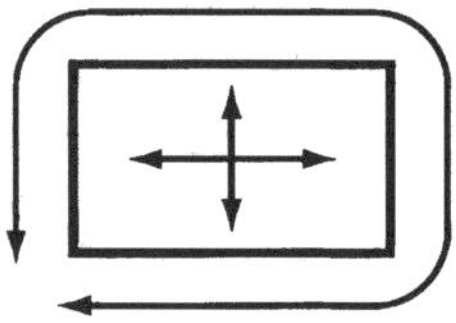	**Enclosure** Limits of pitch defined; players segregated from spectators.
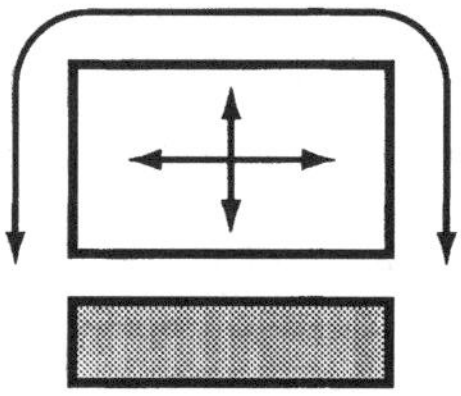	**Partitioning** Embankments, terraces, grandstands; payment for entry; segregation of spectators by social class; start of segregation within crowd; specialised land use.
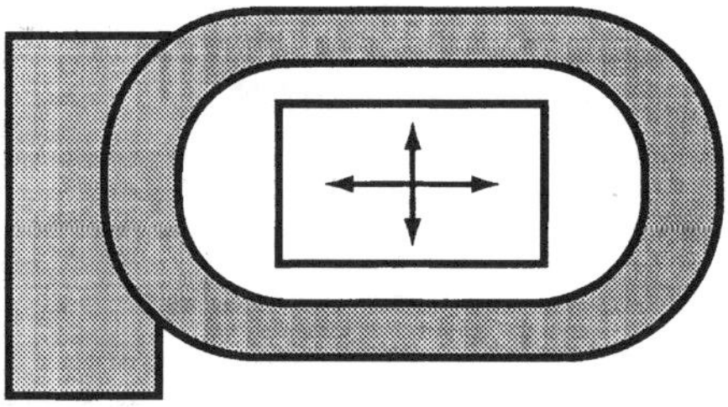	**Surveillance** Enclosed ground; synthetic pitch and concrete bowl; TV replay screen; total segregation within crowd; panopticism; diversified land use. **Rules of exclusion; strong impermeable boundaries**

Figure 7.2 A four-stage model of stadium change, 1800–2000.

costing $500,000. After about 1908 the largest US cities began to abandon the wooden edifices and the more modern stadium had arrived (Riess 1991). Stadium capacity grew rapidly once money changed hands at the turnstiles. In the USA average stadium seating capacity for a sample of 135 college stadiums grew from under 7,000 in 1920 to over 17,000 a decade later (Nielson 1986). In the inter-war years, stadiums on both sides of the Atlantic were erected to hold between 70,000 and 150,000 specta-tors, while the post-Second World War period has witnessed the building of the largest stadium in the world, the Maracana in Rio de Janeiro. Yet in many ordinary stadiums spectators were still allowed considerable spatial freedom.

In recent decades there have been significant changes in stadium devel-opment and technology has imposed itself on the stadium in several ways (stage 4). By the early 1950s the synthetic running track had appeared and the first Astroturf pitch was constructed in 1966. Glassed-in boxes have enclosed the most exclusive spectators; video screens have provided action replays, advertisements and even exhortations to cheer; synthetic playing surfaces have, to varying degrees, replaced grass; floodlights have become ubiquitous. Less benignly, in Britain less exclusive spectators, since the Taylor Report into the Hillsborough disaster, have also been confined to individual seats. Additionally, video-surveillance has arguably sought to convert the fan(atic) into a passive spectator – a 'docile body' in the words of Michel Foucault (1977). The late modern stadium readily invites the metaphor of the prison though, as noted in Chapters 2 and 6, there are other ways of 'reading' it.

In the concrete structures that have replaced the wooden grandstands, it has been averred that 'the closed circle of the bowl breaks the visual con-nection between the stadium and the town. The temporal and historical associations that say, "Here is a place connected to a landscape that grew out of a particular process" are severed' (Nielson 1986). The place becomes a 'non-place', almost identical to others of its type. It could be argued that the kind of concrete bowl – in Britain paralleled by stadiums that are said to be indistinguishable from superstores – that reflect 'place-lessness' have been superseded by postmodern structures, labelled by some (as noted earlier) as 'tradiums' rather than stadiums. Such a tag reflects the fact that the postmodern stadium is focused on trade. Such trade is far from concerned with the selling of a single sport. Rather, it is multifunctional, multi-sport and flexible. The Skydome in Toronto, for example, can accommodate many different activities – from achievement sport to play, from conferences to carnivals. It has a hotel, a conference centre, several restaurants, and a roof that can cover the arena serving to neutralise the physical environment. In Britain, the Millennium Dome in Cardiff is, in some ways, similar (Figure 7.3). The stadium has returned to its pre-modern form – a multi-functional use of space – a gigantic

Figure 7.3 The Millennium Stadium, Cardiff, is more than a 'sports ground'. It is also a focus for spending on 'experience', tours and merchandise.

The Globe [is a] market-place where commodified bodies are used to market other commodities, where the jerseys and pants of ice-hockey players are covered with advertisements for global firms that market cars and household electronic goods in Sweden (Opel, Pioneer), with advertisements for Swedish firms that globally market steel, cars, trucks, food products and insurance, with the advertisements of Swedish retail chains and coffee firms with global sources. The Globe [is a] showplace where athletic performers become little more than sandwich-board men who were once a common sight in downtown streets – and at the same time become somewhat akin to prostitutes, being commodities and sellers at once.

The interior of the Globe is highly flexible, is designed to accommodate 'as many different activities as possible', is capable of being reconfigured to serve a variety of purposes, to serve a variety of entertainment-consumption markets, to meet the particular distinction-reinforcement demands of different groups, to satisfy audiences with different tastes. The Globe can be adjusted to hold anywhere between 3,000 to 16,000 spectators through the use of retractable stands at its lower levels, of removable chairs at its floor level, of a spotlight framework that can be automatically hoisted up and down and fixed at different heights, of dismountable stages, of drapery stage wings and of ice-covered rugs. Within the space of a few hours it may be converted from any one of the following configurations to any one of the others: ice-hockey or ice-show arena; rock-music concert hall; boxing stadium; meeting or convention hall; basketball arena; choral or opera concert hall; tennis stadium; premiere-evening movie theater; circus ring; track-and-field arena. The physical flexibility and architectural design of the Globe are such that, regardless of configuration, the entire attending (consumer-) audience has a sense of being close-up, right in the middle of 'the action', in intimate proximity to the performing commodity it has purchased.

Vignette 7 One reading of the late modern 'sports arena': The Globe, Stockholm (Pred 1995).

entertainment hall (see Vignette 7). Given the variety of uses to which such facilities can be put, and because they are highly ambiguous (e.g. domes like those in Toronto or Cardiff with retractable roofs can become either indoor or outdoor at the flick of a switch), perhaps 'postmodern' is an appropriate term by which to describe them.

Ski spaces

In ski jumping, technology has made equally significant impacts on the landscapes of individual, rather than team, sports. Ski jumping initially took place for fun on natural slopes or from the roofs of houses. The changes induced by the introduction of first wooden and later concrete structures can be illustrated by the example of the famous Holmenkollen ski jump in Norway (Bergsland and Seim-Haugen 1983). Here, on the northern outskirts of Oslo, the first ski jump was set up on the natural slope of the land in 1892, the only minor modification of the natural slope being the 'take off'. This initial jump was 9.5 m high. The subsequent development of Holmenkollen has proceeded through a number of stages (Figure 7.4), culminating with a massive artificial slope constructed of concrete, 121 metres high and dominating the Oslo townscape, being visible from many miles away. Today the ski slope can only be used for ski jumping. It attracts many thousands of tourists per year and has become part of a tourist complex, possessing a neighbouring ski museum and providing tours of the ski jump and adjoining area. Technological change has, of course, been accompanied by improved performances; whereas the best distance achieved on the initial slope was 33 metres the present record stands at over 100 metres.

Other ski-landscapes have been affected by technology in other ways. Where appropriately low temperatures and suitable slopes exist in the absence of snow, manufactured snow is produced at night by snow cannons. These eject water under high pressure which turns to snow on contact with the cold air, forming a narrow strip of snow surrounded by rocks and grass. Where neither slopes nor snow exist, artificial, plastic ski-slopes are constructed for so-called dry-skiing (Tivers 1997). When there is no daylight, forest ski trails in much of Scandinavia are floodlit so that cross-country skiing may continue in what would otherwise be sub-Arctic darkness. In Finland 'indoor' skiing can take place in a tunnel. Known as

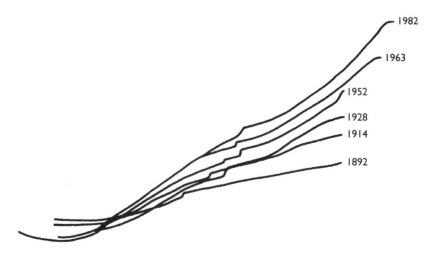

Figure 7.4 The changing long profile of the Holmenkollen ski jump, Oslo, Norway (adapted from Bergsland and Seim-Haugen 1983).

the 'ski-tube', such tunnels of 2 to 3 kilometres are planned for the future. These will enable all-year skiing in southern Finland where the demand for skiing is considerable but snowfall is not. Similarly, the huge shed containing a dry ski-slope recently opened in Milton Keynes is an example of a seriously altered urban environment. It is also possible to keep fit by skiing at home on machinery designed to simulate skiing as movement but, at the same time, to gain in fitness. 'Nordic Track' is described as the world's best aerobic exerciser. The machine becomes an extension of the body, the human being assuming the form of a cyborg (McCormack 1999). 'Indoor' skiing in its various guises reflects an extreme example of the interiorisation of sport. However, the various ways in which nature has been neutralised in the construction of skiing landscapes has not been without controversy, as noted in the previous chapter.

The golf course

A substantial amount of land today is consumed by monocultural golf courses. In the UK the estimated total is 80,000 ha (about 200,000 acres) while in the USA the area taken up by golf courses exceeds that of the state of Rhode Island (Adams and Rooney 1985). In the early days of golf, courses were smaller than at present, but with the arrival of the rubber core golf ball players were able to drive the ball further and courses increased in size as a consequence. Initially golf courses utilised quite natural terrain, coastal sand dunes covered by grass (i.e. links) being the natural home of the sport. Undulating landscapes, natural bunkers, smooth turf and well-drained soil provided the ideal environment out of which golf could grow. These conditions were ideally found in east-central Scotland – the home of British golf (Pryce 1989).

At the end of the nineteenth century there were 61 golf courses in Scotland compared with 46 in the whole of England. In the 1880s inland golf was still played on what the chronicler of the sport, Bernard Darwin (1951), described as 'glorified meadows of extreme muddiness'; inland golf was regarded as a very poor substitute for the real thing. However, by the 1890s it was discovered that landscapes of heather, bracken and sandy heath could be manufactured into inland golf courses. The tremendous demand for the sport meant that these landscapes were insufficient and arable land began to be taken over for golf course construction; the average course of 100 acres was about the size of a small farm. Previously enclosed fields and woodland were metamorphosed into carefully simulated heathland. Contests were held in golf course design. In the example shown as Figure 7.5, the hole was devised to make the player use his [sic] own judgement, according to his driving ability and weather, as to which of the five routes he would adopt. The golf architect had emerged as a kind of sub-Capability Brown figure. Sometimes problems arose when golfers

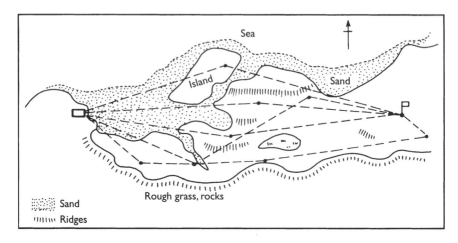

Figure 7.5 Prize design for a hole by Dr A. Mackenzie, 1914 (Darwin 1951).

encroached on common land, usually with disdain and without permission. Violence between 'commoners' and golfers was not unknown and the solution was sometimes to 'incorporate' the commoners into an Artisans' club, though this occurred less frequently than would ideally have been the case; in England (if not in Scotland) golf remains very much an upper and middle-class sport (Lowerson and Myerscough 1977).

Golf course design gradually became a sophisticated science – a long way from the situation in Yonkers, New York in 1892 when the St. Andrews golfers moved from their original location and laid out their new six-hole course in a single day (Durrant and Betterman 1952). Between 1920 and 1930 the number of golf courses in Britain was growing at a rate of 50 per year (Hawtree 1983), while in the USA between 1916 and 1930 the total grew from 742 to 5,856 (Steiner 1933). The growth of golf and the variety of landforms it colonised showed the mastery of technology over nature. In Scotland, for example, the original linkslands courses were supplemented by courses on a wide range of geomorphological features, ranging from hillsides to drumlins and from raised beaches to river terraces (Pryce 1989). Today's golf course architects have produced landscapes of fairway and green in parts of the Florida Everglades, the Nevada Desert, on a mountainside in Texas and on a strip coal mine in West Virginia. Robert Trent Jones and Peter Dye, two of the premier golf course architects of recent decades, have left their own distinctive sportscape signatures on their courses; the former provides 'lush velvet fairways, manicured roughs, tees the length of football pitches and giant undulating greens protected by lakes and contoured bunkers' (Barnes 1984). Dye, on the other hand, has tried to return to the more rugged Scottish flavour that characterised the early British courses, though some have argued that by their severity they are more penal than rugged. In urban and suburban areas, where they are mainly located, golf courses affect the nature of not only the land use but also the adjacent residential development. In the inter-war period the presence of a golf course often influenced the siting of the more affluent suburbs, large detached 'Tudor' style housing frequently abutting the suburban English course. Furthermore, golf courses are known to raise the value of houses sited next to them by around 11 per cent, as noted in the previous chapter.

Recent years have witnessed increased costs of golf course construction as the most appropriate types of landscapes become increasingly scarce. The traditional way of keeping costs down in cases where the prime motive of the developer was to construct a golf course was to build compact courses with a minimum of unused space (Figure 7.6). However, in order to counter costs several major changes in golf course design have taken place. Initially developed in the USA is the golf course that is an integral part of real estate development – or *vice versa* (Figure 7.7). By the mid 1980s about half the golf courses in the USA were of this type and are

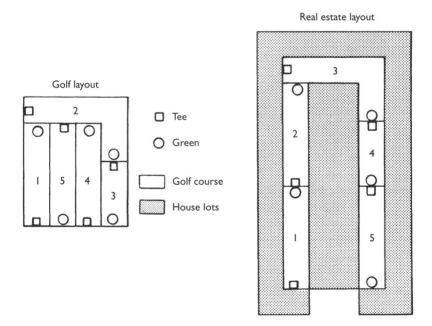

Figure 7.6 Traditional and real estate golf course models. Numbers refer to fairways. Whereas the traditional course was space-extensive, the real estate model seeks to provide maximum residential frontage (adapted from Adams and Rooney 1984).

Figure 7.7 Welcome to a residential golf community near Tarpon Springs, Florida.

currently developing in other parts of the world. According to geographer Bob Adams (1983), 'in such cases the developer uses the golf course as a tool to enhance the attractiveness and value of the real estate, with golf itself being of secondary importance'. However, an alternative perspective is that 'fairway housing' is the most lucrative opportunity to the golf course developer, since the profit from the sale of (often) up-market housing covers the cost of building the course and solves cash flow problems associated with the long delay between the building of the course and the return on investment. Either way, such developments are invariably greater users of space than the traditional course and cause considerable problems for planning authorities.

A second way to responding to increases in the production costs of golf courses is to change the design of the course. The traditional golf course was designed according to what has been termed the 'turf-farm' concept – large areas of manicured grass requiring substantial irrigation systems and mammoth materials, equipment and labour budgets to maintain. In the USA a cost-saving tactic is to reduce the in-course area needing expensive maintenance by restricting the fairway and the maintained rough to an area where golfers should be hitting their shots. In this way the area requiring expensive maintenance is reduced (Figure 7.8).

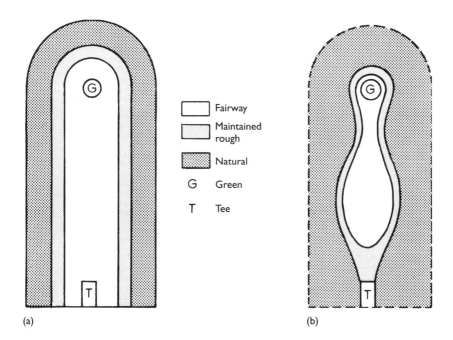

Figure 7.8 Golf course design concepts: (a) turf farm concept; (b) target concept (Adams and Rooney 1984).

Another development is likely to be the emergence of what has become known as the Cayman facility – a new, more spatially efficient form of golf first tested by Jack Nicklaus's Golden Bear Corporation in the Cayman Islands. Cayman golf employs a ball which, when hit, travels only half the distance of a regulation ball. Hence, the course using this ball needs to be only half as long as a regulation course. In addition, the Cayman course is less expensive to build, a game takes nearly half as long and the course achieves a more intense use of land than the regulation course (Hegarty 1985).

A further development in the landscape of golf is the construction of what might be termed 'grandstand' courses. On many golf courses it is difficult for spectators to get a good view of the game. With an improvement in this situation in mind, American initiatives have recently involved the construction of tiered spectator facilities alongside greens and fairways. What is more, football stadiums have recently accommodated golf in an attempt to provide fans with constant action. In 1985 Johannesburg's 70,000 seater Ellis Park Stadium temporarily became a golf course on which eight professionals played nine greens, with sand traps and water hazards cut into the turf to form eighteen par 3 holes. Tees were placed on platforms in the stands and while one foursome walked down the green the other teed off. Stadium golf is likely to be followed by synthetic putting greens and even synthetic courses.

In a sense, many courses are already synthetic, given the vast amounts of chemicals that are used in maintaining fairways and greens. In Europe and the USA, but notably in parts of south-east Asia, 'golf pollution' has become a major problem. In Japan over one per cent of the nation's forests have been cleared to accommodate golf course expansion. The removal of forests on hillsides leads to soil erosion. Huge amounts of herbicides, germicides and pesticides, colouring agents, organic chlorine and other chemicals are used on courses. Water quality has been adversely affected where water drains from golf courses into rivers and lakes. Damage to wildlife has also been reported (McCormack 1991). Advice to golfers today may include: wash hands and forearms at the end of a round; wear long pants whenever the weather allows; never play golf in your bare feet; never place golf balls or tees in your mouth; find out what chemicals have been applied to the course (Burnside 2000).

Whereas golf courses were once part of pasture or common land, with freedom of access to all, today it is not uncommon to see signs asking people to 'keep off' or impenetrable railings prohibiting entry. Golf courses are used today not merely to play golf but to sell real estate, industrial locations, hotel and conference facilities. Golf courses occupy sites which were once sites of agricultural production; today they are sights of consumption. The indoor computerised golf course has also emerged (Vignette 8), a postmodern phenomenon where the simulation appears to be better than the reality.

Writing in the 1930s, the architect Clough Williams Ellis felt that the golf course was one of the things which most threatened the distinctiveness of the English scene. The sameness, the artifice, the enclosure, or what Relph (1976) called 'disneyfication' is certainly a characteristic of many sportscapes of the modern world. The synthetic running track, the standardised 50-metre swimming pool, the synthetic Astroturf, the chemically maintained golf course, ice rinks and indoor sports halls make one sporting environment much the same as another. Add the rule-bound nature of sports and one can conclude that in few activities has there been so much pressure to make one place exactly the same as another. As sport has become a major user of land, the need for planning standards and the compatibility of land uses has arisen, the subject to which I now turn.

Finding space for sport

The inter-war years witnessed the emergence of a growing number of sports of a space-extensive nature which were to make an emphatic impression on the landscape. Motor racing, cycling, skiing and, later, orienteering, all required a considerable amount of space and, apart from the

If you drive along Highway 4 near London, Ontario, you will discover, among factories and warehouses by the side of the highway, an unimpressive containerised structure, typical of such facilities in north America and western Europe. It is called 'CaddyShacks' and once inside you can play 'real' golf. Golfers get out of their parked cars carrying golf bags containing a variety of clubs. The outdoor temperature is about −7°C and a biting wind is sweeping across the Ontario lowlands. Entering the warmth of 'CaddyShacks' you encounter a cash desk, and on one side of the building a pool table and a row of seats and tables where people are enjoying a drink or snack under sunshades and umbrellas which keep off the simulated sunlight. Facing them are six booths about 10 metres long, each with an area for teeing off at one end and, at the other, a large, wall-sized television screen above a synthetic 'putting green' with one hole. It is within this area – about 10 metres by 5 metres – that an 18 hole game of competitive golf can be played. This is done by players selecting which of a number of famous golf courses they want to 'play on' and having paid the fee a picture appears on the screen, showing the view from the first tee on the course of their choice. In turn, they place their golf balls on a tee and drive them towards the view on the screen. On hitting the screen, built-in sensors calculate the velocity and the trajectory of each ball and its flight continues, shown in simulated form by a white line on the screen. The second shot is then taken, with the appropriate club, from the point where the ball (would have) landed and the new scene on the screen shows the view from the second shot. The game proceeds in this way until the first hole is reached. When it is time to putt the ball into the hole a message on the screen informs the player where to place the ball near the actual hole in front of the screen. This is done by being told to select one of a series of numbers painted around the hole on the 'green'. Following a successful putt, the view from the second tee appears and the game continues like this for eighteen holes, if required.

Outwardly the place could be a tacky striptease joint; inside the kitsch décor and individualised booths do nothing to reduce the impression that such a 'golf experience' is analogous to the world of pornography. Just as porn offers 'the simulacrum of a pan-erotic world where sex is always available' (Stam 1988), so CaddyShacks provides a simulacrum of a world of sport where you can always play golf.

Vignette 8 Where golf is always available (Bale 1994).

last named, created to varying degrees distinctive sportscapes out of pre-existing landscapes. At the same time both recreational and serious sports have increased their demands for urban and rural land.

Land requirements differ among the many space-extensive sports. For example, orienteering requires about 750 hectares of, ideally, undulating wooded landscape with lakes, rivers and streams for variety. Uncultivated fields, commons, paths and parkland can also be utilised. On the other hand, downhill skiing needs a long gully at least 18 metres wide and 800 metres long, with a drop in altitude over that stretch of about 300 metres. The maximum and minimum slopes should be 25° and 2° respectively. Differing degrees of compatibility obviously exist, once particular requirements are prescribed for particular sports, even though they may be intrinsically capable of using the same area (Hockin *et al.* 1980). Compatible activities are those which can use the same area (of land or water) at the same time (e.g. canoeing and rowing); partially compatible sports can use the same area but not at the same time (e.g. orienteering and cyclocross) (Table 7.1); incompatible sports cannot use the same area of land and hence land zoning is required. Compatibility of sports frequently leads to conflicts in the countryside about which sport should have the right of use. Resolving such conflicts may be easy enough when the land in question is managed by an independent agent (e.g. as in the case of country parks), but becomes more problematic when the owner of the land favours one particular sport (Patmore 1983).

The less serious and less competitive the level of sporting activity, the more compatible with other sports it becomes. At the purely recreational (non-competitive) level, boating is compatible with canoeing; at the national championship level it is obviously not. In the case of serious top-class sport the sites and the sports have become so specialised that they are, at best, only partially compatible with other uses. In such cases, true sportscapes will exist.

Increasingly, various bodies set up what are regarded as 'standard' levels of provision for sport. For example, the ideal area for a football pitch is regarded as 0.9 hectares (2.25 acres). In Britain the Sports Council suggested that an urban area of about 60,000 people should have about 141 acres devoted to sports use. About 50 acres would be given over to

Table 7.1 Ranked relative compatibility of selected recreational sports

Sport	Ranked (overall) compatibility*
Orienteering	61
Cross-country skiing	54
Downhill skiing	46
Cyclocross	45
Modern pentathlon	43
Grass skiing	40
Motor car sports	25
Motor cycle sports	25
Golf	9
Field archery	0

Source: Hockin *et al.* 1980.

*High scores (over 50) indicate highly compatible sports; score under 25 indicate sports that are totally incompatible with at least half of the other activities in the list.

soccer pitches alone, 20 for cricket and the remainder to rugby, hockey and netball (Patmore 1970). Given these conditions, vast tracts of urban land are today given over to mass-appeal sports and from some vantage points come to totally dominate the urban scene. The Sports Council also recommended sport centre provision at a rate of about one per 50,000. However, as Patmore (1983) has pointed out, the rigid application of national norms may stifle much latent demand. Indeed, the figure of one per 50,000 may look somewhat low when compared with the present national provision of one per 75,000.

New sports, as they appear, affect the landscape in different ways. The marathon and distance running boom, with race fields exceeding 20,000 in some cases, has put pressure on municipal authorities to control and redirect traffic on race days. As geographer-marathoner Christopher Winters (1980) puts it, running in the USA can be understood in part as a reaction to, and an attempt to fit into, a landscape designed for the automobile (Figure 7.9). Sports like hang gliding create pressure on rural hill and scarp country, surfing on beach areas, skiing has placed ecological pressure on mountain regions and water sports compete with

Figure 7.9 Mass participation road running, as in the Potteries marathon shown here, can be read as putting pressure on a landscape designed for motor transport. Another reading is of people claiming back the streets.

one another for precious room on the limited amount of suitable inland water space.

Much sports action, especially of the space-extensive variety, inevitably takes place at the urban fringe, so much so that a peri-urban zone may be emerging – what Sommer (1975) called a 'zone of repose'. Within this girdle of recreational land he sees a futuristic belt accommodating nature trails, nudist camps, winter sports and big stadium complexes – the suburbia of Hedonopolis. Such developments will inevitably create conflict and the response will vary according to the strength of planning controls.

Sport, environment and the senses

It has been suggested that as the sporting landscape has changed over time, the potential for gratification (by both 'players' and spectators) from the sporting experience has become progressively reduced, the result of the increasing sameness in the sports landscape. In this section we consider two basic frameworks which might assist us in exploring experiential aspects of sport–landscape relations. The first is associated with what is known as prospect–refuge theory, but this has been less developed in a sports context than the second approach which views the sports landscape in terms of elements and ensembles.

It has been suggested by geographer Jay Appleton (1975) that it is an inborn necessity to hide and to seek. In the course of seeking, various views (prospects) are encountered, while in the process of hiding a satisfactory refuge has to be found. Appleton argued that the capacity of a landscape to ensure the achievement of seeing (prospect) without being seen (refuge) is a source of aesthetic satisfaction. So what has prospect–refuge theory got to do with the sport landscape and the gratification derived from it? Although running, swimming, walking and interacting in other ways with the environment (from prospect to refuge) provide sources of satisfaction when leading to survival, they persist as a source of pleasure and gratification when the biological prerequisite for survival no longer applies. There are a large number of sporting activities 'which involve the fitting of bodily movements into a context in which they can more effectively evoke the satisfaction which comes with the creature's successful participation in his [sic] entire environment' (Appleton 1975). In some sports environments such as a swimming pool, running track, gymnasium or boxing ring, the milieu may be subservient to the bodily movements as a source of satisfaction. Though satisfaction may be obtained in such relatively homogenised spaces from the spatial arrangement of the spectators vis-à-vis the 'players' (intimacy is frequently cited as contributing to the overall experience), when compared with sports like skiing or orienteering the environment is relatively unimportant as a source of enjoyment.

Although some enjoyment would probably be obtained from skiing on a featureless, sloping surface in a laboratory, satisfaction is greatly enhanced by the environment within which skiing normally takes place. In such landscapes the 'primitive' significance of the prospect becomes symbolically represented by the views, often from an elevated site (especially so in ski-jumping), the absence of hiding places in the open landscape, and the falling ground. The run transfers the skier from the world of prospect to that of refuge and rapid movement in such environments provides an exhilarating (hazardous) experience. Analogies might be made with sports like orienteering, cross-country running, hang-gliding and other such 'green' activities. Golf might seem quite different from downhill skiing but the notions of prospect and refuge can be invoked symbolically to aid an understanding of the sport–environment experience. An extended quotation from Appleton's work illustrates this further.

> A study of any golf course will reveal an extremely close parallel between the game and the experience of landscape as expressed in the terminology of prospect-refuge theory. The player takes his stance on the tee, an open and often somewhat elevated platform commanding a clear view (over falling ground) of the field through which he (represented by his ball) has to pass. From this prospect the goal can be seen as a clearing in a matrix of 'rough' to which a fairway (cf. vista) allows direct approach. Impediment hazards are introduced to right and left and very likely beyond the target. Other natural phenomena may influence his (or rather the ball's) passage, such as the wind, the wetness of the grass, the slope of the ground. That the player will reach his goal is almost certain – even a poor player is only occasionally denied that ultimate satisfaction – but the process may be achieved with a greater or lesser degree of efficiency which can be measured arithmetically by a simple criterion. When eventually he reaches this objective, he, through the medium of his representative, disappears into that most fundamental of refuges, a hole in the ground. Golf is a parody of primitive environmental experience in which the basic relationship of man to habitat is expressed in a system of stylised equivalents whose identity is very thinly disguised.
>
> (Appleton 1975, 178)

Though claimed by some to be an example of biological determinism, Appleton's prospect–refuge theory is an attempt to produce a comprehensive approach to the sports landscape and, indeed, implies a specifically geographical theory of sport.

The second approach that I will illustrate in this section comes from the cultural geographer Karl Raitz who has argued that the sporting landscape is made up of a number of 'landscape elements' which, in total, contribute to a 'landscape ensemble' (1985). He argues that the overall sporting experience is influenced by this ensemble, each element within it contributing to the sense of place experienced by the participants. The ensemble of a community baseball park in a small midwestern town might have elements which include:

> ...the playing surface with a grass outfield and chalk-lined infield; the dugouts along the first and third base fences; the bleachers or grandstand; the concession stands; the board fence with painted advertisements that demarcate the limit of the outfield; the parking lot; the adjacent streets and houses.
>
> (Raitz 1985)

The elimination of one or more elements subtracts from the distinctiveness or uniqueness of the place experience and the total replacement of the elements with what Nielson (1986) calls a 'sports saucer' (or concrete bowl) results in a break between the sport and the broader landscape of which it is part. The argument is that if the landscape elements are reduced in number and one sport place becomes much the same as another, the overall experience will be reduced too because there will be less variety to experience. The English poet and cricket enthusiast, Edmund Blunden (1985), was aware that in village cricket the landscape elements could, indeed, become more significant than the game itself. He recognised, however, that in top-class cricket 'where errors matter' there was a case to be made for 'austere cricket grounds, untouched by mysticism' so that players would not be distracted from their 'function'.

The aim of such austerity and standardisation of the sports environment is, of course, to benefit participants both on the field of play and in the grandstands, terraces or bleachers. The treatment of the sports milieu is another example of the application of scientific humanism which we see around us in shopping malls, housing estates, holiday resorts and international airports. But as we have already noted, some observers suggest that artificial environments actually detract from the sports experience. Eichberg (1982) asked: 'Is the windowless hall, made of plastic and concrete, really something progressive when compared with the wilderness in which Jahn's gymnasts wrestled?' His question is rhetorical and he provides no evidence from those who have experienced such environments. Were such evidence unavailable we could interpret such questions as élitist or atavistic, but sports participants do comment on the apparent paradox of humanistic landscapes, i.e. that though the intention is to improve efficiency and comfort a sense of dissatisfaction somehow results. Let us consider some responses to the tendencies of confinement, artifice and standardisation, first from 'players' and second from spectators.

Michael Oriard (1976), one-time American footballer, refers to the dehumanising aspects of the modern sports environment as 'the seeming lack of air in the semi-domed stadium in Dallas impressed on me a sense of unnatural stillness that was eerie as well as stifling. But playing in the Astrodome produced my ultimate non-experience.' Oriard felt a sense of constriction and an unsettling air of unreality, in great contrast to the feeling of freedom and the connotations of pastoralism in the city which had been generated by the more traditional forms of stadium. Howie Reed, a former pitcher with the Montreal Expos, told James Michener (1976, 423–3):

> I've pitched in those big, sterile stadiums in the States and believe me, it's much better to play a ball game in Jarry [a small, uneconomical ball park in Montreal]. Intimacy is an asset. I'd not hesitate in calling it the best place in the world to play baseball. It actually adds to the enjoyment of the game.

In Britain, Inglis's (1983) survey of the attitudes of British soccer players to different grounds revealed that 'the larger, more open grounds were all disliked'. Likewise, a survey of fans' favourite baseball stadiums in the USA revealed that the top five favourite ballparks were all built before 1930. The Metrodome at Minneapolis and the Kingdome in Seattle were rated 25th and 26th respectively (Douglas 1987).

In the case of golf, the American observer of the game, Herbert Warren Wind (1973), noted that 'a new breed of golfers had forgotten that much of the game's satisfaction results from dealing resourcefully with the hazards' of nature. The US tree-lined course reduced the wind hazard and encouraged a distinctively American style of play, different from that needed on the more 'natural' British course. I have shown that the golf landscape has gradually been transformed into an artificial sportscape within which modern technology is an integral part of the scene. Where bricks and mortar (the 'Condo canyon' type course) are introduced the pleasure gained from playing is certainly reduced; when the golfmobile (Figure 7.10) or, as in Japan, the monorail designed to carry clubs around the course, are introduced it is highly arguable whether such an activity remains 'sport', though 'playing' and 'recreation' may continue. Could such phenomena be sporting analogues of the commuter train, escalator or conveyer belt?

Some sportscapes may be dehumanising because they permit – indeed they may be specifically constructed for – highly specialised, regularised and rationalised training methods. Some sports take place in such environments in order to coerce the athlete into 'continued repetition of the same precisely fixed and isolated narrow tasks' (Rigauer 1981). Synthetic running tracks, for example, are designed not to make training easier but to avoid deterioration in bad weather; they are designed not to interrupt

Figure 7.10 Golfscape of modern America.

the training regimen. Although Astroturf is intended to provide benefits, sliding tackles produce unpleasant 'astroburns', the rate of injury on synthetic turf being 50 per cent higher than on natural grass in the case of American football. Given that two-thirds of gridiron 'fields' in the USA are made of plastic, horrible degrees of wear and tear on joints and tendons are the inevitable result. Heating of artificial surfaces also tends to increase player discomfort, artificial surfaces having on average summer temperatures 4.5°C higher than those of grass. Not surprisingly, players generally dislike such surfaces. Track and field athletics at the highest level are today exclusively confined to synthetic tracks, but the stiffness in these materials has again been implicated in joint and tendon injuries (Riley 1981). Grass, though less efficient, provides a more gentle surface. The marathon runner, Alberto Salazar, expressed a desire to get away from road and track and return to cross-country running, but even here artifice intrudes; at the world cross-country championships artificial 'hills' are temporarily constructed and city streets sometimes changed into 'country' by temporarily laying turf over them.

    In the modern artificial sportscape, the feelings of the fan may also be changed; 'the plushness of the theater seats and the extravagance of electronic scoreboards make the fan a passive observer of spectacle, rather than a vicarious participant in the reenactment of ancient virtues' (Oriard

1976). The traditional baseball park 'with its grassy spaciousness and sunlit diamond' can be seen – perhaps over-romantically – as 'a vestigial remnant of the rural landscape within the crowded, dirty, asphalt city' (Oriard 1976). Such a sense of attachment to, and affection for, sports places – and the kind of political activism in support of their survival (see Chapter 6) – contribute to what geographer Yi-Fu Tuan (1974) has termed 'topophilia' or a love of place. Topophilic baseball environments provide the fan with feelings of 'peace and contentment, and intimations of unity with his [sic] environment' (Oriard 1976). The growing rationalisation of sport and the appliance of science to the sport environment may have made spectating more safe and comfortable but in some way less satisfying.

Several pressures have contributed to the desire to improve the comfort and safety of stadiums, notably in Britain where many football and cricket grounds are approaching a century of service. Three pressures in particular can be identified. First, there has been a desire to slow down, or halt, the declining number of spectators at soccer in particular, by increasing the proportion of seated accommodation. Second, there has been the implementation of certain safety standards and the reduction of capacity following very serious injuries and deaths resulting from fire and crowding. The Bradford fire in 1985 and the Heysel and Hillsborough disasters, of 1985 and 1989 respectively, were the most serious. Third, there has been increased segregation of supporters on the terraces, visiting fans being separated from those of the home team and all fans being forced to sit. This practice is not restricted to Britain; it is common in several European countries. The economist Scitovsky (1976) suggests that improved comfort should not be confused with a higher standard of living or, it might be added, progress. From the spectators' perspective, sitting in a box may be more comfortable but lacks the greater sense of community that is obtained from standing on the more exposed and tiring terraces. It should be stressed that this is not a condemnation of comfort *per se* but an indication that dissatisfaction can result from more comfortable forms.

With glassed-in suites, closed-circuit television, domed stadiums and synthetic pitches which eliminate the chance elements of nature, sport is reduced to theatrical spectacle. Indeed, 'improved' designs in football stadiums may have had the effect of alienating support. Simon Inglis (1983) was told that at some English football grounds, 'the most ardent supporters complained for years how cramped and inadequate the old stands were but once these were replaced by efficient but soulless steel structures, fans pined for the old wooden stand'. Inglis believes that 'the history of ground design is full of clubs who declined rapidly after building a new stand'. He rhetorically asks: 'Would we really want to see our local team perform in soulless concrete bowls that look much like any other concrete bowl?' So, a visit to a bland new stadium may result in the imposition of a 'more standardised experience on the crowd who become more rational units within a functional space' (Kelsall 2000).

The closer people are to the sport action the greater their arousal and excitement, but the bigger the stadium the smaller the proportion of the total number of spectators who are exposed to the fine detail of what is happening on the field (Raitz 1985). This is one of the prices we pay for giant stadiums which have had the effect of changing the relationship between spectators and the sport. Figure 7.11 illustrates:

(a) The Aztec Stadium that was built especially for football yet still suffers from too many spectators too far from the action. It is built in the quadric plan, whereby each side is not parallel to the touchline, but curved slightly to allow better sight lines. The Greeks curved the seats of the arena with a chord of 3 m in a 200 m arc, a calculation also used at the Aztec Stadium in Mexico City.
(b) Elliptical grounds such as Wembley show that the majority of spectators are outside the optimum viewing circle, and maybe one-fifth (20,000) are beyond the maximum viewing circle. Wembley also suffered from being a single-deck stadium, and having a wide perimeter track.
(c) The ideal football ground follows the quadric plan but keeps all the stands within the optimum viewing circle. If space is limited the West Side should be larger, so that more view the game with the sun behind them. In Figure 7.11 the solid circle line is 90 m radius from the centre spot, or 150 m from the furthest corner – the optimum viewing distance. The broken line is 190 m from the furthest corner – the maximum viewing distance. This optimal viewing distance for spectators was largely satisfied in the traditional English stadium with stands close to the pitch and the ground designed to a quadric plan. Newer stadiums, for example the Aztec Stadium, may have been built specially for football but suffers from the fact that too many spectators are outside the optimal viewing circle.

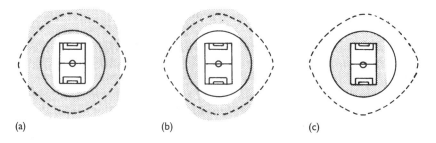

(a)   (b)   (c)

Figure 7.11 Layouts of stadiums and optimal viewing situations (Inglis 1983).

Despite the undoubted technical improvements associated with modern stadiums the spectators, while being more comfortable, are physically and emotionally distanced from the game they come to see. As Relph (1981) would say, these stadiums have 'almost nothing in them that has not been concerned and planned so that it will serve those human needs which can be assessed in terms of efficiency and improved material conditions'. But spontaneity and the expression of human emotions are quietly and unobtrusively diminished, reducing the overall quality of the sport experience. As yet, however, they have not been totally eliminated.

In some sports it might be argued that each stadium has its own idiosyncrasies, hence defying the imposition of a general model. Such an assertion has been made for English cricket, for example (Sampson 1981). To an extent this is obviously true, yet even in the gentle game of cricket, pressures for spatial confinement and artifice are undeniably present. In Australia commercial imperatives have led to the game being played under floodlights (in England, as an experiment, this was tried in downtown soccer stadiums) and in Australia there has been the substantial growth of indoor cricket. Such air-conditioned 'cricket centres' are often set amid industrial buildings, warehouses or filling stations (Figure 7.12); the industrial landscape within which such places are located is reflected in the 'industrialisation' of the sport environment.

The application of technology to sport does not inevitably reduce the

Figure 7.12 Brisbane Indoor Cricket Centre in its industrial environment.

sensations gained from relating closely to the environment. Indeed, those 'technosports' which take place in the open air (e.g. hang gliding, water skiing, motorbike racing) may heighten environmental awareness through the utilisation of air currents, wind, waves, etc. The humanistic geographer, J.B. Jackson (1957/8), drew attention to the fact that sport at speed 'shows nature shorn of gentler and human traits ... To the perceptive individual there can be an almost mystical quality to the experience.' But a heightened awareness and alertness to the surrounding environmental conditions may be best achieved in the absence of technology. Sports like running, skiing, cycling and orienteering 'directly exploit the pleasure-giving potential of nature by intimately incorporating the perceptual experience of the natural environment within the activity itself' (Appleton 1982). On a still, warm summer evening, running in the countryside in preparation for a long-distance race can provide an almost sensual feeling of oneness with nature. Similar effects may be experienced by participants in other 'green' sports. The Scandinavian sport of orienteering, argues Appleton (1982), integrates physical activity and environment to the farthest limits so far achieved in any recreational activity. Similarly Janet Dunleavey (1981) says that 'on cross country skis the human animal becomes a creature of wood and plain, kin to the deer, the ruffed goose, the otter, the snowshoe hare and other creatures who share the winter landscape'. At a time of year when other humans are indoors, the cross-country skier emerges, 'rejoicing in the rhythmic coordination of arms and legs, the spontaneous generation of ever-increasing energy, the exhilaration of breathing deeply in well oxygenated air,... the sense of physical well-being with no hint of exhaustion, that is the skier's bounty'. Such stimulation of the senses contributes to Tuan's notion of 'topophilia' or a love of place.

The rational landscapes of the stadium have not necessarily turned the spectators into passive and docile bodies. Although the participation of the crowd may have become increasingly controlled and orchestrated, the boundary between players and spectators is not totally impermeable and remains 'liminal' (neither one thing or the other, or betwixt and between) in character. The significance of people and 'place' is revealed in the survival of the home field advantage (Chapter 2) and the continuing aural and spontaneous involvement of spectators in the game itself. Because spectators can continue to influence the outcome of a game, it could be argued that 'pure sport' will have arrived only when the 'live' spectators have been removed and viewing is via television only (Bale 1998).

Picnic racing anywhere is one of the great Aussie institutions. There are little meetings on summer days all over Australia, in places with names like Tatura, Towong, and Yanko Creek. There is the Great Western meeting held where they make the local champagne; the racegoers usually go on winery tours first and afterwards behave accordingly. And there is a place called Bong-Bong, where the racing has passed into folklore as a byword.

Hanging Rock, though, is famously good-tempered. Perhaps people are inspired by the setting: the volcanic pinnacles of the rock towering above them, the gum trees and hills of Victoria stretching ahead of them, and the sheer brooding resonance of the place, which is sacred to the Wurrunjerrie (or River Gum Grub) tribe as well as to the Australian film industry.

More likely, everyone behaves because the big meeting is held on New Year's Day, and they are all much too subdued after the night before to get too raucously drunk.

Technically, Hanging Rock is not really a picnic meeting because the jockeys are pros (if not exactly the local Edderys and Carsons); and the whole thing is run by the official stewards. But everyone thinks of it as picnic racing, a day out in the country, an hour's drive from Melbourne.

And if it were a normal meeting it would have been killed off years ago by bureaucratic officials as uneconomic, outdated and even dangerous – it's a very tight track and nasty and greasy if it rains. The meeting has been kept going by its enormous popularity and its sense of tradition.

Vignette 9 Picnic racing in rural Australia. Although some of the races are professional (as in the case of those at Hanging Rock), the pleasure is in large part obtained from the natural environment in which such events are held (extracted from Engel 1987).

Reading the sports landscape

Before concluding this chapter I want to take a final approach to looking at the landscapes of sport. In recent decades, geographers have sought to read the landscape as a text – that is, something to be analysed – in much the same way as one might analyse writing for hidden meanings. I want to take two examples of such an approach. The first is to consider the useful-ness of metaphors in understanding the sports landscape, following on from the work of Tuan (1984) in his book, *Dominance and Affection*. I draw on this work because of Tuan's treatment of the garden as a botani-cal version of the pet. Earlier in this chapter I alluded to the dominance of human beings over nature and the fact that some observers regarded sport as being anti-nature. A less emphatic and much more ambiguous interpre-tation is the use of the metaphor of the garden to describe the sports land-scape. Consider, for example, a lawn tennis court. There is little doubt that humankind dominates nature in constructing such a facility. But at the same time consider the loving care with which the ground staff lovingly maintain the court, covering it when it is raining, tending it when it gets worn, nurturing it throughout the season. The tennis court, football, baseball and cricket fields, and golf courses are therefore products of dominance and affection, much in the same way as a garden is. Like the garden the stadium is a blending of horticulture and architecture. On the one hand they consist of growing things; on the other of terraces, walls and sometimes statues. In some stadiums domination is taken to extremes and natural surfaces are totally eliminated. Grass is replaced by plastic, timber by concrete. However, as Tuan would point out, domination in architecture can be carried out playfully so that the stadium becomes somewhat magical. The football stadium in Monaco could be seen as an example, as could the SkyDome in Toronto with its playful mural decorations.

In a garden water is controlled in the form of fountains or artificially designed water courses or waterfalls. Human dominance over water is widely found in sports, artificial courses for canoes, rowing and kayaks being examples. Swimming baths also control water in typically modern form. As the novelist Joan Didion commented, the 'swimming pool is, for many of us in the West, a symbol not of affluence but of order, of control over the uncontrollable. A pool is water, made available and useful...' (quoted in Bale 1994). These examples illustrate how the garden metaphor, when applied to the sports environment, provides a more ambiguous picture of human relations with nature than a hard-line environmentalist view. It shows how sports landscapes result from dominance, to be sure, but dominance that often has a human face.

My second example of reading the sports landscape is taken from a study of how the sports facilities of a particular university campus might be read. A study by Carolyn Gallaher (1997) focused on activist Protestant fundamentalism in the context of Liberty University, founded in 1971 by fundamentalist televangelist, Jerry Falwell. It is regarded by Gallaher as a 'training ground for fundamentalist young adults'. Alcohol is banned on campus, living arrangements are strictly segregated on the basis of gender, no gay or feminist curricula exist, and a strict dress code is enforced. From these examples it can seen that Liberty represents the radical right wing of American religious politics. How might such an institution be legitimated in mainstream America? Gallaher draws attention to lavish sports facilities on the Liberty campus. It has a 9,500-spectator basketball arena, a 12,000-seat football stadium, training facilities are lavish; and all of Liberty's teams compete in Division I of the NCAA. Gallaher notes:

> Liberty's NCAA regulation sporting arenas ... forge a representation of normalcy and similarity with well-respected public universities through the copying of these mainstream symbols of growth and success in public universities. Liberty's internet home page ... has an

entire section devoted entirely to its athletic program. The program is lauded, legitimated and rendered as on a par with division I public universities through the appropriation of certain key symbols of success ... e.g. the university's ... ability to hire a former NFL football coach. These sporting arenas also bespeak a masculinist form of solidarity building, and of the creation of a group and institutional memory which serves to reinforce the cohesion of fundamentalist identity.

Gallaher sees these elements of the campus environment as a means of 'hiding hate in the landscape'. Generally, Americans see intercollegiate sports as a 'good thing' and sport provides a common cultural currency. Well-respected universities have similar facilities to those at Liberty. The identity of a rabidly radical institution is in this way naturalised.

Conclusion

As sport emerged from its folk game origins it had a number of effects upon the landscape. In some central areas of cities and in some suburbs it is fair to say that sport has been the dominant factor influencing the character and shape of the landscape. At more periodic intervals we have seen how massive flows of fans change the landscapes of our cities. As technology has increasingly been embraced by sports, new forms of monoculture have emerged. Although developed and designed with improved satisfaction and performance in mind, it has been suggested that in some senses the overall sports experience is diminished in such environments and a partial response to this may have been a renewed greening of sports and a return to non-sportised physical activities requiring no specialised sites. In such situation 'place' can be seen as being reclaimed from the 'pure space' which the norms of sport often seem to predict. Like the entertainment industry of which it is part, much achievement sport possesses landscapes that are perhaps the most artificial, and therefore the most human, of environments. As such, it is worth recalling the words of Pierce Lewis (1979), that the landscape is part of our 'unwitting biography, reflecting our values, our aspirations, and even our fears in tangible, visible form'.

Further reading

Two overviews of sports landscapes are John Bale (1994), *Landscapes of Modern Sport* and Karl Raitz (ed.) (1996), *The Theater of Sport*. A brilliant exploration of two iconic American sports landscapes is presented in Charles Springwood (1996), *Cooperstown to Dyersville: A Geography of Baseball Nostalgia* (1996). Highly stimulating ideas on the growing spatial confinement and rationalisation of the sports landscape are found in Chapters 3 and 4 of Henning Eichberg (1998), *Body Cultures*. Sensitive descriptions of the unique qualities of the milieux of particular sports are typified by Aylwin Sampson (1981), *Grounds of Appeal; the Homes of First Class Cricket*, Simon Inglis, *The Football Grounds of England and Wales* (1983), and the latter's more idiosyncratic book *Sightlines: A Stadium Odyssey* (2000). Two quite different views of the baseball stadium are provided by Philip Lowry (1992), *Green Cathedrals* and Bartlett Giamatti (1989), *Take Time for Paradise: Americans and their Games*. On the changing nature of English soccer stadiums and spectating, see the highly personal essay by Gary Kelsall (2000), 'From the Victoria Ground to the Britannia Stadium'.

Chapter 8

Imaginative geographies of sport

Introduction

The psychological association of certain sports with particular places is well known. Mention Texas and football comes to mind; talk of South Wales evokes images of rugby; Scotland and golf go together as much as do Canada and ice hockey. Despite our obvious familiarity with such sports–regional stereotypes, we know rather little about the public's cognitive involvement in sports. Little has been done, for example, to examine the strength of regional sports imagery or of the degree of congruence between the sports images people have of places and the sporting reality. Psychological representations of places or regions are known as mental maps. This chapter alludes to mental maps or perceived environments of sports and proceeds to examine a more recent development in cultural geography, that of imaginative geographies. These differ from mental sports maps in that they draw attention to the lack of innocence of representations of sports, something ignored in mental maps. Imaginative geographies are more than perceptions.

Mental sports maps

Sports-place images are communicated by a variety of media, including the press, television, radio, novels and even poetry (Figure 8.1). Because we cannot visit personally all places and regions at which sports are practised we are dependent upon such secondary sources for images of the sporting character of many parts of our own country and the world. Bias frequently characterises the media coverage of sports; certain regions and places receive greater coverage of certain sports than others; sports commentators on radio and television often link certain places to certain sporting attributes, labelling entire regions such as 'Africa' as homogeneous entities with essential characteristics. Sports geography has tended to neglect the importance of these images, the sporting worlds inside our heads, our cognitive geographies of sports

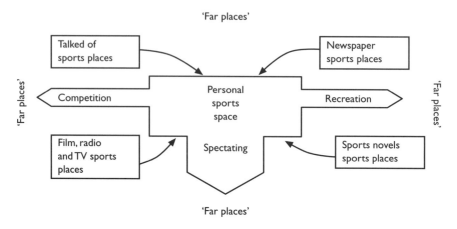

Figure 8.1 Sources of information about sport-place images (Bale 1986).

and the imaginative worlds of sport that are actually written and reproduced.

The way in which sports are organised, i.e. on a team basis, stimulates local rivalries and local and national identities. Nationalism, regionalism and localism, already built into many sports, are reinforced by one of the basic tools of sports coverage, namely the need to identify points of reference for the audience. As Gary Whannell (1992) has put it, 'television does not simply relay sport to us. It presents a particular view of sport.' Successful clubs often obtain greater media coverage than their unsuccessful colleagues, hence obtaining free advertising which helps develop the link between sport and place. Places with teams which regularly win major events build up mental links in people's minds between sport and place. Even novels about sport carry regional connotations. David Storey's *The Sporting Life*, of necessity, had to be set in the north of England, as rugby league is concentrated in that area. But Hugh de Selincourt's *The Cricket Match* did not have to be set in the south-east of England since cricket is played nationwide. De Selincourt chose the south-east and in doing so passed on a sport-place association. Likewise Jilly Cooper, in her book *Class*, chose Esher (in Surrey) to connote rugby union. But each Saturday night the readers of the *South Wales Echo* have been reminded in the cartoon strip by 'Gren' that the valleys of Glamorgan and Gwent are rugby's heartlands (Figure 8.2). In other words, a variety of media communicate sport-place images to the public which receives them as vernacular sports regions.

These regions are not demarcated from their neighbours in any 'scientific' way; they are the taken-for-granted or perceptual regions which people carry around in their heads. Attempts to objectify the subjective

Figure 8.2 An imagined landscape of Welsh Rugby.

can be presented as 'mental maps', examples of which are shown in Figure 8.3. These represent the mapped responses of undergraduate students who were asked to indicate the areas of Britain that they associated with particular sports. Areas identified with each sport by 60 per cent of the respondents are enclosed by isolines (or, perhaps, 'isopercepts'). For example, it can be seen that football (soccer) is most strongly associated with England's industrial heartland – the 'axial belt' stretching from the metropolis, through the midlands to the north-east. Golf, on the other hand, is seen as a dominantly Scottish sport with an outlier in the south-east of England. Tennis is strongly associated with the south-east of England, no other part of the country being associated with the sport by more than 20 per cent of the respondents. If tennis has a south-eastern image, rugby has a South Wales image with a minor outlier in southern Scotland (30 per cent). Cricket approaches a bi-modal pattern in terms of its vernacular regionalisation, with the south-east of England and much of Yorkshire being strongly associated with the game.

Likewise, over 100 geography teachers from all over Australia were asked to undertake a mental mapping exercise of selected sports. The resulting map revealed that the 60 per cent 'isopercept' showed cricket as perceived as being widely identified with the most populated areas of Australia. Australian Rules football, on the other hand, was viewed as being associated with Victoria and much of New South Wales while soccer was identified strongly with the former state only. The extent to which these maps reflect 'reality' (either in terms of the absolute number of participants, clubs, star players, or their per capita equivalents) remains to be researched. The examples noted here reflect the perceptions of a reasonably broad sample of the population. However, sports fans, for example,

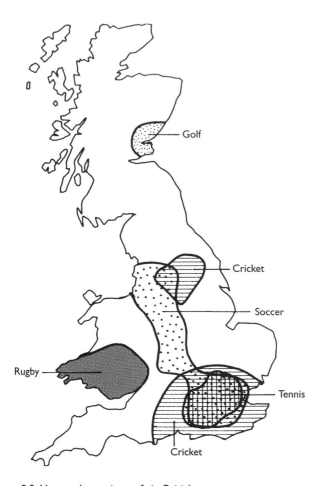

Figure 8.3 Vernacular regions of six British sports.

are likely to have different mental sports maps from those members of the population for whom sport is anything but a passion.

Following the reception of mental sports maps it is not unusual for such images to be utilised by the places involved in order to boost their images in the form of promotional literature. Sport, therefore, helps advertising and, perhaps, assists the creation of new employment. A leaflet designed to attract industry to Wakefield, for example, suggested that the labour force gave as much on the shop floor as the town's rugby team did on the sports field (Burgess 1982). Sometimes places are so strongly associated with sport that they have to stress that they do have other things to offer. Trafford, in Manchester, published an advertisement stressing that it was as good for industry as it was for cricket and soccer. In Brazil in 1970 the government announced plans for the development of the Trans-Amazonian Highway by utilising the national mania for football by producing posters with the pro-government slogan 'There's No Holding Brazil' and a picture of the celebration of a goal by the soccer genius Pele (Humphrey 1986).

Sport is also prominent among the factors that contribute to national stereotyping and identity. An early example comes from the work of J.P. Cole (1972) who, in the early 1970s, asked a small sample of middle-class Mexican respondents to name the five aspects which first came to mind when the names of different countries were mentioned. For Britain, as many people mentioned Wembley Stadium as Trafalgar Square, as many Bobby Charlton as Sir Francis Drake. For Brazil Pele received twenty-three times as many mentions as any other Brazilian. Identical surveys requesting people's responses to China, USSR and France interestingly resulted in no mentions possessing sporting connotations. The fact that some countries seem to possess sporting connotations while others do not may indicate the differing impacts which sports have on societies and the ability of those sports to communicate 'favourable' images overseas.

What is more, it seems probable that if sports stars are the only members of a particular nation (or region or city for that matter) known to people from other places, the sportsmen or women in question may be taken to be representative of the whole nationality. Events like the World Cup or the Olympic Games may mould people's impressions of participating nations and nationalities. For example, Figure 8.4 shows that football fans (if a sample of school students is typical) appear to view Brazilians as more skilful, creative and intelligent than non-fans, who view them as more aggressive, unfriendly, nasty and dull. It is interesting that for those interested in football, Brazil is often regarded as synonymous with skill and excitement (Walton 1984). In other words, the perceived characteristics of nations may be derived from those of the sporting individuals who represent them. What people *think* places, regions and countries are like is what is important in the way they form judgements of such places.

Mental maps are basically attempts to objectively map subjective views of space and place. They draw on the traditions of geography outlined in Chapters 3 to 5, being simple ways of quantifying perceptions of places. An approach which has attracted more recent attention is one that draws on literary studies, to which I now turn.

Imaginative sports geographies

The literary critic Edward Said (1974) noted that all geographies are imaginative. Such a comment reflects the concerns of anthropologists, literary theorists and more recently geographers and sports sociologists, who have

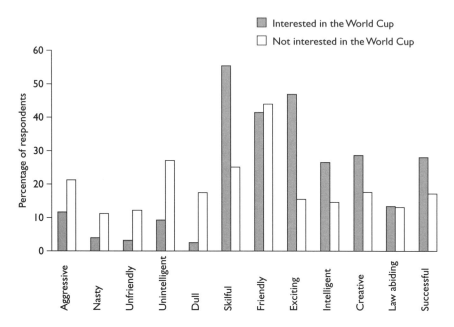

Figure 8.4 Impressions of Brazilian people held by soccer fans and non-fans (adapted from Walton 1984).

recognised the problem of how the world can be re-presented. At its simplest, it is now widely recognised that a photograph or a piece of writing about a football game is a representation of a football game, not a football game itself. In other words, sports are mediated by the ways in which they are represented. This clearly creates problems for any 'objective' view of sport; hence, it is widely argued that the social sciences and humanities are witnessing a 'crisis of representation'.

Imaginative sports geographies are different from mental maps. They are 'made' rather than simply recorded. Imaginative sports geographies are worlds constructed by texts of various kinds, including writing, photography, movies and art. Studies of imaginative geographies have generally stressed their lack of 'innocence' and the way in which they collude with power relations. This section explores the ways in which some of these media may construct imaginative geographies of sports.

First, consider the huge amount of written work that exists in connection with cricket, the quintessential English summer sport. A recurring message from such writing on English cricket is that it is (a) set in a rural environment, and (b) located in the south of the country. Consider how the following poems construct cricket as a rural sport. In 'The Cricket Pitch 1944', Brian Jones refers to the field 'ringed with elms'; in 'The

Cricketers' Neil Powell watched the game 'from the woodland edge';
Edmund Blunden's 'The Season Opens' starts as follows:

> A tower we must have, and a clock in the tower,
> Looking over the tombs, the tithe barn, the bower,
> The inn and the mill, the forge and the hall,
> And the loamy sweet level that loves bat and ball.

These extracts from cricket-centred poems (quoted from Bale 1994) are
matched by a large number of more literary allusions to cricket as being
rural. One example will suffice. The classic view is that 'of cricket set
against a background of green trees, haystacks, barns, and a landscape of
peace and plenty, remote from a world of busy getting and spending'
(Arlott and Cardus 1969; see also vignette 10).

Visual images of cricket also construct the rural (Bale 1994). On the
back of an English £10 note is a picture based on an episode from Charles
Dickens's *Pickwick Papers*. The scene is rural, sited at Dingley Dell with
trees and church on the skyline. Cricket, the rural and England are con-
joined in a taken-for-granted imaginative geography. Almost all coffee-
table books on cricket have cover illustrations that present a rural image.
The recurring icons of village pub, church, trees and gently rolling chalk
downland are popular images. So too is their southern location. Most
cricket writing and cricket illustrations are set in the south. Indeed, the
south is the 'defining reality' of cricket. The next step in the analysis of
sports texts is their deconstruction. By this is meant an attempt to desta-
bilise and undercut the claims of the text, just as in Chapter 6 the notion of
deconstruction was employed to explore the 'meanings' of sports landscapes. In other words, what alternative meanings are lurking below the
surface of the written work? What are these rural scenes of a particular
kind of 'Englishness' saying?

According to the cultural theorist Fred Inglis (1992), the propagation of
a rural idyll, surrounding a highly mathematical and geometric sport,
played on a surface produced by 'turf science', is an example of the 'official imaginative life' offered to the British public by those forming 'the
version of the English landscape which is so powerful a component of
ruling class culture'. Social and class divisions are dissolved in such images
which often represent 'Merrie England', a land presented as unscathed by
technology, industry and commerce – an antidote to the 'dreadful present'
as geographer David Lowenthal (1985) put it. In such images cricket
carries the message of the industrial as rural and the rational as rustic. The
function of these images seems, in part, to provide a world of peace and
harmony, devoid of social and political strife. The rural environments
represented in the writing noted above does not hint at problems of rural
deprivation or crime. Cricket almost becomes a sign of an essential

At twelve-thirty it was decided not to wait for the missing pair, and the nine cricketers started off. At two-thirty, after halts at Catford, the White Hart at Sevenoaks, the Angel at Tunbridge Wells, and three smaller inns at tiny villages, the charabanc drew up triumphantly beside the cricket ground of the Kentish village of Fordenden. Donald was enchanted at his first sight of rural England. And rural England is the real England, unspoilt by factories and financiers and tourists and hustle. He sprang out of the charabanc ... and gazed eagerly round. The sight was worth an eager gaze or two. It was a hot summer's afternoon. There was no wind, and the smoke from the red roofed cottages curled slowly up into the golden haze. The clock on the flint tower of the church struck the half hour, and the vibrations spread slowly across the shimmering hedge rows, spangled with white blossom of the convolvulus, and lost themselves tremulously among the orchards. Bees lazily drifted. White butterflies flopped their aimless way among the gardens. Delphiniums, larkspur, tiger-lilies, evening primrose, monk's hood, sweet peas, swaggered brilliantly above the box hedges, the wooden palings and the rickety gates. The cricket field itself was a mass of daisies and buttercups and dandelions, tall grasses and purple vetches and thistledown, and great clumps of dark red sorrel, except, of course, for the oblong patch in the centre – mown, rolled, watered – a smooth, shining emerald of grass, the Pride of Fordenden, the Wicket.

Vignette 10 Cricket in Kent. This extract conjures a rustic image of cricket in the 'Garden of England'. Indeed, the climax of this 'English country gardens' paragraph is the wicket itself. In fact, more cricket clubs per capita are found in the northern industrial areas of Yorkshire (Macdonnell 1935).

Englishness that would be recognised by English Conservatives such as Norman Tebbit and John Major (Bale 1994). Clearly, these imaginative geographies are far from innocent and seek to provide a mythological view of sports places.

I now want to consider a second example of imaginative geographies of sport by considering one dimension of geographer Martyn Bowden's (1994) deconstruction of the two British movies, *The Loneliness of the Long Distance Runner* and *Chariots of Fire*. Each of these movies focused on running but again have 'the rural' as an important focus. The former was based on the novella by Allan Sillitoe (1959) and featured the cross-country runner, Colin Smith. The second represented partly fictionalised accounts of the track athletes of the 1920s, Harold Abrahams and Eric Liddell who, respectively, won gold medals in the 100 and 400 metre events at the 1924 Olympics. Sillitoe's book, on which the film was based, can be read as a neo-marxist critique of sport. Smith is an inmate in a young offenders' institution; the encouragement of his running ability by agents of the prison system are presented as a form of social control.

However, well ahead of the field in an important race, he pulls up in the final stretch just before the finishing line, withdrawing from the race, unwilling to 'play the game', unwilling to satisfy the ego of the prison authorities who had encouraged him to run in the first place. By transgressing the norms of achievement sport, and (literally) stepping outside of sport's space, this can be read as a form of resistance against the repression of 'the system' of both sport and society. Likewise, in *Chariots of Fire*, the main theme is the battle between two athletes and the power élite. Abrahams (a Jew) is browbeaten not only by polite antisemitism but by demands to reject his professional coach, while Liddell (an evangelical Christian) is pressured to deny his religious principles and run on a Sunday. In other words, achievement-running itself can be read as a site for resistance, transgressing the social space of polite society.

The other pervasive theme in each of the films is the central presence of the dystopian urban/industrial and the idyllic rural in the words of William Blake in the hymn 'Jerusalem', a metaphor for an ideal place and the antithesis of England's 'dark satanic mills'. In both films the liberating qualities of the beach are added to the countryside (the rural). Both are presented as places of liberation, escape and innocence, unspoiled by the industrial revolution. Although Bowden's essay looks at much more than the rural symbolism in the films, it is that upon which I will concentrate here.

Colin Smith comes from the working-class inner-city environment of Nottingham and frequently yearns for a life away from its squalor and industrial pollution. Before his incarceration, he can escape the grime and crime of the urban sprawl by running on the beach and in the sand dunes of Skegness on the North Sea coast. During his incarceration he is able to leave the confined space of the institution and take to the woods and fields to which he has access during cross-country races and training. As Bowden (1994, 77) puts it:

> He runs free in his early-morning training sessions through a carefully landscaped garden. His lonely figure plods over dewy pastures closely cropped by sheep and deer. A tall Scots pine or two and the occasional clump of beeches and elms dot the landscape. And then he is across the stream and into the trees.
>
> These are Colin's only happy memories – away from the dark satanic mills; 'England's green and pleasant land works wonders on the city boy'.

Eric Liddell, the Scottish Christian missionary whose preaching is aimed at the working classes of the Scottish industrial zones, finds a form of 'heaven' (Jerusalem) in the dramatic landscape of the Scottish Highlands where he is seen training, or in the bracing air above the urban blight of Edinburgh. Harold Abrahams is also seen training on a tree-lined road leading to an aristocratic estate. He runs with the hounds in the English countryside. For Abrahams and his Oxford chums, even the site of a track meet is 'bounded by grass and tall deciduous trees in open country'. In *Chariots*, the rural idyll in an English setting also features in the lives of the aristocratic élite. The film depicts a fictional adaptation of Lord Burghley, the 1928 Olympic 400 metres hurdles champion, who trains on an immaculately kept lawn in the rural splendour of Highbeck House. He places a glass of champagne on each hurdle and aims to perfect his style by clearing each without spilling a drop. The rural, the idyllic – 'England's green and pleasant land' – is central to the film's imagery. And in the memorable final scene, while the credits roll, a large team of runners, including the two adversaries, Liddell and Abrahams, run barefoot at the water's edge, along a grey-skied, windswept, deserted beach – next to nature. Bowden argues that the 'character and style of each of the major runners are determined by the pastoral environment in which each trains. And the training of all four runners in the English and Scottish countryside is critical to their victories.'

The third example of an imaginative geography shows how the athletic representations of the colonial (or pre-colonial) world were ambiguous and equivocal. This is an example that might be termed a postcolonial geography of sport in that it interrogates and provides alternative readings of colonial representations of African athleticism. For some colonialists, Africa was a place in which natural athletes were thought to exist and could be recruited to serve the interests of the West. Popular sports magazines, coaching manuals, geographical journals and travel writing textually 'produced' the African as athlete. However, I want to show that when the native was photographed performing feats of (what were perceived as) athletic excellence, it was represented in an equivocal way. I want to show how an athletic image could be read in numerous ways.

During the period between 1907 and 1960 many writers, photographers and anthropologists recorded the athleticism of the people of Rwanda. Among these were those who were particularly attracted to the performances of what they termed the 'high jumpers' from Rwanda. The first major anthropological study of Rwanda was undertaken by the Duke of Mecklenburg's expedition in 1907. As far as is known, Mecklenburg's photographer was the first European to photograph and describe a kind of indigenous high jumping practised by young Rwandan men. Athletes jumped off a mound and landed feet first. It was not necessarily competitive and the Rwandans did not take measurements of the heights cleared. The surface off which such jumping took place was not standardised nor necessarily flat. It differed considerably, therefore, from the sportised model of jumping practised in Europe and North America.

My purpose here is to illustrate the ambiguity of the visual representation shown in the photograph taken on the Mecklenburg expedition and reproduced many times (Bale 2002). It is shown as Figure 8.5. An important initial point here is that the caption tells the readers what they are supposed to see. We are told that it is a Tutsi high jumper, not a Hutu or a Twa, the two other groups in Rwanda. The Tutsi were a minority group who held power in Rwanda at the time of the Duke's visit and, for the first half of the twentieth century, were generally favoured and supported by the colonial powers. We are also told that the height cleared was 2.50 metres and in a footnote we learn that this is significantly better than the existing world record for the Western form of high jumping. The identification of a Tutsi apparently achieving a performance better than the world record can be read as reinforcing a positive image of Tutsi *per se*.

The content of the photograph itself may be read at several levels and is too ambiguous to convey a simple, single message. With the help of the caption it certainly *denotes* an African clearing a rope above the heads of two Europeans. The text accompanying the image tells the reader that they are the Duke of Mecklenburg on the right and his uniformed adjutant on the left. But (if the caption is ignored) what does it *connote*? Is it a sign of an African or a European triumph – or both? There is no one meaning and many possible meanings could be taken from it. Consider some further ways in which the photograph can be read.

First, the photograph could be read as illustrating a landscape of discipline and hierarchy. The clear demarcation of the Africans and the Europeans suggest an emphasis on 'difference'; the photograph stresses the binary opposites of white and black, European and African, dressed and semi-naked. This reinforces the view that while nakedness signified 'uncivilised', clothing was an obvious appendage of 'civilisation'. The attraction for the viewer, of the European photographed *with* the Rwandan, may have lain in these contrasts. The Europeans command the centre even if they were not the objects of the photograph. The athlete is said to be a Tutsi. The man next to the upright (seemingly questioning the entire episode) appears to be some kind of 'assistant' (whether to the Germans or the jumper is not clear). He is certainly not in charge: he knows his place. But this 'assistant' could be read as being part of a cultural or even 'racial' hierarchy. The athlete is said to be a Tutsi; those at the centre are Europeans. Is the passive attendant (an imperfect body compared with the perfection of the Tutsi, and located at the margins of the action) a stereotypical Hutu? If so, the hierarchy of Rwandan colonial society is summarised in the activities shown; the centrally powerful Europeans, the athletic and active Tutsi and the passive Hutu. It is also possible to read a progressive decline of 'culture' away from the Europeans at the centre. Beyond them are the Africans and beyond them nature itself.

Bringing the Tutsi and the European together, the photograph connotes feelings of power which would be absent in two individual representations. As the Germans distance themselves from local life by their attitude and

Figure 8.5 The original caption for this photograph was 'Tutsi high jump (2.50 meters)'.

posture, they also demonstrate European power, contained centrally within the image. The positioning of the camera enables the jumper to be outlined against the sky, hence (literally) heightening the dramatic effects of his performance, but it cannot be said unequivocally that he is given primacy over the German visitors. Although the performance is regarded as the object of the image, the Europeans' centrality, upright posture and military uniform carry messages of power and control. Without the caption, it is unclear who the photographer wished to privilege.

It is an image of order; African corporeality is confined to a cleared space. There is ample room for the event and it takes place in an atmo-sphere of structure, and possibly rehearsal. The audience are orderly and well controlled. Their semi-nudity and their exotic activity identify the Africans but the photographic capture and the European-imposed order domesticate them. But power and oppression are not the sole properties of this image and I cannot deny that the photograph also idealises – even promotes – 'the Tutsi'. It projects corporeal achievement.

Finally, and staying with a postcolonial approach, I want to outline what can be termed the 'imaginative geographies' of African footballers using an approach inspired by the writing of David Spurr (1994). The impor-tance of postcolonial studies can be argued to lie in their application to the present and here I want to explore how African footballers – mainly those from Cameroon – are both 'received' and 'constructed' in Western media. I seek to demonstrate how well-worn colonial rhetorics continue to be employed in the post/neo-colonial representation of African sports workers. I mainly rework a variety of texts that allude to African football workers and suggest the value of an awareness of the question (or 'crisis') of representation in sports studies. I want to outline the continuing validity of Spurr's (1994) schema of colonial writing that encourages a move away from monolithic studies of, say, stereotyping. Instead, I focus on four cate-gories of writing or, as Spurr puts it, rhetorical modes – surveillance, naturalisation, idealisation and negation. These reveal the discourse on the African footballer as being fractured and often contradictory.

In colonial texts African athletes were often represented as fantastic natural athletes, but lying alongside the rhetoric of the 'noble savage' was often that of the 'idle native'. The same applies today. However, there seems to be one important difference between the rhetoric used to repre-sent athletic Africans in colonial texts and those used to represent many African football workers of the twenty-first century. When Europeans ventured into central Africa in the late nineteenth and early twentieth cen-turies, no modern sports existed there. Yet it has been shown how native peoples were often rhetorically appropriated and constructed as potential world-class sportsmen (the gendered noun is deliberate) in an idealised, yet equivocal, way (Bale 2002). Conversely, at the start of the twenty-first century, popular representations of black athletes who have, in actuality, achieved world-class status in the world of achievement sports, are often rhetorically 'reduced' to their (pre-)colonial state by the application of modes of debasement and negation, again equivocally. Certainly, the modes of surveillance, naturalisation and idealisation continue, but negating of the African seems to me to be the most pernicious mode of representation in an ambivalent and ambiguous discourse. Let me briefly illustrate four rhetorical modes employed in writing 'the African footballer'.

Surveillance in modern sport is a pervasive global phenomenon and is much more prevalent today than in the first half of the twentieth century. The quantitative recording of sport has become more spatially extensive and more sophisticated. Ranking and ordering of individuals and teams are central features of the global sportised gaze. The universal currencies of achievement sports – the record and the statistic – enable the employers of sports labour to stand back and take an 'objective' view of the sports potential among young people the world over. The videotape is an essential form of representation that has enabled the European recruiter to gaze at the African prospect from afar. Through the collection of quantitative data (e.g. Ricci 2000) the West is able to record the extent of potential recruitment and monitor the success of the neo-colonial project of sport 'development'. The quantitative data which facilitate the classification of individuals and of nations permit a mapping of the new global sports empires, in a similar way to the recording of the anthropologists' categorisations of 'native games and customs' in past decades. Underlying such forms of surveillance is the domination and power of those in authority and privilege.

The rhetorical mode of *appropriation* is displayed in the words of a German football coach, Dettmar Cramer, who has stated that 'we can systematically comb thoroughly one continent after another and help our friends in every country to leap in order to smooth their path towards the top of world football. This is their aim. That they may reach it, this is our task' (quoted in Eichberg 1994). Global sports organisations today see the people of neo-colonial states as belonging to the achievement sport movement, rather than to traditional folk-games. The emphasis here is to eliminate difference and to gather African and other athletes from the world's economic 'periphery' into the fold of modern sport – a new 'family of man' – on the West's terms. Football seems to have been projected as a necessary and fundamental human experience. However, the universalistic claims and ambitions of world football should be placed against the irony of Western colonialism and racism.

The appropriative language used to describe African soccer players often reveals them as versions of a European ideal. Though projected in less blatant terms than those of Cramer it can be illustrated by examples taken from work by British media analysts who examined European newspaper coverage of the 1990 World Cup in Spain (Blain, Boyle and O'Donnell 1993). In this, and in the paragraphs that follow, I will concentrate on their findings concerning the representation of the Cameroon national team. For example, the Cameroon player Oman Biyik was referred to as 'a black van Basten', an 'African Gerd Müller' or a 'black Horst Hrubesch'. Africans are here defined in relation to Europeans. The Cameroon team was also viewed as a hybrid – 'well-versed in modern tactics [but] it plays its game without abandoning its indigenous style'. A 'native style' is not seen as enough and, at least, it needs to possess modern techniques.

Idealisation is an equally familiar mode of neo-colonial representation with idealised statements being juxtaposed with those of appropriation noted above. The survey of images of the 1990 World Cup revealed that the players from Cameroon were written has having 'football in their blood'; they 'obtained their skills as whippersnappers on the streets'; their play brought 'magic to the game'; they were 'instinctive footballers', 'refreshingly attacking' and 'not at all inhibited'. European soccer, on the other hand, was represented by 'modern' images – those of 'the artificial' and 'the machine' (Blain, Boyle and O'Donnell 1993). Among the implications of these idealised kinds of reporting of black athletes is the desire for a more 'pure' kind of sport, one not blemished by artifice or tactics, reflecting atavistic tendencies on the part of the writers: a romantic nostalgia, a view that sees in the African an untutored and ideal sportsman – what the European might have been, but for his loss of innocence and his gain in refinement. In a lengthy article in the German soccer magazine *Kicker*, Karl-Heinz Heimann noted that

> ... in Cameroon, everywhere in Africa and Asia the ball is the favourite toy of millions of children, they know no other. Neither surf board nor mountainbike, neither tennis courts or even computers are at hand to distract them from playing with the ball.
>
> There is no longer any 'street football' here in our country (Germany). Should children join a club, usually when they are considerably older, the first thing the trainer has to do is to apply his efforts to teaching them ball control. In most cases it's already too late. And tactics are already given too much importance in the youth work of our clubs.
>
> (Quoted in Blain, Boyle and O'Donnell 1993, 74)

Heimann yearns for kids playing soccer in bare feet, kicking a ball around for fun and pleasure, for a 'purification' of modern soccer through play rather than tactics. A mythical, idealised, romantic world of yesteryear – or of Africa – would ideally replace the corrupted and debased world of modern sports.

In the course of naturalising the African sports worker, the mode of *negation* evidently parallels it. The African athlete (not just footballers) has often been projected as a negative stereotype – 'great speed but little stamina' has traditionally been a widespread appellation (Wiggins 1989). During the 1990 World Cup competition, the Cameroon team could be labelled, in Western journalism, as 'harmless wild men', 'irrational' and 'less intellectual'; the soccer set-up in Cameroon was described as 'chaotic' with a 'deficient system'. The team 'knows nothing about tactics' and 'they need to hear the applause of the crowd more than the instructions of the trainer' (quoted in Blain, Boyle and O'Donnell 1993, 73–6). African sports workers are often negated by alluding to their 'natural' talent. It is said that their performances are unfairly enhanced as a result of their supposed innate ability, something that Adolf Hitler recognised as a reason for banning 'the Negro' from the Olympic Games. It is still possible in the modern world to see colonial modes of rhetoric such as negation and idealisation, quantification and naturalisation, lying alongside each other.

Conclusion

This chapter has exemplified two kinds of geographies of sport that reside in the mind's eye. Mental maps are images that are received from various stimuli; imaginative geographies are those that are constructed. To a degree, this chapter has encapsulated the broad pattern of this book, a move from an emphasis on numbers to one on words. The early chapters tended to focus on models and generalisations, backed up with maps, graphs and figures. This chapter, while continuing a tendency towards measurement in its focus on mental maps, finished with ideas drawn from literary studies rather than from social science. This trend is likely to continue but will, at the same time, be paralleled by other approaches.

The contents of this book more or less reflect the conceptual balance of work undertaken under the umbrella term, 'the geography of sport'. Future developments in the sub-discipline will, I believe, be reflected in more geographers becoming involved in sports studies and more students of sports taking – or at least acknowledging – a geographical approach. As sport continues to feature in social, political, ethical and cultural matters, geographers will be able to find a fertile field of study that is not only relevant in itself but also illustrative of broader geographical themes. Such work will embrace the broad cloth of geographical work – from sports applications of Geographical Information Systems to the excavation and a huge range of texts about sports.

This book has been written to alert students in sports studies and geography to the existence of a fertile field of academic enquiry. The book's contents have charted a route; it is hoped that others will explore newer frontiers and horizons.

Further reading

For a very thorough media analysis of national sporting stereotypes see Neil Blain, Raymond Boyle and Hugh O'Donnell, *Sport and National Identity in the European Media* (1993). Excellent examples of the deconstruction of sports-geographic texts can be found in the classic essays by Roland Barthes on the Tour de France and on wrestling, in respectively, 'The Tour de France as Epic' in *The Eiffel Tower and Other Mythologies* (1997) and 'The world of wrestling', in *Mythologies* (1973). For a much more extended treatment of the construction of sport through texts, see Michael Oriard, *Reading Football* (1993). On further work on sports and texts see several of the essays in Geneviève Rail (ed.), *Sport and Postmodern Times* (1998).

Bibliography

Adams, R. (1983) 'A geographic analysis of US golf facilities', paper read at Annual Meeting of the Society for the North American Cultural Survey, Lexington, Ky.

Adams, R. and J. Rooney (1984) 'Condo Canyon: an examination of emerging golf landscapes in America', *North American Culture*, 1, 65–75.

Adams, R. and J. Rooney (1985) 'Evolution of American golf facilities', *The Geographical Review*, 75, 419–38.

Appleton, J. (1982) *The Experience of Landscape*, Wiley, Chichester.

Arlott, J. (1976) *The Oxford Companion to Sports and Games*, Oxford University Press, Oxford.

Arlott, J. and N. Cardus (1969) *The Noblest Game*, Harrap, London.

Armstrong, G. (1998), *Football Hooliganism*, Berg, Oxford.

Ashworth, G. (1984) *Recreation and Tourism*, Bell and Hyman, London.

Baade, R. (1995) 'Stadiums, professional sports and city economies: an analysis of the United States Experience', in J. Bale and O. Moen *The Stadium and the City*, Keele University Press, Keele, 277–94.

Badenhorst, C. and C. Rogerson (1985) 'Teach the native to play: social control and organized black sport on the Witwatersrand, 1920–1939', *GeoJournal*, 12, 197–202.

Bale, J. (1979) 'Track and field regions of Europe', *Physical Education Review*, 2, 87–90.

Bale, J. (1980) 'The adoption of football in Europe: an historical-geographic perspective', *Canadian Journal of History of Sport*, 11, 56–66.

Bale, J. (1981) 'Cricket in pre-Victorian England', *Area*, 13, 119–22.

Bale, J. (1982) *Sport and Place: a Geography of Sport in England, Scotland and Wales*, Hurst, London.

Bale, J. (1983) 'Changing regional origins of an occupation: the case of professional footballers in 1950 and 1980', *Geography*, 140–8.

Bale, J. (1984) 'International sports history as innovation diffusion', *Canadian Journal of History of Sport*, 15, 38–63.

Bale, J. (1985) 'Towards a geography of international sport', *Occasional Paper 8*, Department of Geography, Loughborough University.

Bale, J. (1990) 'In the shadow of the stadium: football grounds as urban nuisances', *Geography*, 75, 325–44.

Bale, J. (1991) *The Brawn Drain: Foreign Student-Athletes in American Universities*, University of Illinois Press, Urbana.

Bale, J. (1994) *Landscapes of Modern Sport*, Leicester University Press, London.

Bale, J. (1998) 'Virtual fandoms: futurescapes of football', in A. Brown (ed.), *Fanatics: Power, Identity and Fandom in Football*, Routledge, London.

Bale, J. (2000) 'Geography at the Olympics: An evaluation of the work of Ernst Jokl', *Journal of Science and Medicine in Sport*, 3, 223–9.

Bale, J. (2001) [1993] *Sport, Space and the City*, Routledge, London.

Bale, J. (2001) 'African footballers and Europe: migration, exploitation and post-colonialism', paper read at annual conference of British International Studies Association, University of Bradford.

Bale, J. (2002) *Imagined Olympians: Body Culture and Colonial Representation in Rwanda*, University of Minnesota Press, Minneapolis.

Bale, J. and J. Maguire (eds) (1994) *The Global Sports Arena*, Cass, London.

Bale, J. and O. Moen (eds) (1995) *The Stadium and the City*, Keele University Press, Keele.

Bale, J. and J. Sang (1996) *Kenyan Running: Movement Culture, Geography and Global Change*, Cass, London.

Balmer, N., A. Nevill and A. Williams (2001) 'Home advantage in the Winter Olympics (1908–1998)', *Journal of Sports Science*, 19, 129–39.

Barnes, J. (1984) 'The hole world in their hands', *Sunday Times Magazine*, 22 July, 32–5.

Barth, G. (1980) *City People*, Oxford University Press, New York.

Barthes, R. (1973) *Mythologies*, Paladin, London.

Barthes, R. (1997) *The Eiffel Tower and Other Mythologies*, University of California Press, Berkeley.

Baumeister, R. and A. Steinhilber (1984) 'Paradoxical effects of supportive audiences on performance under pressure: the home advantage in sports championships', *Journal of Personality and Social Psychology*, 47, 85–93.

Bergsland, E. and O. Seim-Haugen (1983) 'Holmenkollbakken og Holmenkollrenne, *Sno og Ski*, 1, 97–108.

Betts, J. (1974) *America's Sporting Heritage*, Addison Wesley, Reading, Mass.

Bishop, J. and R. Booth (1974) 'People's images of Chelsea Football Club', *Working Paper 10*, Architectural Psychology Research Unit.

Blake, A. (1996) *The Body Language: The Meaning of Modern Sport*, Lawrence and Wishart, London.

Blain, N., R. Boyle and H. O'Donnell (1993) *Sport and National Identity in the European Media*, Leicester University Press, Leicester.

Blunden, E. (1985) *Cricket Country*, Pavilion, London.

Boal, F. (1970) 'Social space in the Belfast urban area', in N. Stephens and R. Glasscock (eds) *Irish Geographical Essays in Honour of E. Estyn Evans*, Queens University, Belfast.

Bowden, M. (1994) 'Jerusalem, Dover Beach and King's Cross: imagined places as metaphors of the British class struggle in *Chariots of Fire* and *The Loneliness of the Long Distance Runner*', in S. Aitken and L. Zonn (eds) *Place, Power, Situation and Spectacle: A Geography of Film*, Rowman and Littefield, Lanham, Mass., 69–100.

Bowen, M. (1974) 'Outdoor recreation around large cities', in J. Johnson (ed.) *Suburban Growth*, Wiley, London, 225–48.

Brailsford, D. (1987) 'The geography of eighteenth century spectator sport', *Sport Place*, 1, 41–56.

Burgess, J. (1982) 'Selling places: environmental images for the executive', *Regional Studies*, 16, 1017.

Burnside, J. (2000) 'Bunkered by Mr. Big', *The Guardian, Saturday Review*, 28 July 1–2.

Butcher, J. (1979) *The British in Malaya, 1880–1941*, Oxford University Press, Kuala Lumpur.

Cady, D. (1978) *The Big Game*, University of Tennessee Press, Knoxville.

Carr, G. (1974) 'The use of sport in the German Democratic Republic for the promotion of national consciousness and international prestige', *Journal of Sport History*, 1, 123–36.

Chase, J. and M. Healey (1995) 'The spatial externality effects of football matches and rock concerts', *Applied Geography*, 15, 18–34.

Clawson, M. and J. Knetsch (1966) *The Economics of Outdoor Recreation*, Johns Hopkins University Press, Baltimore.

Cloke, P., P. Crang and M. Goodwin (eds) (1999) *Introducing Human Geography*, Arnold, London.

Coakley, J. and E. Dunning (eds) (2000) *Handbook of Sports Studies*, Sage, London.

Cole, J. (1972) 'A Mexican view of Mexico and the World', *Ideas in Geography*, 45.

Coleman, J. (1960) 'Athletics in high school', *Annals of the American Academy of Political and Social Science*, 338, 33–43.

Comer, J. and T. Newsome (1996) 'Recent patterns of professional sports facility construction in North America', *Sport Place*, 10, 22–39.

Connell, J. (1985) 'Football and regional decline, some reflections', *Geography*, 70, 240–2.

Cox, K. (1979) *Location and Public Policy*, Blackwell, Oxford.

Cratty, B. (1973) *Psychology in Contemporary Society*, Prentice Hall, Englewood Cliffs.

Cromwell, D. and A. Wesson (1941) *Championship Techniques in Track and Field*, McGraw Hill, New York.

Curtis, J. and J. Birch (1987) 'Size of community of origin and recruitment to professional and Olympic hockey in North America, *Sociology of Sport Journal*, 4, 229–44.

Darwin, B. (1951) *British Golf*, Collins, London.

Dear, M. (1988) 'The postmodern challenge: reconstructing human geography', *Transactions of the Institute of British Geographers*, 13, 262–74.

Denney, R. (1957) *The Astonished Muse*, University of Chicago Press, Chicago.

Derrick, E. and J. McRory (1973) 'Cup in hand: Sunderland's self-image after the Cup', *Working Paper 8*, Centre for Urban and Regional Studies, University of Birmingham.

Deville-Danthu, B. (1997) *Le Sport en Noir et Blanc*, L'Harmattan, Paris.

Donaghu, M. and R. Barff (1990), 'Nike just did it: international subcontracting and flexibility in athletic footwear production', *Regional Studies*, 24, 537–52.

Douglas, B. (1987) 'Fans rate major league baseball parks', *Sport Place*, 1, 36.

Dunleavy, J. (1981) 'Skiing: the worship of Ullr in America', *Journal of Popular Culture*, 4, 74–85.

Dunning, E. (1971) 'The development of modern football', in E. Dunning (ed.) *The Sociology of Sport*, Cass, London.

Dunning, E. (1981) 'Social bonding and the socio-genesis of violence', in A. Tomlinson (ed.) *The Sociological Study of Sport*, Brighton Polytechnic, London.

Dunning, E. (1983) 'Social bonding and violence in sport: a theoretical-empirical analysis', in G. Goldstein (ed.) *Sports Violence*, Springer Verlag, New York.

Dunning, E. and K. Sheard (1979) *Barbarians, Gentlemen and Players*, Martin Robertson, Oxford.

Durrant, J. and O. Betterman (1952) *Pictorial History of American Sports*, Barnes, New York.

Edwards, J. (1979) 'The home field advantage', in J. Goldstein (ed.) *Sport, Games and Play: Social and Psychological Perspectives*, Erlbaum, Hillside, NJ.

Eichberg, H. (1982) 'Stopwatch, horizontal bar, gymnasium: the technologizing of sport in the eighteenth and early nineteenth centuries', *Journal of the Philosophy of Sport*, 9, 43–59.

Eichberg, H. (1994) 'Travelling, comparing, emigrating: configurations of sport mobility', in J. Bale and J. Maguire (eds) *The Global Sports Arena*, Cass, London, 256–80.

Eichberg, H. (1998) *Body Cultures*, Routledge, London.

Engel, M. (1987) 'Horseplay at Hanging Rock', *The Guardian*, 10 January.

Euchner, C. (1993) *Playing the Field*, Johns Hopkins University Press, Baltimore.

Everitt, T. (1991) *Battle for the Valley*, Voice of the Valley, London.

Federation of Stadium Communities (1999) *Stadium Communities Handbook*, FSC, Stoke-on-Trent.

Foucault, M. (1977) *Discipline and Punish*, Penguin, Harmondsworth.

Frankenberg, R. (1957) *Village on the Border: A Social Study of Religion, Politics and Football in a North Wales Community*, Cohen and West, London.

Gallaher, C. (1997) 'Identity politics and the religious right: hiding in the landscape', *Antipode*, 29, 256–77.

Galtung, J. (1984) 'Sport and international understanding: sport as a carrier of deep culture and structure', in M. Ilmarinen (ed.) *Sport and International Understanding*, Springer-Verlag, Berlin, 12–19.

Gaspar, J. *et al.* (1982) 'Transformaçães recentes na geografia do futbol en Portugal', *Finisterra*, 17, 301–24.

Gattrell, A. and P. Gould (1979) 'A micro-geography of team games; graphical explorations of structural relations', *Area*, 11, 275–8.

Geddert, R. and K. Semple (1987) 'A National Hockey League franchise: the modified central place theory', *Leisure Sciences*, 9, 1–13.

Geipel, R. (1981) 'Which Munich for whom?', in A. Pred (ed.) *Space and Time in Geography*, Gleerup, Lund, 160–82.

Gelber, S. (1983) 'Working at playing: the culture of the workplace and the rise of baseball', *Journal of Social History*, 16, 3–32.

Giamatti, B. (1989) *Take Time for Paradise: Americans and their Games*, Summit Books, New York.

Gillman, H. (1982) 'Home run weather', paper presented at annual meeting of the Association of American Geographers, San Antonio.

Gillmeister, H. (1981) 'The origin of European ball games, a re-evaluation and linguistic analysis', *Stadion*, 7, 19–51.

Gillmeister, H. (1997) *Tennis: A Cultural History*, Leicester University Press, London.

Goksøyr, M. (1990) ' "One certainly expected a good deal more from the savages." The anthropology days at St. Louis, 1904 and their aftermath', *International Journal of the History of Sport*, 7, 296, 3–6.

Gottman, J. (1974) 'The dynamics of large cities', *Geographical Journal*, 140, 254–62.

Gould, P. (1999) 'Skiing with Euler at Beaver Creek', in *Becoming a Geographer*, Syracuse University Press, Syracuse.

Gould, P. and N. Greenwalt (1981) 'Some methodological perspectives on the analysis of team games', *Journal of Sport Psychology*, 4, 283–304.

Gratton, C. and P. Taylor (1985) *Sport and Recreation: An Economic Analysis*, Spon, London.

Guttmann, A. (1978) *From Ritual to Record*, Columbia University Press, New York.

Guttmann, A. (1994) *Games and Empires*, Columbia University Press, New York.

Haggett, P. (2001) *Geography: A World Synthesis*, Prentice-Hall, Harlow.

Hague, E. and J. Mercer (1998) 'Geographical memory and urban identity in Scotland: Raith Rovers FC and Kirkaldy, Fife', *Geography*, 83, 105–16.

Hallinan, C. (1991) 'Aborigines and positional segregation in Australian Rugby League', *International Review for the Sociology of Sport*, 26, 69–81.

Harrison, E. (1913) *The Fighting Spirit of Japan*, Fisher Unwin, London.

Harvey, D. (2000) *Spaces of Hope*, Edinburgh University Press, Edinburgh.

Hawtree, F. (1983) *The Golf Course*, Spon, London.

Hayashi, N. (1972) 'Judo', in H. Jessup (ed.) *The Little Known Olympic Sports*, AAHPER, Washington.

Hegarty, C. (1985) *An Analysis of the Geography of United States Golf with Particular Reference to a New Form of Golf, the Cayman Facility*, unpublished master's dissertation, Oklahoma State University.

Hildebrand, J. (1919) 'The geography of games', *National Geographic Magazine*, 34, 98–143.

Hockin, R., B. Goodall and J. Whittow (1980) 'The site requirements for landing outdoor recreation events', *Geographical Papers*, 43, University of Reading, Reading.

Holt, R. (1981) *Sport and Society in Modern France*, Cambridge University Press, Cambridge.

Humphrey, J. (1986) 'No holding Brazil: football, nationalism and politics', in A. Tomlinson and G. Whannell (eds) *Off the Ball*, Pluto, London.

Humphreys, D., C. Mason and S. Pinch (1983) 'The externality fields of football grounds: a case study of The Dell, Southampton', *Geoforum*, 14, 401–11.

Huntington, E. (1915) *Civilization and Climate*, Yale University Press, New Haven.

Ingham A. and S. Hardy (1984) 'Sport: structuration, subjugation and hegemony', *Theory, Culture and Society*, 2, 85–103.

Ingham, A., J. Howell and T. Schilperoot (1987) 'Professional sports and community: a review and exegesis', *Exercise and Sport Science Reviews*, 15, 427–65.

Inglis, F. (1992) 'Intellectual history and popular culture: the case of sport', *British Society of Sports History Bulletin*, 12, 1–22.

Inglis, S. (1983) *The Football Grounds of England and Wales*, Collins Willow, London.

Inglis, S. (2000) *Sightlines: A Stadium Odyssey*, Yellow Jersey Press, London.

Jackson, J.B. (1957/8) 'The abstract world of the hot-rodder', *Landscape*, 7, 22–7.

Jackson, J. (1989) 'State intervention in sport and leisure in Britain between the wars', *Journal of Contemporary History*, 22, 163–82.

Jett, S. (1971) 'Diffusion versus independent development: the bases of controversy', in C. Riley *et al.* (eds) *Man Across the Sea*, University of Texas Press, Austin.

Johnston, R.J., D. Gregory and D. Smith (eds) (1994) *Dictionary of Human Geography*, Blackwell, Oxford.

Jokl, E. (1964) *Medical Sociology and Cultural Anthropology of Sport and Physical Education*, Thomas, Springfield.

Jones, C. (2001) 'A level playing field? Sports stadium infrastructure and urban development in the United Kingdom', *Environment and Planning A*, 33, 845–61.

Jones, S. (1987) 'State intervention in sport and leisure in Britain between the wars', *Journal of Contemporary History*, 22, 163–82.

Jordan, T. and L. Rowntree (1982) *The Human Mosaic*, Harper and Row, New York.

Kelsall, G. (2000) 'From the Victoria Ground to the Britannia Stadium: Remembering and Reinventing the Experience and Identity of Place', in T. Edensor (ed.), *Reclaiming Stoke-on-Trent: Leisure, Space and Identity in The Potteries*, Staffordshire University Press, Stoke, 85–104.

Kidd, B. (1970) 'Canada's national sport', in I. Lumsden (ed.) *The Americanization of Canada*, University of Toronto Press, Toronto, 257–74.

Kidd, B. (1979) *The Political Economy of Sport*, CAPHER, Ottawa.

Kirby, Andrew (1985) 'Leisure as commodity: the role of the state in leisure provision', *Progress in Human Geography*, 9, 64–84.

Kna, H. (1929) 'Die Watussi als Springkünstler', *Erdball*, 12, 459–62.

Korr, C. (1978) 'West Ham United Football Club and the beginnings of professional football in east London, 1895–1914', *Journal of Contemporary History*, 13, 211–32.

Krüger, A. (1999) 'Strength through joy: the culture of consent under fascism, Nazism and Francoism', in J. Riordan and A. Krüger (eds) *The International Politics of Sport in the Twentieth Century*, Spon, London, 67– 89.

Lanfranchi, P. and M. Taylor (2001) *Moving with the Ball: The Migration of Professional Footballers*, Berg, Oxford.

Lay, D. (1984) *The Migration of Scottish Footballers to the English Football League*, unpublished undergraduate dissertation, Department of Geography, Southampton University.

Lehman, H. (1940) 'The geographic origin of professional baseball players', *Journal of Educational Research*, 34, 130–8.

Lenskyj, H. (2000) *Inside the Olympic Industry*, State University of New York Press, Albany.

Lever, J. (1981) *Soccer Madness*, University of Chicago Press, Chicago.

Lewis, C. and M. McCarthy (1977) 'The horse racing industry in Ireland', *Irish Geography*, 10, 72–89.

Lewis, G. (1968) 'On the beginnings of an era of American sport', *Proceedings*, Annual Meeting of the National College PE Association for Men.

Lewis, P. (1979) 'Axioms for reading the landscape', in D. Meinig (ed.) *The Interpretation of Ordinary Landscapes*, Oxford University Press, New York, 11–32.

Ley, D. (1983) *A Social Geography of the City*, Harper and Row, New York.

Ley, D. (1985) 'Cultural–humanistic geography', *Progress in Human Geography*, 9, 415–23.

Lipsitz, G. (1984) 'Sports stadia and urban development: a tale of three cities', *Journal of Sport and Social Issues*, 8, 1–18.

Lipsyte, R. (1974) *Sportsworld: An American Dreamland*, Quadrangle Books, New York.

Lobozewicz, T. (1981) *Meteorologie im Sport*, Sportverlag, Berlin.

Loken, N. (1949) *Trampolining*, Overbeck, Ann Arbor.

Lowe, B. (1977) 'Sport prestige: the politicization of winning in international sport', *Arena Newsletter*, 1, 11–13.

Lowenthal, D. (1985) *The Past is a Foreign Country*, Cambridge University Press, Cambridge.

Lowerson, J. and J. Myerscough (1977) *Time to Spare in Victorian England*, Harvester, Hassocks.

Lowry, P. (1992) *Green Cathedrals*, Addison Wesley, Reading, Mass.

Loy, J. and J. McElvogue (1970) 'Racial segregation in American sport', *International Review of Sport Sociology*, 5, 5–23.

Loy, J., B. McPherson and G. Kenyan (1978) *Sport and Social Systems*, Addison-Wesley, Reading, Mass.

MacAloon, J. (1981) *This Great Symbol: Pierre de Coubertin and the Origins of the Modern Olympic Games*, University of Chicago Press, Chicago.

Macdonnell, A. (1935) *England, their England*, Macmillan, London.

Mackay, D. (1976) 'Environment', in J. Williams and P. Sperryn (eds) *Sports Medicine*, Arnold, London.

Maguire, J. (1988) 'Race and position assignment in English soccer', *Sociology of Sport Journal*, 5, 257–69.

Maguire, J. (1999) *Global Sport*, Polity Press, Cambridge.

Maguire, J. and D. Stead (1996) 'Far pavilions? Cricket migrants, foreign sojourn and contested identities', *International Review for the Sociology of Sport*, 31, 1–24.

Malcolm, D. (1997) 'Stacking in cricket: a figurational sociological reappraisal of centrality', *Sociology of Sport Journal*, 12, 263–82.

Mandell, R. (1971) *The Nazi Olympics*, Ballantine Books, New York.

Mandell, R. (1984) *Sport: A Cultural History*, Columbia University Press, New York.

Mandle, W. (1979) 'Sports as politics: the Gaelic athletic association, 1884–1916', in R. Cashman and M. McKernan (eds) *Sport in History*, University of Queensland Press, St. Lucia.

Mangan, J. (1986) *The Games Ethic and Imperialism*, Viking Penguin, Harmondsworth.

Marsh, J. (1984) 'The economic impact of a small city annual sporting event', *Recreational Research Review*, 11, 48–55.

Mason, C. and A. Moncrieff (1993) 'The effect of relocation on the externality fields of football stadia: the case of St. Johnstone Football Club', *Scottish Geographical Magazine*, 109, 97–105.

Mathieu, D. and J. Praicheux (eds) (1987) *Sports en France*, Fayard-Reclus, Paris.

Maurice, J. (1994) *The Impact of Selected Recreation Facilities on Residential Neighbourhoods in the City of Peterborough, Ontario*, unpublished undergraduate dissertation, Department of Geography, Trent University, Peterborough, Ont.

McCormack, D. (1999) 'Body shopping: reconfiguring geographies of fitness', *Gender, Place and Culture*, 6, 155–77.

McCormack, G. (1991) 'The price of affluence: the political economy of Japanese leisure', *New Left Review*, 188, 121–34.

Metcalfe, A. (1976) 'Sport and athletics: a case study of lacrosse in Canada', *Journal of Sports History*, 3, 1–19.

Michener, J. (1976) *Sport in America*, Random House, New York.

Miller, T., G. Lawrence, J. McKay and D. Rowe (2001) *Globalization and Sport*, Sage, London.

Morgan, R. (1976) 'Rain starts play', *Area*, 8, 257–8.

Morgan, W. (1998) 'Hassiba Boulmerka and Islamic green: international sports, cultural differences and their postmodern interpretation' in G. Rail (ed.) *Sport and Postmodern Times*, State University of New York Press, Albany.

Mrozek, D. (1983) *Sport and the American Mentality, 1880–61*, University of Tennessee Press, Knoxville.

Muller, P. (1981) *Contemporary Suburban America*, Prentice Hall, Englewood Cliffs.

Müller, N. (ed.) (2000) *Pierre de Coubertin 1863–1937: Selected Writings*, International Olympic Committee, Lausanne.

Mumford, L. (1973) 'Sport and the "bitch goddess" ', in J. Talimini and C. Page (eds) *Sport and Society*, Brown, Boston.

Murphy, P. (1985) *Tourism: A Community Approach*, Methuen, London.

Murphy, P. and D. Parker (1986) 'Some relationships between leadership, captaincy, management and playing position in the English Football League', in *Sport, Culture and Society: International Historical and Sociological Perspectives*, Spon, London.

Murphy, P. and R. White (1978) *The Psychic Side of Sports*, Addison-Wesley, Reading, Mass.

NCCA (1996) *NCAA Study of International Student Athletes*, NCAA.

Nielson, B. (1986) 'Dialogue with the city; the evolution of the baseball park', *Landscape*, 29, 39–47.

Noll, R. (1974) 'Attendance and price setting', in R. Noll (ed.) *Government and the Sports Business*, Brookings Institute, Washington, DC, 115–57.

Noll, R. and A. Zimbalist (1997) *Sports, Jobs and Taxes: The Economic Impact of Sports Teams and Stadiums*, Brookings Institute, Washington, DC.

Okner, B. (1974) 'Subsidies on stadiums and arenas', in R. Noll (ed.) *Government and the Sports Business*, Brookings Institute, Washington, DC.

Olds, K. (1998) 'Urban mega-events, evictions and housing rights: the Canadian case', ⟨http:www.breadnotcircuses.org⟩.

Oriard, M. (1976) 'Sport and space', *Landscape*, 21, 32–40.

Oriard, M. (1993) *Reading Football*, University of North Carolina Press, Chapel Hill.

Patmore, A. (1970) *Land and Leisure*, David and Charles, Newton Abbot.

Patmore, A. (1983) *Recreation and Resources*, Blackwell, Oxford.

Paul, A.H. (1972) 'Weather and the daily use of outdoor recreation areas in Canada', in J.A. Taylor (ed.) *Weather Forecasting for Agriculture and Industry*, David and Charles, Newton Abbot, 131–46.

Philo, C. (1994) 'In the same ballpark? Looking in on the new sports geography', in John Bale (ed.) *Community, Landscape and Identity: Horizons in a Geography of Sport*, Keele, Department of Geography Occasional Papers, 20.

Political and Economic Planning (1966) 'The football industry', *Planning*, 32.

Pollard, R. (1986) 'Home advantage in soccer: a retrospective analysis', *Journal of Sports Science*, 4, 237–48.

Pratt, J. and M. Salter (1984) 'A fresh look at football hooliganism', *Leisure Studies*, 3, 201–30.

Pred, A. (1981) 'Production, family and free time projects', *Journal of Historical Geography*, 7, 3–36.

Pred, A. (1995) *Recognizing European Modernities*, Routledge, London.

Pryce, R. (1989) *Scotland's Golf Courses*, Aberdeen University Press, Aberdeen.

Quirk, J. (1973) 'An economic analysis of team movements in professional sports', *Law and Contemporary Problems*, 38, 42–56.

Rail, G. (ed.) (1998) *Sport and Postmodern Times*, State University of New York Press, Albany.

Raitz, K. (1985) 'Places, spaces and environment in America's leisure landscapes', *Journal of Cultural Geography*, 8, 49–62.

Raitz, K. (1996) *The Theater of Sport*, Baltimore, Johns Hopkins University Press.

Raevuori, A. (1997) *Paavo Nurmi*, Werner Söderström, Porvoo.

Ravenel, L. (1997) *Le Football de Haut Niveau en France: Espaces et Territoires*, unpublished doctoral thesis, Université d'Avignon et des Pays de Vaucluse (vol. I).

Reclus, E. (1876) *The Universal Geography*, Vol. IV, Virtue, London.

Reisman, D. and R. Denny (1969) 'Football in America: a study in culture diffusion', in J. Loy and G. Kenyan (eds) *Sport, Culture and Society*, Macmillan, London.

Relph, E. (1976) *Place and Placelessness*, Pion, London.

Relph, E. (1981) *Rational Landscapes and Humanistic Geography*, Croom Helm, London.

Ricci, F. (2000) *African Football Yearbook, 2000*, Ricci, Rome.

Riess, S. (1991) *City Games: The Evolution of American Urban Society and the Rise of Sports*, University of Illinois Press, Urbana.

Rigauer, B. (1981) *Sport and Work*, Columbia University Press, New York.

Riley, T. (1981) *Sports Fitness and Sports Injuries*, Faber, London.

Rimmer, P. and R. Johnston (1967) 'Areas of community interest in Victoria as indicated by professional sport', *Australian Geographer*, 10, 311–13.

Riordan, J. (1977) *Sport in Soviet Society*, Cambridge University Press, Cambridge.

Rivett, P. (1975) 'The structure of League Football', *Operational Research Quarterly*, 26, 801–12.

Robins, D. (1981) *We Hate Humans*, Penguin, Harmondsworth.

Rodgers, B. (1977) *Rationalising Sports Policies: Sport in its Social Context*, Council of Europe, Strasbourg.

Rohé, F. (1974) *The Zen of Running*, Random House, New York.

Rooney, J. (1974) *A Geography of American Sport: From Cabin Creek to Anaheim*, Addison Wesley, Reading, Mass.

Rooney, J. (1986) 'The demand for golf in the year 2000', in *Golf Projections 2000*, National Golf Foundation, Jupiter, Fl., 1–8.

Rooney, J. and R. Pillsbury (1992) *Atlas of American Sport*, Macmillan, New York.

Rosentraub, M. (1977) 'Financial incentives, locational decision making and professional sports: the case of the Texas rangers baseball network and the city of Arlington', in M. Rosentraub (ed.) *Financing Local Government: New Approaches to Old Problems*, Western Social Sciences Associations, Fort Collins, Col.

Rosentraub, M. and S. Nunn (1978) Suburban city investment in professional sport', *American Behavioral Scientist*, 21, 393–414.

Ross, M. (1973) 'Football and baseball in America', in J. Talimini and C. Page (eds) *Sport and Society*, Brown, Boston.

Rupert, M. (1980) *A Geographic Analysis of Professional Baseball's First Year*

Signings, 1965–1977, unpublished master's dissertation, Oklahoma State University.

Rürup, R. (ed.) (2000) *1936: The Olympic Games and National Socialism*, Stiftung Topographie des Terrros, Berlin.

Sack, R. (1986) *Human Territoriality*, Cambridge University Press, Cambridge.

Sadler, B. (1983) 'Ski area development in the Canadian Rockies', in P. Murphy (ed.) *Tourism in Canada: Selected Issues and Options*, Dept. of Geography, University of Victoria, Victoria, BC, 309–29.

Said, E. (1974) *Orientalism*, Penguin, London.

Salter, M. (1975/6) 'Meteorological play-forms of the eastern woodlands', *History of Physical Education and Sports Research Studies*, 3, 11–25.

Sampson, A. (1981) *Grounds of Appeal: The Homes of First-Class Cricket*, Hale, London.

Sandiford, K. (1984) 'Victorian cricket techniques and industrial technology', *The British Journal of Sports History*, 1, 272–85.

Saunders, L. (1972) 'The characteristics and impact of travel generated by Chelsea Football Club', *Research Memorandum*, 344, Dept. of Planning and Transportation, Greater London Council, London.

Schaffer, W. and L. Davidson (1985) *Economic Impact of the Falcons on Atlanta, 1984*, Atlanta Falcons, Suwanee, Ga.

Scott, J. and P. Simpson-Housley (1989) 'Relativising the relativisers: the postmodern challenge to human geography', *Transactions of the Institute of British Geographers*, 14, 231–6.

Schimmel, K. (1995) 'Growth politics, urban development and sports stadium construction in the United States: a case study', in J. Bale and O. Moen *The Stadium and the City*, Keele University Press, Keele, 111–56.

Schumacher, J. (1936) *Die Finnen: Das Grosse Sportvolk*, Limpert Verlag, Berlin.

Schwartz, B. and S. Barsky (1977) 'The home advantage', *Social Forces*, 55, 641–61.

Scitovsky, T. (1976) *The Joyless Economy*, Oxford University Press, New York.

Semple, E. (1911) *Influences of Geographic Environment on the Basis of Ratzel's System of Anthropo-Geography*, Holt, New York.

Seppänen, P. (1981) 'Olympic success; a cross-national perspective', in G. Luschen and G. Sage, *Handbook of Social Sciences in Sport*, Sipes, Champaign, Ill.

Shaw, E. (1963) 'Geography and baseball', *Journal of Geography*, 62, 74–6.

Shelley, F. and K. Cartin (1984) 'The geography of baseball fan support in the United States', *North American Culture*, 1, 77–95.

Shinnick, P. (1979) 'North-east regional development and the Olympic prison', *Arena Review*, 2, 3–11.

Sillitoe, A. (1959) *The Loneliness of the Long Distance Runner*, W.H. Allen, London.

Sir Norman Chester Centre (1995) *FA Premier League Fan Surveys 1994/95*, Sir Norman Chester Centre for Football Research, Leicester University, Leicester.

Sloane, P. (1960) 'Sport in the market? The economic causes and consequences of the Packer Revolution', *Hobart Paper*, 85, Institute of Economic Affairs, London.

Smith, D. (1977) *Human Geography: A Welfare Approach*, Arnold, London.

Smith, J. (1972) 'The Native American ball games', in M. Hart (ed.) *Sport in the Socio-Cultural Process*, Brown, Dubuque.

Sommer, J. (1975) 'Fat city and Hedonopolis: the American urban future', in R. Abler, D. Janelle, A. Philbrick and J. Sommer (eds.) *Human Geography in a Shrinking World*, Duxbury Press, North Scituate, Mss.

Springwood, C. (1996) *Coopertown to Dyersville: A Geography of Baseball Nostalgia*, Westview Press, Boulder.

Spurr, D. (1994) *The Rhetoric of Empire*, Duke University Press, Durham.

Stefani, M. (1985) 'Observed betting tendencies and suggested betting strategies for European football pools', *The Statistician*, 32, 1985.

Steiner, J. (1933) *America at Play*, McGraw Hill, New York.

Stepney, P. (1983) 'Towards a politics of football; the case of Bradford Park Avenue', in A. Tomlinson (ed.) *Explorations in Football Culture*, Brighton Polytechnic, Brighton.

Stovkis, R. (1982) 'Conservative and progressive alternatives in the organisation of sport', *International Social Science Journal*, 92, 197–220.

Szymanski, S. and T. Kuypers (2000) *Winners and Losers: The Business Strategy of Football*, Penguin, London.

Taylor, Lord Justice (1990) *Hillsborough Stadium Disaster: Final Report*, HMSO, London.

Tennyson, C. (1959) 'They taught the world to play', *Victorian Studies*, 2.

Thornes, J. (1977) 'The effect of weather on sport', *Weather*, 32, 258–67.

Thornes, J. (1983) 'The effect of weather on attendance at sporting events', in J. Bale and C. Jenkins (eds) *Geographical Perspectives on Sport*, Department of PE, Birmingham University, Birmingham, 182–90.

Thrift, N. (1981) 'Owners time and own time: the making of a capitalist time-consciousness', in A. Pred (ed.) *Time and Space in Geography*, Gleerup, Lund.

Tivers, J. (1997) 'From artificiality to authenticity? The development of dry ski slopes in England and Wales', *Area*, 29, 344–56.

Tomlinson, R. (1986) 'A geography of flat racing in Great Britain', *Geography*, 71, 228–39.

Tuan, Y-F. (1974) *Topophilia*, Prentice-Hall, Englewood Cliffs, NJ.

Tuan, Y-F. (1984) *Dominance and Affection: The Making of Pets*, Yale University Press, New Haven.

Turner, I. (1979) 'The emergence of "Aussie Rules"', in R. Cashman and M. McKernan (eds) *Sport in History*, University of Queensland Press, St. Lucia.

Tylor, E. (1880) 'Remarks on the geographical distribution of games', *Journal of the Anthropological Society of Great Britain and Ireland*, 9, 23–30.

Vennum, T. (1994) *American Indian Lacrosse: Little Brother of War*, Smithsonian Institution Press, Washington.

Wagner, P. (1981) 'Sport: culture and environment', in A. Pred (ed.) *Time and Space in Geography*, Gleerup, Lund.

Walker, B. (1986) 'The demand for professional football and the success of league teams: some city size effects', *Urban Studies*, 23, 209–20.

Walton, M. (1984) 'The influence of the World Cup on international stereotypes', *Teaching Geography*, 9, 203–7.

Walvin, J. (1975) *The People's Game*, Allen Lane, London.

Waylen, P. and A. Snook (1990) 'Patterns of regional success in the Football League, 1921–1988', *Area*, 22, 353–67.

Webb, R. (1982) *The Concept of Territoriality: The Home Ground Advantage in Selected British Sports*, unpublished undergraduate dissertation, Keele University.

Whannell, G. (1992) *Fields in Vision*, Routledge, London.

Wiggins, D. (1989) 'Great speed but little stamina: the historical debate over black athletic superiority', *Journal of Sport History*, 16, 158–85.

Williams, G. (1983) 'From grand slam to grand slump; economy, society and rugby football in Wales during the depression', *The Welsh History Review*, 11, 338–57.

Williams, J., E. Dunning and P. Murphy (1984) 'Come on you whites', *New Society*, 68, 310–11.

Williams, M. and W. Zelinsky (1970) 'On some patterns of international tourist flows', *Economic Geography*, 46, 549–67.

Wind, H. (1973) 'The lure of golf', in J. Talamini and C. Page (eds) *Sport and Society*, Little, Brown, Boston, 397–412.

Winningham, G. and A. Reinart (1979) *Rites of Fall: High School Football in Texas*, University of Texas Press, Austin.

Winters, C. (1980), 'Running', *Landscape*, 24, 19–22.

Wiseman, N. (1977) 'The economics of football', *Lloyds Bank Review*, 123, 29–43.

Woeltz, R. (1977) 'Sport, culture and society in late imperial Weimar Germany', *Journal of Sport History*, 4, 295–315.

Wright, G. (1999) 'Globalisation and sport'. ⟨http://cat.org.au/aoa/documents/g-wright.html⟩.

Yetman, H. and S. Eitzen (1973) 'Some social and demographic correlates of football productivity', *The Geographical Review*, 63.

Young, T. (1986) 'The sociology of sport: structural marxist and cultural marxist approaches', *Sociological Perspectives*, 29, 3–28.

Zeldin, T. (1977) *France 1848–1945* (vol. 2), Oxford University Press, Oxford.

Zelinsky, W. (1988) 'Where every town is above average: welcoming signs along America's highways', *Landscape*, 30, 1–10.

Zeller, R. and T. Jurkovac (1989) 'A domed stadium: docs it help the home team in the National Football League?' *Sport Place*, 3, 36–9.

Author index

Subject index